CAPITAL PUNISHMENT IN JAPAN

BRILL'S JAPANESE STUDIES LIBRARY

EDITED BY

H. BOLITHO AND K.W. RADTKE

VOLUME 17

CAPITAL PUNISHMENT IN JAPAN

BY

PETRA SCHMIDT

TUTA SUB AEGIDE PALLAS · 1683 ·

BRILL
LEIDEN · BOSTON · KÖLN
2002

This book is printed on acid-free paper.

Die Deutsche Bibliothek - CIP-Einheitsaufnahme

Schmidt, Petra:
Capital punishment in Japan / by Petra Schmidt. – Leiden ; Boston ;
Köln : Brill, 2001
(Brill's Japanese studies library ; Vol 15)
ISBN 90-04-12421-7

Library of Congress Cataloging-in-Publication Data

Library of Congress Cataloging-in-Publication Data is also available.

ISSN 0925-6512
ISBN 90 04 12421 7

PRINTED IN THE NETHERLANDS

For Philip Sarbutt

For Waltraud Schmidt

CONTENTS

INTRODUCTION

INTRODUCTION

More than ten people get sentenced to death in Japan every year. Three or four death-row inmates, sometimes more, will be led to the gallows to hang for the crimes they have committed. Japanese law provides for the death penalty for a number of crimes. And Japan's courts apply this punishment in a recently increasing number of cases of homicide, robbery-murder and rape-murder.

Whether capital punishment is morally justifiable or not is ultimately a philosophical question, which can hardly be conclusively decided. Today most industrial nations have removed the death penalty from their criminal codes for a variety of considerations. Only the United States and Japan still impose and execute death sentences. Following a steady decline of the number of finalised death sentences as well as of executions since the *Meiji* Period, the abolition of capital punishment in Japan seemed imminent after a stay on executions, which lasted for more than three years. The 'bloody Friday' on 26 March 1993, however, brought an end to the moratorium with three executions, and ruined in one day all hopes and expectations of the opponents of capital punishment. The executions ushered in a period during which so far more people have been brought to the gallows than in the entire preceding decade.

Historically, capital punishment in Japan shows a unique development. From its beginnings in the era of the mythological gods until the 20th century, it was intertwined with religion, philosophy and the state system. The death penalty was variously used as a means to enforce the 'way of the warrior', to rule the country, to educate the people or to do away with unpleasant political opponents. Japan was the first nation in the world to abolish capital punishment in the *Heian* Period, but later, in the Middle Ages, reached new heights in cruelty and contempt for human life in its re-application. During the *Tokugawa* Period, the death penalty served as a tool to implement Confucian values in family and state life. Even after the thorough Westernisation of Japanese law in the late 19th century, capital punishment, especially from the 1910s, was applied in a way as to uphold the 'beautiful mores and good customs' of Japan, as interpreted by the ultra-nationalistic and militaristic ruling elite. Similarly, the present-day discussion on capital punishment in Japan shows some remarkable differences to the debates elsewhere. Arguing for and against the death penalty has a long tradition in Europe and the United States, beginning with Beccaria's and Bentham's utilitarian theories of abolition. Scholars of criminal law and politicians, philosophers and clerics have been discussing arguments for and against capital punishment for centuries. In Japan first timid beginnings of this discussion can only be found from about the middle of the *Meiji* Period, but these hints at Western tendencies of abolition and punishment's character as education did not fall on fertile ground in prewar and wartime Japan.

Only the nation's extensive democratisation after the Second World War provided the proponents of an abolition of capital punishment with the security and self-confidence needed for the discussion, and Japan's new constitution (*Nihon-koku kenpô*) of November 1946 paved the way for a new line of arguments. The constitutional prohibition of cruel punishment, the need to protect lawful procedure or basic values such as the 'right to life', 'individual dignity' or the 'common weal', have all been raised by some of Japan's most prominent legal scholars and other individual commentators of the death penalty. The judiciary however upheld the constitutionality of this life-taking punishment.

Besides constitutional issues, focus is laid on several other arguments, which are also applied elsewhere in the discussion: for example, some proponents of the death penalty attempt to legitimise its existence from the social contract. In the centre of a heated debate stands the possibility of general prevention, meaning deterrence from and prevention of crimes through imposition and execution of death sentences. Closely related to this is the attempt to define the 'typical criminal', to measure and compare the deterrent effect of capital and other forms of punishment, to provide alternatives, or to present statistical evidence for or against the superior deterrence of the death penalty. Retaliation, the ancient *lex talionis* with its stipulation of 'an eye for an eye, a tooth for a tooth', is equally brought forward in the Japanese discussion, as are the victims' feelings, which, aver the proponents of the death penalty, can only be appeased by taking the life of a murderer.

Forming the core of the Japanese discussion in the past decade, is the issue of mistrials, of miscarriages of justice. Ever since the

1980s, when four men were found not guilty in retrials of their cases after decades on death row, the government's assurance that justice was done in all cases involving capital punishment has begun to waver. Has there really not been a single error among the thousands of death sentences and executions since the *Meiji* Period? Were the cases of four men released after decades on death row in the 1980s isolated occurrences, caused by the postwar turmoils? Can such mistakes be prevented from recurring? And finally, the question remains about the role of religion, morality and ethics in the Japanese discussion on capital punishment. Are there differences between the approaches and opinions in the Judeo-Christian West and in Japan with its multitude of religious beliefs and moral philosophies? Does, as some have postulated since the early 1970s, the special 'national character' of the Japanese people demand a retention of the death penalty? The defenders of the death penalty in Japan have been attempting to justify their views with the help of the 'people's will', as shown in opinion polls. Their opponents, however, equally use opinion polls as seemingly the only 'scientific' way to determine the right or wrong of the death penalty. Dozens of polls have been conducted in the past half-century, invariably providing the outcome desired by the pollers. But what is the real public opinion in Japan? Is it the will of the average Japanese, or of a person with expert knowledge on capital punishment? Do the Japanese people have interest, knowledge and opinion the issue? Can it be conclusively proven?

This book will illuminate the practical side of capital punishment in Japan: who is sentenced to death for which crime and why? Statistics show a clear decrease in sentencing and executions since the 19th century, and a reverse course since 1993. The criteria for death sentences are unclear. Several case studies will attempt to discern a pattern behind the Japanese courts' choice of the death sentence. Which crime will be punished by death? Which courts are more likely to exempt the life of a violent criminal? Is there a way to 'standardise' the criteria for sentencing?

Equally shrouded in mystery is the process leading to an execution. How does a death row convict become chosen to be sent to the gallows? How does the machinery of the omnipotent Ministry of Justice work? Does the Minister of Justice have a duty to sign execution orders? A closer look at past practice shows that previous ministers had very divergent attitudes towards this task.

Of special interest is the question of why the Justice Ministry throws a veil of secrecy over the issue of executions of death sentences. While insisting that capital punishment must be retained for its invaluable deterrent effect, the Ministry refuses to release any information about who is executed when and where.

If these organs back capital punishment, who opposes it? A closer look will be cast at the groups who support an abolition, their sociology and activities, if there are such. For decades under conservative Liberal-Democratic rule, the opposition parties maintained the abolition of capital punishment as party policy. But as soon as they took over the helm in 1993, they adhered to the existing system, even increasing the number of executions.

Opinions and trends in political parties and the Japanese Diet will be examined, as will the role of the sensation-seeking media in the continuation and direction of the discussion.

Unlike many other countries, opposition against capital punishment in Japan is rather unorganised. Who are the few small groups and individuals who keep fighting for an abolition?

In light of the recent dramatic increase in violent crime in the former safe-haven of Japan, beginning with the Aum cult's sarin gas attack on the Tokyo subway system in March 1995 to the murder of eight primary school children in Osaka in June 2001, an answer will be sought to the question: why has the death penalty not been abolished in Japan? Why has there even been an increase in its application? What does the future hold in store?

PART A:
THE HISTORY OF CAPITAL PUNISHMENT IN JAPAN

PART A

THE HISTORY OF CAPITAL PUNISHMENT IN JAPAN

The history of punishment is the history of the death penalty. Early man knew no difference between 'revenge' or 'retaliation' and capital punishment. Death as a means of avenging disturbances of the social order has since ancient times formed the core of criminal law, the oldest and original law.[1] Like all primitive law, the law of ancient Japan was unwritten and characterised by occult and religious elements. Law, morality and religion were not separated yet, and all norms were referred to as *nori* - an oracle, a sign of the will of the gods, which also functioned as the declaration of those, who held power or authority.[2] Thus, prehistoric Japan's sacral legal system was based on superstition.[3] Certain disturbances of the order were righted by sacrificing the perpetrator, later by corporal punishment, ablution, property confiscation and banishment.[4]

From about the fourth century, Chinese concepts of punishment began to penetrate Japan's legal system: torture was applied to extract confessions; for misdeeds such as murder, theft or

---

1 TAKIGAWA MASAJIRÔ, Nihon hôsei-shi jô (Japanese Legal History, pt. I) p. 103 (Tokyo 1985); ONO SEIICHIRÔ, *Keibatsu no honshitsu ni tsuite, sono ta (On the Nature of Punishment)*, in Takigawa sensei kanreki kinen – gendai keihô-gaku no kadai I (Festschrift for the Sixtieth Birthday of Professor Takigawa – Problems of Contemporary Criminal Law) p. 343 (Tokyo 1955)

2 *nori* = law = justice = oracle; according to YOSIYUKI NODA, Introduction to Japanese Law p. 21 (Tokyo 1976), the term *nori* derives from the verb *noru*: ‚[L]aw was the will of the gods as declared by the person interceding between the gods and the people.'

3 HANS HELLMUTH RUETE, Der Einfluß des Abendländischen Rechts auf die Rechtsgestaltung in Japan und China (The Influence of Occidental Law on the Formation of Law in Japan and China) p. 65 (Bonn 1940); MORIKAWA TETSURÔ, Nihon shikei-shi (The History of Capital Punishment in Japan) p. 26 (Tokyo 1970)

4 Among many, see, for example, SAEKI CHIHIRO, Keihô kôgi rôron (Lectures on Criminal Law, General Part) p. 10 (Tokyo 1968); TAKAYANAGI KENZÔ, Nori no imi to ishiki 1 (Meaning and Conscience of nori, Pt. 1), in 13-9 Hôgaku 1 p. 7 (1944)

kidnapping, a broad variety of punishments existed, such as death, incarceration, banishment or beatings.[5] The law at that time was still strongly based on the idea of retaliation, although great importance was placed on deterrence; some punishments even had the character of care and correction.[6] In the spirit of Chinese humanism, the cruel and mutilating punishments of the previous period disappeared. But the law was 'rough and inflexible', by systematically determining the 'correct' punishment of a culprit and his crime. Its foremost aim was to strengthen the system of dependencies on which the Chinese state was based and the Japanese state was meant to be based.[7]

The punishments at that time were divided into regular (*shokei*) and extraordinary ones (*junkei*). The five kinds of *shokei* were: flogging (*chi*), beating with the lesser stick (*jô*), imprisonment (*zu*), banishment (*ru*) and death (*shi*). Capital punishment was executed either by hanging (*kô*) or beheading (*zan*), with the latter one being considered the more severe form.[8]

The history of capital punishment in Japan took an unprecedented turn during the *Heian* Period. While Chinese influence continued to grow – in general and on criminal law- the cruel variety of capital punishment – the Chinese knew more than two hundred different forms of execution! – was not adopted. Japan under Kanmu Tennô (781-806) applied only two methods: hanging and decapitation, a fact often explained as due to both the generosity of the Emperor and the gentle character of the Japanese.[9] Already during the *Nara*

---

5 MIHARA KENZÔ, Shikei haishi no kenkyû (Studies on the Abolition of Capital Punishment) p. 26 (Tokyo 1990); UK-TJONG ZONG, *Zur Geschichte der Kodifikation des Strafrechts in Ostasien (On the History of Codification of Criminal Law in East Asia)*, in 84 ZStW pp. 434, 446 (1972)

6 NODA note 2 p. 23; RUETE note 3 pp. 66-67

7 RUETE note 102 pp. 66-67; GÜNTHER VON OTTO, Geschichte des Japanischen Strafrechts (The History of Japanese Criminal Law) pp. 44, 46 (Leipzig Diss. 1913)

8 The reason for beheading being regarded as a heavier punishment, is based on the Chinese idea of resurrection: if the head had been severed from the torso, it was believed, resurrection would be impossible. SUGIYAMA HARUYASU, Nihon hôsei-shi gairon (The History of Japanese Law) p. 122 (Tokyo 1980). For a different, albeit unconvincing, interpretation, see OTTO note 7 p. 30

In the occident, too, it was believed that resurrection 'on Doomsday' would be impossible with broken bones or an incomplete skeletton. Details: KARL BRUNO LEDER, Todesstrafe – Ursprung, Geschichte, Opfer (Capital Punishment – Origin, History, Victims) p. 106 (Wien 1980).

9 MASAKI AKIRA, Shikei – kieyuku saigo no yaban (Capital Punishment – The Last Barbarity) pp. 3-4 (Tokyo 1964). Using the *ritsuryô* system, the Imperial

Period (710-794), Shômu Tennô (724-749) allegedly had gone further: the faithful Buddhist decreed that all executions be stayed.[10] While this can not be proven as a historic fact, a similar occurrence is shown for the following *Heian* Period. At a time, when the Japanese penal system in general became more lenient, Saga Tennô (809-823) in 818 decided that all capital punishment for theft be mitigated into incarceration.[11] Cases of robbery soon received the same treatment, and eventually capital punishment no longer was applied. This was indeed the first abolition or non-application in the world, lasting until in 1156 when Minamoto no Tameyoshi, leader of the unlucky side in the *Hôgen* Insurrection, was executed.[12]

The theories about the causes for the non-application vary widely. While some try to explain the phenomenon as due to the mild character of the Japanese and the warm climate and safe nature surrounding them,[13] others point to the Buddhist politics of the *Nara* and *Heian* Periods, with much importance placed on mercy and the

---

government in the meantime had unified all power in its hands. The legal and political position of the Tennô now was almost equal to that of the Chinese Son of Heaven, a despotic monarch. The Tennô was now regarded a living diety. NODA note 105 p. 25

10 Shômu, deeply moved and impressed by a Buddhist sermon, had converted to Buddhism. Shômu was enthroned in 724 and changed the period name to *Jinki*. In the second year of this period he invited 600 Buddhist priests and for the prevention of fires he made 3,000 men priests and lay priests. The Tennô was a deeply religious man and had temples erected throughout the country. Due to a large number of natural disasters, Buddhism also gradually took root among the general public. Therefore it may be assumed that indeed the influence of Buddhism was fundamental for the worldwide first abolition of capital punishment. MIHARA note 5 p. 42

11 ISHII RYÔSUKE, Nihon hôsei-shi gaiyô (Japanese Legal History) p. 50 (Tokyo 1978); MASAKI note 9 pp. 5-7

12 Tameyoshi (1096-1156) had fought for the ex-Emperor during the *Hôgen* insurrection. After the defeat he was executed upon the order of Taira no Kiyomori. See ISHII RYÔSUKE, Hôsei-shi (Legal History) pp. 75, 76 (Tokyo 1964). It is of interest that the dishonourable punishment of skewering the severed head of a decapitated criminal, which normally was executed in addition to capital punishment, during the whole period was applied - after the natural demise of a culprit or after death by torture. MAESAKA TOSHIYUKI, Shikei (Capital Punishment) p. 127 (Tokyo 1991)

13 RIKÔ MITSUO, Ritsuryô no kenkyû (Studies on Ritsuryô) pp. 312-313 (Tokyo 1981); also see DANDÔ SHIGEMITSU, Shikei haishi-ron (On the Abolition of Capital Punishment) p. 464 (Tokyo 5th ed. 1997)

prohibition of killing.[14] Also mentioned is the concept of karma, of *inga*, that is the belief that in the next incarnation one will be rewarded for each good deed done in a previous existence, but punished for all evil ones.[15] Yet another argument often brought forward is the *Heian* nobility's fear of revengeful spirits (*goryô*).[16] It is also conceivable that the reason was an imitation of *Tang* China[17] or the extensive use of banishment as a punishment with the same concept of 'divine justice' as capital punishment.[18] Finally, the primitive sensation of horror must be mentioned, which made the Japanese from the earliest times see death as impure, as ignoble.[19]

Whatever the reason may have been, it prevented for more than three centuries the execution of death sentences in Japan – until the civil war between the *Heike* (*Taira*) and *Genji* (*Minamoto*) rang in one of the most cruel and blood-thirsty periods in Japanese history. War and capital punishment became commonplace during the *Kamakura* Period (1192-1333). The warriors (*buke)* fought each other; their education mainly consisted of the teaching of contempt for human life and for death. In this world of the warriors, capital punishment soon became the main tool to suppress crime. It was not applied to cause fear, but clearly as pure punishment. The tendency

---

14 MURANO KAORU, Nihon no shikei (Capital Punishment in Japan) p. 40 (Tokyo 1990)

15 AOYAGI FUMIO, *Shikei seido wa sonzoku subeki de aru (The Death Penalty Must be Retained*), in 33-12 Jiyû to seigi pp. 16, 17 (1982). According to the Lotus Sutra (*Myôhô renge-kyô*), a good cause produces a good effect, and a bad cause a bad effect, and thus cause and effect naturally level each other. To make the idea of this causality more stringent, is anchored in the Buddhist code of morality. The concept entails that by a good deed in the present and future incarnation, concrete advantages can be gained. This was very beneficial for the spread of Buddhism. RIKÔ note 111 p. 26-27

16 E.g. RIKÔ note 111 pp. 28-29. The evil spirits of revenge were mentioned for the first time in the NIHONGI upon the death of monk Genbô in 746: 'Word spread that the spiritual effect of Fujiwara no Hirotsugu had caused him harm.' Hirotsugu, whose rebellion in 740 ended with his death, at the time had demanded the removal of Genbô from court. NELLY NAUMANN, Die Einheimische Religion Japans – Teil I: Bis Zum Ende der *Heian*-Zeit (The Indigenous Religion of Japan, pt.i: Until the End of the *Heian* Period) p. 210 (Leiden … 1988)

17 E.g. RIKÔ MITSUO, *Heian jidai ni okeru shikei teishi ni tsuite (On the Suspension of Capital Punishment During the Heian Period*), in 53-9 Hôgaku kenkyû pp. 316, 322-323 (1974)

18 ISHIO YOSHIHIRA, Nihon kôdai-hô no kenkyû (The Law of Japanese Antiquity) p. 47 (Kyoto 1959)

19 RIKÔ note 17 p. 53

became increasingly cruel until, after a delay of several centuries, finally the full cruel variety of Chinese penal laws was introduced, which was to form the foundation of Japan's penal system until the end of the *Tokugawa* (*Edo)* Period (1600-1867).[20]

A complicated system of various methods of executions according to the social rank of victim and culprit developed. The variety of execution forms during the *Kamakura* Period included, among many others, hanging, slaying, decapitation, crucifixion, burning, boiling and so on. Samurai occasionally were permitted to disembowel themselves in order to be spared the shame and dishonour of hanging or decapitation.

Once the *buke* had gained a firm grip on power in Japan, the Confucian ideal of a virtuous government became unfashionable. The *buke* felt contempt for life. To calmly accept death was the guiding principle of the *bushidô*, the way of the warrior. In the sphere of criminal law and procedure, this philosophy led to the introduction of extreme and brutal punishments, for the two terms '*bushi*' and 'respect for life' were incompatible. Punishment saw a general increase in severity, which was deemed necessary in a time of rapacity and unlawfulness.[21]

Following the Chinese concept that a punishment had to fit the crime, *Kamakura* law provided different punishments for similar crimes, depending on the social status of the culprit and the victim. While, for example, killing by a samurai was followed by confiscation of property or banishment, the same crime committed by a person of a lower rank was avenged by incarceration.[22]

During the following *Ashikaga* or *Muromachi* Period (1392-1490), a time described by George Sansom[23] as one of 'much law and little justice', the death penalty clearly became the punishment of choice. In general, punishment had become very rigorous; from the period of the warring states (*sengoku jidai*), punishment had assumed a more private nature, sought by revengeful individuals rather than the state. Forms of executions now included crucifixion (*haritsuke*),

---

20 See e.g. MASAKI note 9 pp. 3-5, 7-8

21 AMNESTY INTERNATIONAL (A.I.), Die Todesstrafe in Japan p. 3 (Bonn 1983). MAESAKA note 12 p. 127

22 See, for example, CARL STEENSTRUP, A History of Law in Japan until 1868 p. 97 (Leiden... 1991)

23 GEORGE SANSOM, A History of Japan: 1334-1615 p. 85 (Tokyo 1974)

crucifixion upside down (*sakasaharitsuke*), spearing (*kushizashi*), sawing (*nokohiki*), being torn by oxen (*ushizaki*) or by carts (*kurumazaki*), burning (*hiaburi*), boiling (*kama-iri*), burning bound on wood (*taimatsuaburi*), hanging (*shibarikubi*), decapitating (*funkei*) and many more.[24]

Punishment had become extremely harsh, but no new legislation was created, except for house laws (*kahô*), enacted by feudal lords (*daimyô*) and limited to their own domains (*ryugoku*). Those who quarrelled were punished, no matter who had started the fight. Wives, children, even neighbours often were punished together with the culprit (*enza*). Deterrence was the aim, and even lightest offences were punished by death, often aggravated by torture. Capital and corporal punishment were so cruel that one clearly can speak of a brutalisation of the penal system, which continued until the unification of the country in the late 16th century.[25]

The details of execution methods demonstrate their full cruelty: if the sentence was decapitation, the culprit was handed over to the victim or the pariah (*eta)*, tied to a pillar and finally decapitated. Death by slaying meant that after decapitation, the corpse could be used for trying out new swords and thereafter was cast away. Skewering of the head (*gokumon*) was executed after the culprit had been paraded around town on horseback (*hikimawashi*). A culprit might be decapitated and his severed head displayed for three days and two nights next to a sign informing the public about the nature his crime. Execution by crucifixion included first of all *hikimawashi;* then the unfortunate was tied to a cross made from one vertical and two horizontal poles. The cross was raised, the convict speared several times from two sides, and eventually killed with a final thrust through the throat. The corpse was left on the cross for three days. If one condemned to crucifixion died in prison, his body was pickled and the punishment executed on the dead body. Under Toyotomi Hideyoshi, one of the great 16th century unifiers, crucifixion upside down was frequently used. Water crucifixion (*mizuharitsuke*) awaited mostly Christians: a cross was raised at low tide; when high tide came, the convict was submerged under water

---

24 SUGIYAMA note 8 p. 231

25 STEENSTRUP note 22 pp. 86, 105; KATSUMATA SHIGEO & MARTIN COLLCUTT, *The Development of Sengoku Law*, in: Japan before Tokugawa – Political Consolidation and Economic Growth, 1500 TO 1650 pp. 103-104, 107 (John Whitney Hall et.al. eds., Princeton 1981)

up to the head, prolonging death for many days. If sentenced to burning, after *hikimawashi* the unfortunate was bound to a pillar atop a pile of bamboo and was set alight. The punishment of sawing (*nokogiribiki*) was mostly applied under Oda Nobunaga and Hideyoshi and later was provided for in the *Tokugawa* Period *Osadamegaki* code. The criminal was buried up to the head, which was sawed off while he was alive. If he had committed suicide, the punishment was carried out on the dead body. Self-disembowelment (*seppuku*) was reserved for the warrior class and executed within prison or the convict's home in the presence of an official.[26]

The described above execution methods were applied until the *Tokugawa* era, some even until the early years of the *Meiji* Period (1868-1911). Some methods vanished at the end of the era, such as hanging (*kôshu*), decapitation in the form of *hanshiuchi,* spearing, tearing by oxen or by carts, boiling in oil or in water (*kamayude* or *kamaire)*, drowning (*fuzuke*) and death by starvation (*koushikoroshi).*

Once Tokugawa Ieyasu had unified the country, a time of peace and stability began for Japan from the 1600s. The Tokugawa Shogunate ruled the fate of the nation for over two and a half centuries. In the field of law, not much changed during this period. 17th century *bakufu* law still was a product of the *Sengoku* Period. Criminals were frequently punished together with their kin, even trivial offences were avenged by death or extremely cruel corporal punishment such as cutting off nose and ears. But once the old *Sengoku* warriors had died, Confucian ideas gained the upper hand over torture and mutilation. During the 18th century, mutilating punishments disappeared, the number of executions decreased. The Tokugawa preferred to fight crime with deterrence and moral exhortation. This period marked the heyday of Confucianism in Japanese history. The total adherence to the teachings of the ancient Chinese moral philosopher was, among others, expressed in the law. A person who disregarded the principles of respect for the ruler, the master, and the older, was punished by way of example, and in grave cases together with his kin.[27]

---

26 ISHII note 11 p. 156; SATO TOMOYUKI, Shikei no nihon-shi (The History of Capital Punishment in Japan) 105 et seq (Tokyo 1994)

27 STEENSTRUP note 22 pp. 150, 151

The main code of the period, the *Osadamegaki Hyakkajô* of 1742,[28] a meticulously specified collection of precedents, provided for a large number of punishments on top of which stood death, carried out in lesser and heavier forms. No less than 35 of the code's 103 provisions dealt with crimes punishable by death. If one considers that each of the individual provisions contained a number of crimes and varieties thereof, it was an impressive collection. For example, 'death' was the prescribed punishment for the killing of one's parents, murder, arson, robbery and violations of the *bakufu* laws. It was also the punishment imposed on a person who obtained a loan using forged documents. A person who forced his way into a warehouse was punished by death, and so was one who stole from the blind, the maimed or from travellers or who sold stolen goods. Death awaited a kidnapper, a blackmailer and one who made false accusations or threatened to burn down another's house. A parent who killed his child or one who killed a younger sibling, niece or nephew was punished by death, and so was one who instigated a murder or a person who hid a criminal. One who fled his place of banishment or prison had to avenge with death, which also awaited a guard, who found money and kept it or who failed to report a foundling. A former adoptive son-in-law, who after divorce and expulsion from his adoptive house kidnapped his former wife, faced death.

Crimes considered most despicable were punished by crucifixion. A person who had sneaked by a roadblock or assisted such a crime was crucified, as was one who let a foundling die. An adulterous wife who killed her husband was crucified. False accusers of their own master or parents ended at the cross, as did the forger of gold or silver coins. Crucifixion also was the punishment for someone who attempted to kill or who wounded his master or parent.

Farmers who had complained to their lord, rioted and escaped were beheaded. The same punishment awaited the captain of a ship who declared his load lost or sunken but sold it or who sold a stolen load. A servant's guarantor who let his protégée run away after receiving part of his wages, lost his head, and so did a father who sold his daughter against his wife's wish. An adulterous wife and

---

28 An English translation of the Code can be found in JOHN CAREY HALL, *Japanese Feudal Laws III – The Tokugawa Legislation*, in 38-III TASJ p. 269 (1911)

her companion were punished by decapitation. A thief or robber faced beheading, and so did a forger of documents or seals. The same fate awaited the seller of poison and one who attempted to lay arson. A person who attempted to wound his present or former master, a relative of the master, a parent, in-laws, ascendants, one's teacher or mayor was decapitated. This also was the punishment for one who killed a commoner without justified reason for trying out his sword. An arsonist was burnt. The killer of his master had his head sawn off before crucifixion.[29]

Principally, crimes of lower against higher-ranking persons were punished more severely than vice versa, and occasionally crimes of socially higher ranked persons against lower ones were not avenged at all. The Confucian tradition of respect for the older, the parents, the teacher, the master and so on, was especially evident in Art. 71 of the *Osadamegaki*, which dealt with crimes against life and limb, such as the denial of assistance in case of fire: if such omission caused the death of one's parents, the punishment was death. If, however, 'only' older siblings, aunts or uncles died, the culprit got away with medium banishment.

All violations of the fundamental rules of the government system were severely punished, such as the prohibition of the wives of regional lords *(daimyô)* from leaving the capital. In such a case there was no avoiding death. Also, one who attempted to enrich himself at the cost of the state had to expect harsh punishment, as had a thief or robber.

The subordinate position of women is shown in the *Osadamegaki's* provision on adultery, which granted a deceived husband the right to kill wife and adulterer. Adultery of a husband, however, did not constitute a punishable crime. It is furthermore remarkable that, unlike in Chinese law, there were no provisions on incest between siblings. Only provisions on sexual relations between parents and children existed.

The concept of criminal responsibility was not known to *Tokugawa* criminal law. The individual had to take responsibility even for accidental events and results exceeding the intent. This was of special importance in case of crimes against life and limb, since there was no independent crime of bodily injury.

---

29 In detail see PETRA SCHMIDT, Die Todesstrafe in Japan (Capital Punishment in Japan) (Hamburg 1996)

From today's concept and principle of culpability, the code contained several interesting provisions on this matter: children under the age of 15 were principally held responsible for their acts, although mitigation was provided for in certain cases. Drunkenness, too, did not influence the punishment for murder or other violent crime. Mental defects did diminish the responsibility under certain circumstances in case of killing or arson, but not in case of the killing of ascendants. Women sometimes faced lesser penalties, and pregnancy seems to have been a cause for mitigation. Motives modifying responsibility were profit seeking, self-interest, greed, thieving intention and vindictiveness. A lack of self-interest or profit seeking was a reason for mitigation. A planned crime was aggravating. An act committed in the heat of the moment, an outburst of rage with a lack of intent or planning or because of sudden desire had mitigating effect. Voluntary self-incrimination seems to have been recognised customarily.

A criminal was only sentenced after a confession was obtained. Since a suspect did not always provide the desired statement voluntarily, first it was tried to coerce him into confession by intimidation. If that was unsuccessful, the long-standing method of torture was applied. Here, too, the Japanese showed astonishing imagination. Gradually, a fixed four-step system developed, which included imaginatively named methods such as 'hugging the stone', 'the cancer' or 'the rack'.

An old Confucian principle said that the people should well know what they had to do and what to avoid doing, but that it would be mistaken to inform them about the consequences resulting from their action or omission; since otherwise individuals could slip through loopholes in the law all too easily. Thus the general populace was informed of prohibitions and orders, but not taught about punishments. As a substitute, punishments were executed in public, and their elaborated cruelty served the purpose of general prevention.[30]

The execution procedure of the death sentence, threatened in various forms as punishment for certain crimes, was detailed in Art. 103 of the *Osadamegaki*.[31] As in the previous period, a criminal

---

30 OTTO note 7 p. 92; SATO note 26 p. 150

31 Details in JOHN CAREY HALL, *Japanese Feudal Laws III. The Tokugawa Legislation Part IV, The Edict in 100 Sections*, in 41 TASJ pp. 683, 791-793, 798 (1913)

sentenced to death by sawing, the gravest method of execution, was placed up to his head inside a box. Both his shoulders were cut with a sword, blood-soaked bamboo saws were put up next to him. For two days, passers-by were permitted to saw. Crucifixion was carried out either in Asakusa or Shinagawa in Edo or at the scene of the crime. Next to a placard informing about the crime, the dead body was put on display for three days before being handed over to the *Eta*. The aggravated form of decapitation followed by spearing of the severed head also normally took place in Asakusa, Shinagawa or at the scene of the crime, as was burning, and beheading. An executioner, a supervisor of the fourth rank (*kachi-metsuke*) and a gendarme (*yoriki*) were to be present and to report to the government.

In the case of 'death' (*shizai*), the corpse after the execution was discarded as a *tameshimono*, meaning it would be used for trying out new swords.

As in the previous period, the main forms of execution were further subdivided, and each method could be aggravated by preceding the execution with public parading (*hikimawashi)* or dishonourable display in chains (*sarashi)*. To give an example, the heaviest punishment provided for in the *Osadamegaki* for the murder of one's master, was a combination of four gruelling elements: *hikimawashi*, *sarashi,* sawing and crucifixion. Such cruel and agonising executions undoubtedly provided vivid visual instruction to the public of what awaited those who broke the – unknown – rules of the law.[32]

After a long period of slow decay and the eventual forced opening of Japan by the West, the *Tokugawa* Period ended in 1867 with the restoration of Imperial rule. The *Meiji* Period had begun. The new government realised the necessity of modernisation in all aspects of Japanese society, but initially did not have the time to draft and enact new legislation. In 1868 it was decided that in the field of penal law, enforcement should proceed as before under the *Osadamegaki* until the proclamation of a new code. Nevertheless, a reform was urgent. In the same year, the *Ka-keiritsu*[33] (Temporary Penal Law) was created based on the *Nara*- and *Heian* Period codifications, the *Taihô*- and *Yôrô*-Codes as well as the *Osadamegaki*.

---

32 OTTO note 7 p. 92

33 In detail on the code see MIHARA note 5 pp. 93 et seq

The *Ka-keiritsu* roughly divided crimes punished by death into rebellion and high treason, sorcerous writings and words, theft of the relics of a grand shrine, theft of Imperial decrees and documents, theft from Imperial or administrative warehouses, aiding and abetting the escape of prisoners, theft of horses or oxen, abduction and sale of women, deprivation of personal liberty, assault on a sword bearer, assault on an official, quarrel between a low ranking person and a *rônin*, assault on one's master, assault on one's teacher, assault on a close relative, assault on parents or grand parents, assault on the spouse, manslaughter, murder of parents or grandparents, murder of a close relative, murder of one's master, murder and adultery, murder of three or more members of a family by poison, inflicting bodily injury by weapons or poison, accidental killing, false accusation, failing to execute a warrant of arrest, rape, rape and murder, rape of family members, causing death by rape, treason, forgery. If these provisions already seem extraordinarily numerous, one must bear in mind that they are merely the headings of chapters, which in turn contain many more, explicitly detailed crimes.

Methods of execution were beheading, hanging (or gibbeting) and, in case of arson, burning.

This code was neither promulgated nor enforced. In practice, administrative provisions were applied in criminal trials, and within this limitation the application of the *Osadamegaki* had been abandoned.[34]

The first standardised penal code for *Meiji* Japan was the *Shinritsu Kôryô* (Outline of the New Penal Laws) of December 1870 (enforced January 1871). The code was meant to clear away feudal traditions and to adapt Japanese penal law to the new circumstances. Once more the drafters relied on Chinese legal tradition and compiled the code after the model of *Ming* and *Qing* dynasty penal laws.[35] As a consequence, the new law was close to the old Imperial law, the *Taihô* Code of one millennium earlier. At the same time it held on to the social distinctions of feudal Japan: *Tokugawa* law formed the core of the code. At least the members of the commission which had been entrusted with the compilation of the

---

34 AOYAGI FUMIO, Keiji tsûron I sôron (Criminal Law I – General Part) p. 46 (Tokyo 1965)

35 1368-1644 and 1644-1911. Code *Ta-qing-lü-li*

new Japanese penal code, realised that the true meaning of punishment did not lie in extreme and relentless cruelty, but in ensuring prosecution and punishment. Thus all barbaric methods of execution, which had been so symptomatic of the *Tokugawa* Period, were banned. The number of crimes punished by death was reduced, merciless and excessive torture as well as flogging abolished, and most crimes now were avenged by imprisonment and compulsory labour.[36] Western influence existed only in so far as a structured general part preceded the code and, for the first time, general regulations of concurrence, subsequent offence and accessory crimes were included.[37]

This code, drafted after the traditional pattern, was soon outdated and in 1873 subjected to a thorough revision. The *Kaitei Ritsurei*[38] (Reformed Penal and Administrative Laws, enforced May 1873) replaced it. Although closely oriented at the *Shinritsu Kôryô*, it paid tribute to new ideas and removed all inadequate provisions of the previous code. The new interpretations, additions and improvements without exception embraced mitigation and reason. Japan's jurists by now were convinced that the aim of punishment should be realised by standardisation and determination of penal provisions, by the removal of arbitrariness and the great personal inequality before the law. A deeper-reaching influence of European and North American legal principles and humanitarian ideals led to a further reduction of crimes threatened by death; corporal punishment was eliminated almost completely. Also imported from Europe was the transition from a strictly moral punishment to a merely legal conception of penal law. Nevertheless, as a whole the *Kaitei Ritsurei* still had a very traditional outlook, standing in the tradition of elaborate, Confucian-inspired case law.[39] Robbery was

---

36 In contrast to the laws of the *Tokugawa* period, the main changes regarding capital punishment included e.g. death as punishment for unchaste monks. However, capital punishment was still the punishment for the killing of the head of a house, theft of valuables, and the death penalty for theft of relics of grand shrines was added.

37 RUETE note 3 pp. 74-75; JOSEPH H. LONGFORD, *A Summary of the Japanese Penal Codes*, in 5-II TASJ p. 1 (1877)

38 An English translation can be found in LONGFORD note 37.

39 OTTO note 7 p. 131; LONGFORD note 37 p. 2. The code in old tradition relied on detailed case law, although for the first time preceded by general provisions. The Confucian character of the law remained without change, with punishment still accorded upon the social rank of a criminal.

distinguished into two categories: violent robbery with and without weapons. A thief who was armed at the time of commission of the crime was, if the robbery was accomplished, sentenced to death by decapitation. This was irrespective of the amount stolen and without distinction of principal and accessory. In case of attempt, the principal was hanged. Had the offender, in addition to robbery, been guilty of murder or wounding, the punishment was decapitation. An unarmed robber who also committed murder faced decapitation. Additional wounding or rape was avenged with hanging. Accidental killing committed during a common robbery was punished by hanging. While it was allowed for an uncle to rob his nephew, the same did not apply vice versa. If, in the latter case, the crime was accompanied with the - even accidental - killing or wounding of the robbed relative, the offender was to be punished under the provision on robbery or homicide which subjected him to the severest penalty. The ringleader of a band of rioters who wrecked, burnt, or plundered property, or caused wounds or death, was to be punished by decapitation. An accessory who committed murder or kindled a fire, by hanging. The ringleaders of a group of people who, due to crop failure, assembled and assaulted farmers, threatened the authorities, plundered the local stores, made an uproar at the government office, or, due to resentment, forsook their occupations and thus brought discredit on the authorities, were to be punished by hanging.

Especially numerous were the provisions on homicide. To give just a few examples, premeditated and wilful murder was defined as having a scheme of revenge, having previously prepared noxious drugs, weapons or implements of any kind, or when a number of persons had united and made a simultaneous assault. In ordinary cases of wilful and deliberate murder, that is, where there was no relationship of any kind between the victim and culprit, decapitation awaited the principal, hanging an accessory. The principal in a case of attempted homicide was hanged. Most severely punished was the murder of grandparents, parents, paternal uncle or aunts, elder siblings, a husband, or husband's ascendants: the culprit had to await decapitation with displaying of the severed head, and even in case of attempt the punishment was hanging. Equally, an accomplished murder of a senior by a junior relative below the third degree of relationship or of a master by his servant was avenged with decapitation. Wilful, but not preconcerted murder was to be punished by decapitation. This type of penalty could occur where death resulted from a wound deliberately inflicted, in the heat of a discussion or quarrel or before the consequent resentment has had time to subside, in an affray or otherwise, and with either the hand, foot or any weapon whatsoever. The punishment of decapitation would be administered so long as the wound was inflicted with the intention of causing a fatal result. Infanticide by relatives was to be treated according to the law of preconcerted or wilful murder, as was murder in self-defence. No punishment awaited a husband who, on discovery of his wife or concubine in the act of committing adultery, killed either or both guilty parties. If he killed after a lapse of time, he was punished according to the provisions on murder in an affray. On the other hand, if a wife or concubine conspired with a lover to murder her husband, she had to await death by decapitation, aggravated by displaying of the severed head; the lover was decapitated. This also was the punishment for a physician whose patient died under improper treatment applied to prolong the illness and thus increase the physician's profit. A person who slew three or more members of one family, whether relatives or servants, or three or more persons who, though not living together, were closely related, either premeditatedly, in connection with an act of incendiarism or robbery, or in any other way, or who deliberately mangled the body of a person he slew, or who committed murder by a slow and painful process, was to be punished by decapitation accompanied with displaying of the head. The same punishment awaited one who terrified another person into the commission of suicide, and if threats were used in connection with an attempted robbery and rape. A common assault on an official of Imperial appointment committed by a person who was not an official was punished by hanging if a cutting wound was inflicted. If the assault caused the death of the official, the punishment was decapitation. If a husband committed wilful murder of his wife or concubine, the crime was avenged by hanging. If a wife assaulted her husband and caused his death, the punishment was decapitation, aggravated with displaying of the head if she wilfully murdered her husband. A husband who wilfully murdered his wife's parents was sentenced to death. Children or grandchildren who assaulted their parents or grandparents, or a wife or concubine who assaulted her husband, were decapitated if the assault caused the death of the victim. The punishment was accompanied by displaying of the head if the crime was wilful murder. The wilful murder of an elder sibling, uncle, aunt or maternal grandparent was punished by decapitation with exposure of the head. Hanging was the punishment for an assault on a senior relative causing his or her death. Wilful murder was avenged by decapitation. The same crime committed by a senior against a junior official was punished by hanging in the case of wilful murder. An official who, instigated by private malice, deliberately committed to prison a person whom he knew was innocent of any offence was punished by hanging, if the falsely accused person died as a result of such imprisonment. If death resulted from torture, the official was decapitated.

There were twenty degrees of punishment, ranging from penal servitude for ten days to death.[40] In several provisions, the various forms of execution of capital punishment were laid down. The death penalty as the most severe punishment was executed either by hanging or decapitation, with the latter being considered more severe. In case of a few very heinous crimes, such as patricide, decapitation was aggravated by public display of the severed head. If a culprit belonged to the samurai class, a death sentence was substituted by imprisonment, unless the crime was of a very hideous nature.

The *Kaitei Ritsurei,* too, soon proved to be incompatible with the general speedy Westernisation of all aspects of Japanese life, and calls for further codification grew louder. The whole Japanese legal system had to be placed on a level equal to European and North American law, if Japan wanted to revoke the so-called unequal treaties, and end extraterritoriality for foreigners. The Imperial government's first justice minister Etô Shinpei's hope to promulgate a translation of the French *Code Pénal* failed due to Etô's execution in 1874 for his participation in an anti-government uprising. Upon the instigation of his successor, Ôta Takato, another attempt was undertaken by Frenchman Gustave Emile Boissonade, who in later years gained a prominent place in Japanese legal history for his codification work in the field of civil law. In July 1875, Boissonade presented a draft of a code of criminal procedure. Deliberations on a new penal code started in 1877. Both drafts, closely following French law, were presented by the minister of justice to a special committee of the Upper House. On 17 July 1880, they were

40 LONGFORD note 37 pp. 4-5

promulgated as Great Council of State decree (*dajô-kan fukoku*), and enforced on 1 January 1882.

In the Penal Code (*Keihô*), Western influence clearly predominated. The penal system was constructed rationally, and the facts of a crime were outlined in a simple and clear way. Punishments were comparatively rational and humane. The Japanese had not simply copied the European codes. Rather, the *Keihô* of 1882 was based on the general principles of European legal science, whose experiences and progress were taken into consideration. The strongest influence had undoubtedly been exerted by the French *Code Pénal.* Adopting the latter's systematic rules, the Japanese code was divided into the chapters 'Crimes and delicts against public rights', 'Crimes against the person and private property', as well as 'Misdemeanours'. The code also comprised the principle *nulla poena sine lege*, constituting the removal of *Edo* Period judicial discretion. Crimes were divided into three categories according to their gravity in *crimes*, *délits* and *contraventions.* However, the formal mistakes, especially the complexity of the penal system and the narrowness of the range of sentences, as well as ambiguities in many provisions, led to considerable uncertainties in the administration of justice. Furthermore, technical problems arose, such as the lack of training of the judges in European law and linguistic obstacles. Finally there was always the issue whether a European penal system was adequate for Japanese sentiments.[41]

Regarding crimes punished by death in this so-called 'Old Penal Code' (*Kyû-Keihô),* the large number of provisions, threatening death for crimes against the Emperor and his family is striking.

---

41 One must bear in mind that the majority of European legal terms had not existed in the Japanese language prior to the reception of Western law, and new terms had to be created.
Although the term *hô,* for example, had been adopted from Chinese law in antiquity, it meant law in the objective sense. For subjective law, the term *kenri* was created. But a word alone did not automatically bring the new institutions into the consciousness of the people, or only even that of the judges. In traditional Japan, the flipside of a duty was not automatically a subjective right, but rather *giri* had to be observed at any time, as what was expected from the other side at any given time. MURAKAMI JUN'ICHI, Einführung in die Grundlagen des japanischen Rechts (Introduction to the Foundations of Japanese Law) pp. 19-22 (Darmstadt 1974)
These issues caused problems in the application of the new criminal law, which still could be overcome, but the code of criminal procedure, closely modelled after the French *Code d'Instruction*, could not be adjusted to Japanese circumstances and thus quickly became a paper tiger. RUETE note 3 p. 78

Art. 116:	Jeopardising the Emperor
Art. 118:	Jeopardising the Imperial Family
Art. 121:	Preparing or conspiring to wage a civil war with the object of overthrowing the government or seizing the territory of the state or otherwise subverting the constitution (leader and accessories)
Art. 123:	Murder committed with the object of overthrowing the government
Art. 126:	Attempt of any of the aforementioned crimes
Art. 130:	Conspiring with a foreign state in times of external war or assisting the enemy
Art. 138:	Murder committed by using explosives or arson laid to buildings, vessels, warehouses etc.
Art. 169:	Murder committed by overturning trains or sinking of vessels
Art. 292:	Premeditated murder
Art. 293:	Murder by poison
Art. 296:	Murder with the object to commit or conceal another crime
Art. 298:	Premeditated murder of the wrong person
Art. 362:	Premeditated patricide
Art. 363:	Assault on parents or grandparents, resulting in death
Art. 381:	Robbery resulting in death
Art. 402:	Arson of structures where people are present

As to the execution of capital punishment, the early years of the *Meiji* Period had already seen a decrease in methods.[42] After lengthy debates in the senate (*Genrô-in*), hanging remained as the only form of execution. Details were provided for in the supplementary provisions: executions were carried out inside the prison grounds. Only the prison guards were permitted to be present at an execution. For the first time, the principle of secrecy had been laid down in the law.

42 In a proclamation dated 4 January 1879, the public display of a head was abolished.

As already shown, the first decades of the *Meiji* Period were marked by a feverish zeal to adapt the whole nation, including its legal system, to Western standards. Although only a few years passed between the various codifications of this period, culturally they represented a development, for which other peoples had taken centuries. In this process, the 1882 Penal Code, too, was not meant to stay in force for long, soon proving to be insufficient and outdated. First revision attempts were undertaken as early as 1883, and eventually culminated in the enforcement on 1 January 1908 of the *Kaisei Keihô* (Reformed Penal Code), which for the most part is still in force to the present day.[43]

Mandatory death sentences in this code were provided for in two cases, both of which once again stood in close relation to the Imperial Household. A large number of other crimes were also threatened by optional death sentences. Death was the punishment for any assault or attempted assault on the Emperor, the Empress-Dowager, the Empress, the Crown Prince or his son. Art. 77 provided for capital punishment for the ringleader of an insurrection or seditious act with the object of overthrowing the government, seizing the state territory or otherwise subverting the constitution. As to crimes related to external war, a mandatory death sentence was the punishment for inducement of such a war (Art. 81). It was optional in case of assistance to the enemy in person or by providing goods, structures etc. for military use, or for someone who spied for the enemy. Art. 119 provided death for the crime of inflicting damage to structures by inundation, causing death. The derailment or destruction of trains, or capsizing or destruction of vessels, causing the death of a person, was punishable by death. So was the crime of poisoning water-works, causing the death of a person. Art. 199 threatened capital punishment in case of homicide, and Art. 200 for the killing of an ascendant. The death sentence could also be handed down for inflicting injury causing death, robbery causing death, or robbery and rape causing death.

As can already be seen from the aforementioned provisions, a substantial simplification and abbreviation of the law as well as an extensive expansion of judicial discretion in sentencing had taken

---

43 On the process leading to the 1908 code, see OTTO 7 106 p. 125; OKADA ASSATARÔ, Vorentwurf zu einem Strafgesetzbuch für das Kaiserlich Japanische Reich (Preliminary Draft for a Penal Code for the Japanese Empire) p. 5 (Berlin 1899); MIHARA note 5 p. 122; MASAKI note 9 p. 59

place. The previous threefold partition of crimes according to the French model was abandoned and a simplification of punishments adopted, reducing their number to six main forms of punishment: capital punishment (*shûkei*), penitentiary (*chô-eki*), confinement (*kinkô*), imprisonment (*kôryû*), monetary penalty (*bakkin*) and correctional fine (*karyô*). Hanging remained as the only form of execution; the principle of secrecy was left unchanged (Art. 11). The execution of capital punishment was carried out upon order by the minister of justice in the presence of a prosecutor and a court clerk.

In the years following the First World War, a tendency of leniency could be observed in the West; Japan chose a different path. A 'Temporary Commission on the Legal System' (*Rinji hôsei shingi-kai*), established in 1922 to consider 'Japan's beautiful morality, good customs and beautiful mores', concluded on a need for a revision of the Penal Code. Against all trends in criminal science, a 1940 draft code did not provide for an abolition of capital punishment;[44] on the contrary, another draft published that same year by the 'Commission for the Inquiry in a Reform of the Prison Law' (*Kangoku-hô kaisei chôsa iin-kai*) increased the number of crimes punishable by death.[45] Although none of these drafts was passed, in the wake of growing nationalism and militarism and in the attempt to suppress any potential subversive movement, various special laws were enacted, such as the Security Law and the Strike

---

44 462 general and special provisions under the heading of 'Provisional Provisions and Resolution of the Committee on the Inquiry into the Penal and Prison Law' (*Keihô-hei kangoku-hô kaisei chôsa iin-kai sôkai ketsugi oyobi ryûho jôkô (keihô chôsa oyobi keihô kakusoku michi*), the so-called 'Provisional Draft of a Reformed Penal Code' (*Kaisei keihô kaan*). KURITA MASAYOSHI, *Kaisei keihô kaan chûgaku (Draft of a Penal Law Reform)*, in 32-8 HÔRITSU JIHÔ p. 334 (1960); MASAKI note 9 pp. 75-76

45 For example, Art. 158 of this draft provided for capital punishment for an assault on the regent or an attempt thereof. Art. 167.1 threatened with death anyone, who committed murder with the object of overthrowing the state. Art. 167.2 provided for the death penalty or imprisonment for life for one who killed with the aim of overthrowing the government, seizing the territory of the state or in any other way subverting the constitution. A person using explosives with the object of disturbing the public peace or causing damage to the life, body or property of people, according to Art. 249 should be punished by death or penal servitude for life or not less than seven years. The same penalty was provided for attempt. Finally, Art. 174 threatened with death one who gathers troops for an enemy nation. For details see SCHMIDT note 29 pp. 140 et seq.

Arbitration Law (1900). Entering the *Taishô* Period (1911-1926), this social-political situation of strengthening security policies and political oppression continued. To fight off the alleged danger, in 1926 the Public Peace and Order Law (*Chian iji-hô*) was enacted, and in 1928 its provisions tightened even further, threatening death as punishment for many attempted crimes.[46] During the war, which began with the Manchurian Incident in 1931 and widened to the Pacific War after Japan's surprise attack on Pearl Harbor in 1941, Japan experienced a period with flourishing capital punishment. The spirit of heroically giving one's life for the Emperor and the country muffled all calls for an abolition of capital punishment. The provisions even increased in number and became ever more severe. During these years of militarism, no active public attempts were made to abolish the death penalty.[47] On the contrary, an increasing number of crimes was threatened with death in special laws such as the Penal Provisions on the Control of Explosives (*Bakuhatsu-mono torishime bassoku*) of 1884, the Duel Law (*Kettô-zai*) of 1889, the Public Peace and Order Preservation Law (*Chian iji-hô*) of 1924, the War Crimes Law (*Senji hanzai shôbatsu no tokurei ni kansuru hôritsu*) of 1942, the Military Penal Code (*Rikugun Keihô*) of 1908, the Navy Penal Code (*Kaigun Keihô*) of 1908, the State Preservation Law (*Kokubô hôan-hô*) of 1908, and the Law on the Protection of Military Installations (*Gunki hogo-hô*) of 1894.

The year 1945 brought Japan's defeat and thorough reforms in all spheres of life. One of the major changes was the abolition of the Emperor system. A new constitution, enforced 3 May 1947, and a variety of further reforms had effects on the legal system, including the penal system and capital punishment. But those who had expected the abolition of the death penalty in the course of Japan's democratisation and the constitutional recognition of fundamental human rights were disappointed. The Penal Code in 1947 underwent

---

46 The Public Peace and Order Law provided that a person, who with the object of overthrowing the state, forms a group or becomes a member of a group or conducts other tasks of a leading figure, was to be punished by death or imprisonment or penitentiary for life or not less than seven years (Art. 1). Art. 2 threatened capital punishment (or alternatively imprisonment or penitentiary for life or not less than five years) to someone who, with the aim of supporting such a group organises a group or conducts the tasks of a functionary or a leader of a group. Art. 3 provided for the same punishment for the case that a person organised a group or carried out the tasks of a functionary or leader thereof.

47 For details see SCHMIDT note 29 pp. 143 et seq fn. 615

the farthest-reaching reforms since its enforcement. Regarding capital punishment, all provisions which threatened death for crimes against the Imperial Family were abolished (Arts. 73-76). Also repealed were provisions on crimes against international relations (Arts. 90, 91). These were the only provisions on capital punishment affected by this reform.[48] The chapter on crimes relating to external war underwent thorough reforms (Arts. 81-89) due to a constitutional amendment, i.e. the creation of Art. 9, the renunciation of war. Also based on this provision, the Army Penal Code, Navy Penal Code, the War Crimes Law, the State Preservation Law, the Law on the Protection of Military Installations and the Public Peace and Order Preservation Law were abolished and thus all provisions therein which provided for capital punishment.[49] After these abolitions or reforms, current Japanese criminal law provides for capital punishment in the following cases:

In the Penal Code:

- Art. 199: Homicide[50]
- Art. 240: Robbery causing death
- Art. 241: Robbery and rape causing death
- Art. 126: Overturning of trains etc. causing death
- Art. 127: Endangering traffic causing death
- Art. 146: Poisoning of water works causing death
- Art. 77: Rebellion
- Art. 81: Inducement of external war
- Art. 82: Assistance to the enemy during external war, including military service for such power
- Art. 108: Arson of structures where persons are present
- Art. 117: Destruction by explosives
- Art. 119: Damage to structures by inundation etc.

---

48 Also, the Juvenile Law (*Shônen-hô*) saw the inclusion of Art. 51, which exempted minors from the application of the death penalty.

49 In detail, the following abolitions and amendments were carried out:
Abolitions:
Arts. 73, 75, 83, 85 Penal Code, Art. 10 Explosives Law, Art. 6 Public Peace and Order Preservation Law, Art. 2, 11 War Crimes Law, Art. 3 State Preservation Law, Art. 3 II Law on the Protection of Military Installations
Reforms:
Art. 73, 75, 81, 82, 83 Penal Code

50 Art. 200, Murder of ascendants, in 1974 was declared unconstitutional by the Supreme Court.

In special laws:

- Law on the Hijacking of Airplanes and Related Crimes (Law No. 68 of 1976): Unlawful hijacking of a plane causing death
- Law on the Endangerment of Air Traffic (Law No. 87 of 1974): Destruction of Airplanes causing Death
- Duel Law (Law No. 34 of 1889): Duel causing Death
- Explosives Control Law (Decree No. 34 of 1884): Use of Explosives
- Law on Hostage-taking (Law No. 48 of 1978): Wilful Killing of a Hostage

PART B:
CAPITAL PUNISHMENT IN JAPAN TODAY

PART B

CAPITAL PUNISHMENT IN JAPAN TODAY

1. *Figures and Facts*

The statistics show a clear tendency of continuous decrease of the number of death sentences and executions from the early *Meiji* Period. From 1873, the number of executions fell below 1,000 per year, and after 1877 there were never again more than 200 executions in a single year. From 1887, the number fell further below 100, and from 1919 below 50. In 1960, for the last time, more than 30 convicts were hanged, and in 1970 for the last time more than 20. Since 1976, the number of executions lies below 10 a year. Naturally, there are variations. After 59 executions in 1913, only five convicts were hanged in 1914, before the number again reached 94 in 1915. After seven executions of death sentences in 1958, a total of 69 persons were hanged during the following two years, but only six in 1961. In 1967, 23 executions were carried out, none in 1968, and 18 in 1969.[1]

The decreasing tendency of the number of executions is especially obvious, when looked at the figures for periods of five years.

1 MURANO part A note 14 pp 122-123. However, in 1982, eleven, and in 1988, ten death sentences were handed down.

Graphs B-1, 2:[2] Death Sentences and Executions

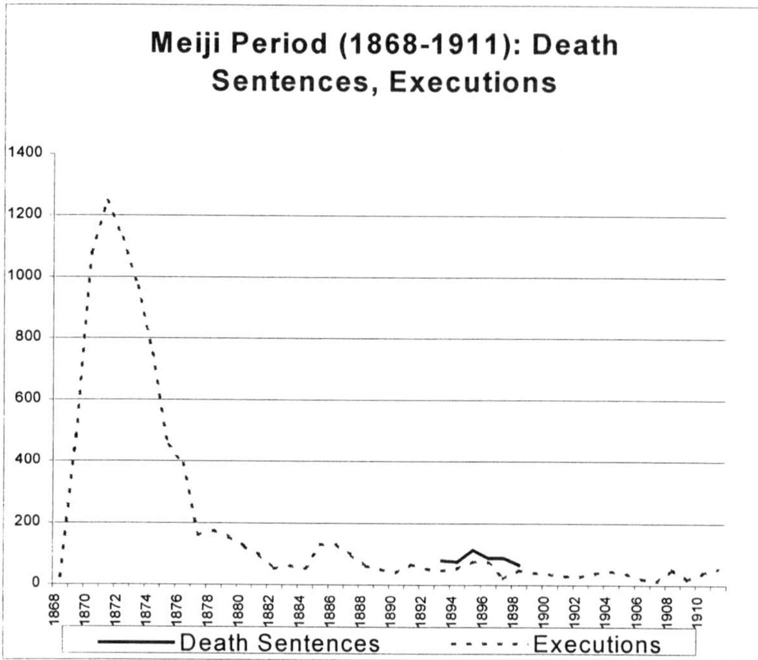

2 Hanzai Hakusho 1993 p. 65; 1997 p. 212. Nationwide Japanese statistics are compiled since 1872. Figures are rather unreliable until about the turn of the century. MURANO part A note 14 p. 53 (Tokyo 1990)) quotes the Genrô-in kaigi hikki, according to which there had been 2,829 death sentences between 1868 and 1871. For the period between 1872 and 1881 he estimates at least 4,400 death sentences. From 1882, figures are more precise. Together with the enforcement of the Old Penal Code on 1 January 1882, statistics on the penal system were introduced. These Kangoku-kyoku nenpô (Yearbooks of the Bureau for the Prison System) in 1899 were replaced by the Gyôkei tôkei nenpô (Statistical Yearbooks of the Penal System). Since 1961, the relevant data are included in the Kyôsei tôkei nenpô (Statistical Yearbooks for the Penal System). For the postwar period, the Hanzai hakusho (Whitebook on Crime) also provides detailed information.
The numbers in the table do not include death sentences and executions handed down or carried out in the Japanese colonies or under special laws.

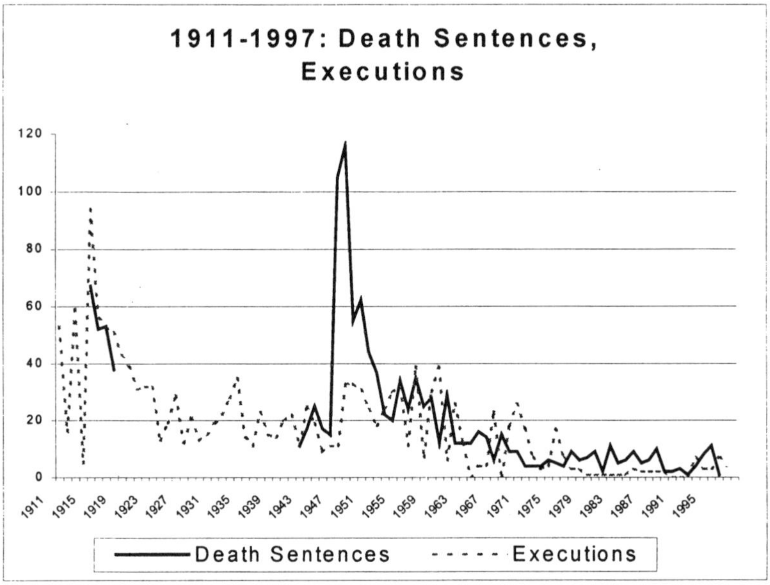

Table B-1: Executions, Five-Year Periods

Years	Exec.	Years	Exec.	Years	Exec.
1868-1872	3,975	**1913-1917**	267	**1958-1962**	108
1873-1877	2,722	**1918-1922**	196	**1963-1967**	68
1878-1882	601	**1923-1927**	105	**1968-1972**	68
1883-1887	471	**1928-1932**	90	**1973-1977**	40
1888-1892	265	**1933-1937**	111	**1978-1982**	7
1893-1897	266	**1938-1942**	82	**1983-1987**	9
1898-1902	178	**1943-1947**	76	**1988-1992**	4
1903-1907	150	**1948-1952**	139	**1993-1997**	22
1908-1912	177	**1953-1957**	136	**1998-2001**	14

Exec.: Executions

Looking at the figures for the various Japanese periods of Imperial reign, during the *Meiji* era (1867-1911), from 1882, a total of 1,529 death sentences were executed, an average of 51 per year. This figure during the *Taishô* Period (1912-1925) fell to 40 executions a year (a total of 558 between 1911 and 1926). In the early phase of the *Shôwa* Period (1926-1945) until the end of the war, 370 persons were executed (an average of 18.5 per year). Since the end of the war until 1997, 616 executions have been carried out, i.e. an average of 12 a year. If one has a closer look at this period, the following are the results: in the third decade of the *Shôwa* Period (1945-1954), every year an average of 24.8 death convicts were executed. In the following decade (1955-1964), the number had already fallen to 17.2. Between 1965 and 1975, the average sank to 11.9, to 4.9 for the decade between 1975 and 1984, and eventually to 2.4 for the period between 1985 and 1994. However, between 1995 and 1997, the number rose again to an average of five.

Accurate figures on death sentences exist only for the postwar period. In the years immediately following the end of the war, an especially strong concentration of death sentences can be seen. This is usually explained by the increase in crime during the turmoils of that period and the resulting rigour of the courts. The following periods, however, saw a decrease in this field, too. However, the annual number of death sentences handed down sank to below 20 only from 1960, and after 1969 below 10.

Since in the first postwar decades especially the number of death sentences often considerably exceeded that of executions, the number of death row convicts waiting in Japanese prisons for their executions increased. Until 1970, this figure regularly lay well above fifty, and in 1968 reached a record high of 82. After a continuous decrease until 1980, their number rose again. Today, a total of more than 50 death row inmates is estimated for Japan.

Table B-2: Number of Death Row Inmates[3]

Year	Number	Year	Number
1950	76	**1975**	41
1955	66	**1980**	26
1960	53	**1985**	26
1965	70	**1990**	46
1970	58	**1995**	54
1975	41	**2001**	54

The number of handed-down but challenged death sentences exceeded that of finalised ones by a wide margin. Japanese prosecutors are dissatisfied with this: between 1975 and 1985, the

3 Hanzai Hakusho 1963 p. 132, 1973 p. 211, 1983 p. 225, 1993 p. 367. KIKUTA KÔICHI, Shikei zonchi to haishi no deai (Meeting pro and con Capital Punishment) 220 (Tokyo 1997)

number of death sentences demanded by the prosecution exceeded that of those actually handed down by two to three times.

Which crimes were punished with death? Current Japanese law provides capital punishment for seventeen different crimes. In practice, however, since 1945 cases of murder and robbery-murder are almost the only crimes avenged with death. Until the mid-1950s, there were also cases of patricide and robbery with rape and murder. Other crimes were punished by death only in exceptional cases. In total, between 1947 and 1983, out of 828 finalised death sentences, 572 (69.2%) were handed down for robbery-murder and 214 (25.8%) for murder, that is, 95% of all death sentences were allotted to murder or robbery causing death.[4]

Although murder and robbery-murder hold the biggest number among all capital crimes, only a small number of all such crimes are punished with death. Between 1983 and 1996, not even 1% of all murderers and robbers who killed were sentenced to death.

Table B-3: Finalised Death Sentences and Number of Murderers and Robber-killers 1983-1996[5]

Year	**FDS**	**Murderers**	**Robber-killers**	**Year**	**FDS**	**Murderers**	**Robber-killers**
1983	1	1,745	65	**1990**	6	1,238	23
1984	3	1,788	68	**1991**	5	1,215	37
1985	2	1,833	64	**1992**	5	1,227	48
1986	0	1,692	72	**1993**	4	1,233	39
1987	8	1,651	65	**1994**	8	1,279	42
1988	11	1,408	39	**1995**	11	1,281	31
1989	5	1,308	41	**1996**	1	1,218	39

FDS: Finalised death sentences

4 Before the war, there had been numerous cases of crimes against the Emperor or the Imperial Family.

5 Hanzai Hakusho 1993 p. 3; MAESAKA part A note 12 p. 92; KIKUTA KÔICHI, *Yaburareta shikei shikkô zero no kiroku – Gotôda Hôsô no shikei shikkô no imi suru mono (The End of Execution Rate Zero – The Meaning of Executions under Minister of Justice Gotôda)*, in 462 Hôgaku seminaa pp. 22, 23 (1993)

Graph B-3: Crimes Punished with Death 1947-1996[6]

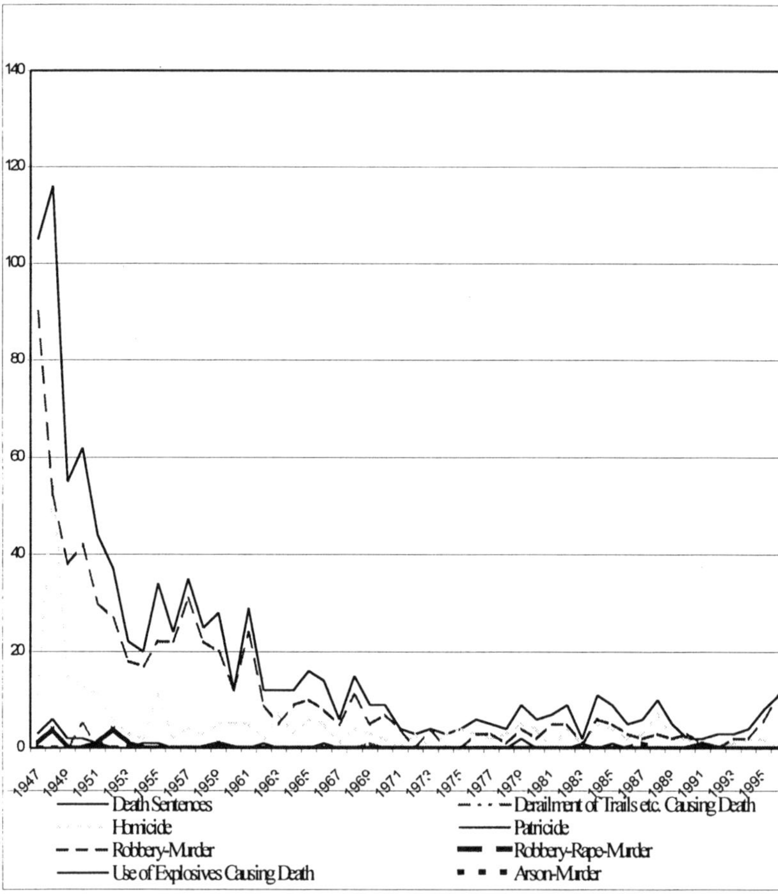

The probability of being sentenced to death is the highest in case of robbery committed in concomitance with murder. Out of 157 such cases between 1954 and 1958, 14.6% ended with a death sentence, 35.7% with penal servitude for life.[7] Before the war, the number of death sentences for robbery-murder was a far higher proportion of all

6 Hanzai Hakusho 1990 pp. 123, 124; 1991 p. 110; 1992 p. 108; 1993 p. 362; 1996 pp. 126, 265; 1997 p. 452; SHIKEI NI KANSURU TÔKEI NARABI NI BENRAN (STB), *Shikei ni kansuru tôkei narabi ni benran* (*On the Preventive Force of Capital Punishment*), in 69-8 KEISEI pp. 77, 78 (1958)

7 0.6% were sentenced to imprisonment for up to 20 years, 22.3% up to 15 years, 15.3 % up to ten years, 7% up to seven years.

death sentences. Between 1932 and 1936, 27.4% of all robbers who killed were sentenced to death, 35.6% to life in prison.[8]

Overall, such crimes form only a small part of all the crimes committed in Japan. The amount of murders after the war regularly lay below 0.2%, that of robbery-murders, below 0.02%.[9]

Table B-4: Share of Homicides and Robberies causing Death of all Crimes[10]

Year	A	H	RM	Year	A	H	RM
1946	1,387,080	1,791	-	**1972**	1,818,072	2,060	-
1947	1,386,020	1,938	-	**1973**	1,728,726	2,048	-
1948	1,603,265	2,495	-	**1974**	1,671,947	1,912	-
1949	1,603,048	2,716	-	**1975**	1,673,727	2,098	-
1950	1,469,662	2,892	-	**1976**	1,691,229	2,111	-
1951	1,399,184	2,865	-	**1977**	1,704,995	2,031	-
1952	1,395,197	2,871	267	**1978**	1,776,801	1,862	-
1953	1,344,482	2,944	-	**1979**	1,738,407	1,853	-
1954	1,360,405	3,081	-	**1980**	1,812,755	1,684	-
1955	1,478,202	3,066	-	**1981**	1,925,796	1,754	-
1956	1,410,441	2,617	227	**1982**	2,005,292	1,764	-
1957	1,426,029	2,524	144	**1983**	2,039,209	1,745	65
1958	1,440,259	2,683	162	**1984**	2,080,323	1,726	61
1959	1,483,258	2,683	189	**1985**	2,121,444	1,780	67
1960	1,495,888	2,648	160	**1986**	2,124,272	1,676	68
1961	1,530,464	2,619	106	**1987**	2,132,617	1,584	61
1962	1,522,480	2,348	-	**1988**	2,207,380	1,441	35
1963	1,557,803	2,283	-	**1989**	2,261,076	1,308	41
1964	1,609,741	2,366	-	**1990**	2,217,559	1,238	23
1965	1,602,430	2,288	-	**1991**	2,284,401	1,215	37
1966	1,590,681	2,198	-	**1992**	2,355,504	1,227	48
1967	1,603,471	2,111	-	**1993**	2,437,252	1,223	39
1968	1,742,479	2,195	-	**1994**	2,426,694	1,279	42
1969	1,848,740	2,098	-	**1995**	2,435,983	1,281	31
1970	1,932,401	1,986	-	**1996**	2,465,503	1,218	39
				1997		1,282	

A: All Crimes; H: Homicides; RM: Robbery-Murders

As with all crime in Japan, the number of cases of homicide and robbery-murder, which are solved, is very high. In 1961, for

8 8.2 % were sentenced to 15 or more years in prison, 15.1% to ten or more years.

9 Hanzai Hakusho 1993 p. 67; 1997 p. 207

10 Hanzai Hakusho 1963 pp. 20-21; 1973 p. 2; 1983 pp. 5-6, 102, 208; 1993 pp. 3, 344-346; 1997 pp. 406, 408

example, 2,565 suspects were arrested in 2,619 cases of murder. This relates to a ratio of 97.6%. In the same year, 1,625 out of 1,873 cases of robbery-murder and robbery in concomitance with rape and murder were solved (88.6%).[11] The success rate in the prosecution of capital crime in Japan has not dropped since. For example, in 1996, a total of 1,218 cases of homicide occurred. The prosecution lodged indictments in 1,197 of these.[12]

In international comparison, Japan generally looks favourable. Japan has fewer crimes, a smaller incidence of violent crime and a higher rate of solution. With violent crime accounting for less than 1.5% of all crimes, Japan is rated one of the 'safest' countries in the world.[13] Although the rate of solution in murder cases is rather high in other countries with regularly around 90%, Japan could produce a figure of 99.1% as of 1982. Even though this figure in recent years has fallen to 90-96%, Japan is still at the top of the class. In absolute figures, in relation to population, too, murder rates in Japan are very low. As compared to the United States with a total population of 260 million, where in 1995 21,500 murders were committed - roughly one homicide per 10,000 people - Japan with its 130 million people had 1,312 homicides – roughly one per 100,000.

11 Hanzai Hakusho 1963 p. 15

12 Hanzai Hakusho 1997 p. 408

13 Japanese courts, as Ramseyer & Nakazato put it, convict 'with a vengeance'. J. MARK RAMSEYER & MINORU NAKAZATO, Japanese Law: An Economic Approach p. 178 (Chicago, London 1999)

Graph B-4: Murder Cases, International Comparison, 1986-1995[14]

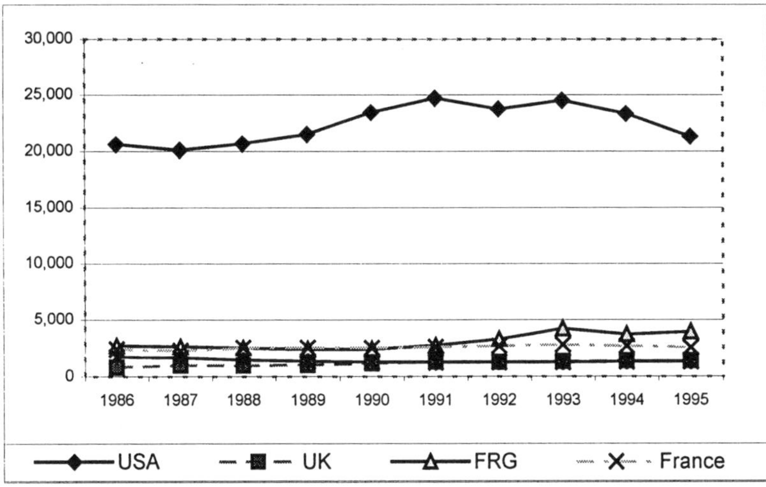

Graph B-5: Share in % of homicides on all crimes, International comparison, 1989-1991[15]

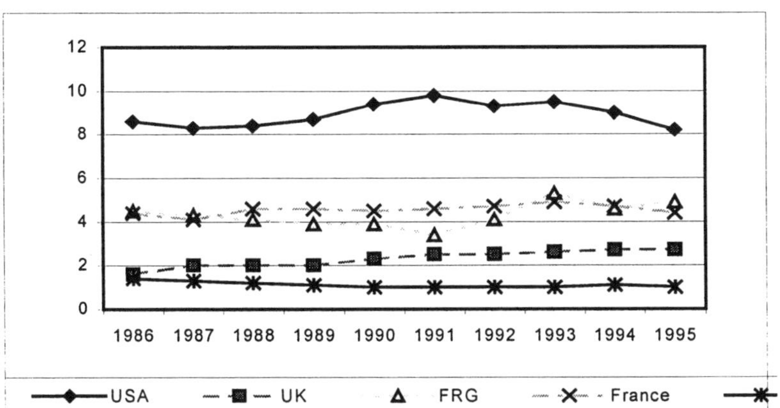

14 Hanzai Hakusho 1993 p. 28; 1997 p. 436; Crime in the United States, Criminal Statistics England and Wales, Polizeiliche Kriminalstatistik, Aspects de la Criminalité et de la délinquance constatées en France

15 Ibid.

Graph B-6: Solution quota (in %), International Comparison, 1989-1991[16]

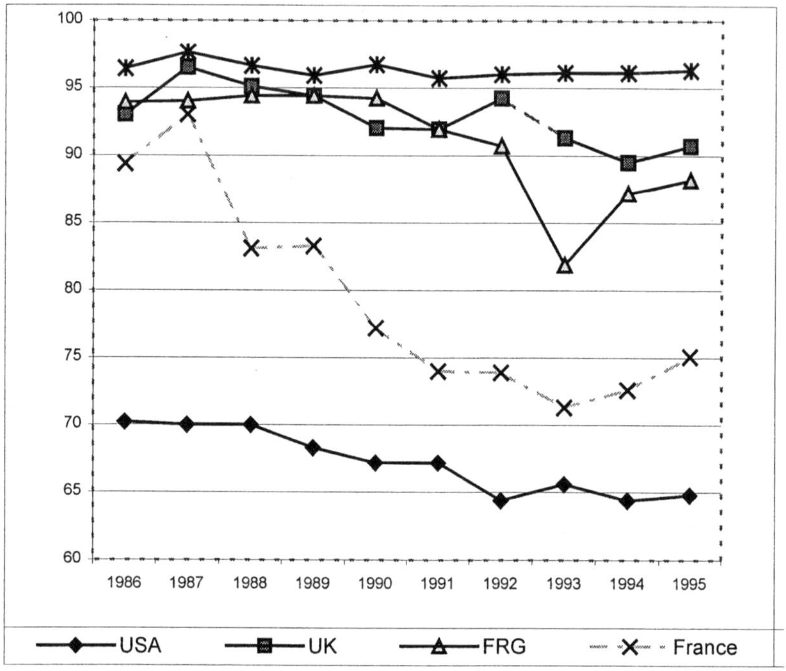

2. *Capital Punishment or Penal Servitude for Life?*

In recent years, only a few death sentences have been handed down and executed in Japan and these exclusively in cases of homicide or robbery-murder. Most of the criminals did not have to atone for their crimes with death. What are the criteria based on which Japanese courts hand down death sentences?

The starting point for the choice of a sentence is the prosecution's demand before the court of original jurisdiction. In case of killing, this choice depends on whether the prosecution defines the crime as homicide, injury causing death or robbery-murder. Even if the law provides for the death penalty for a certain crime, this does not mean

16 Ibid.

that a death sentence will automatically be handed down.[17] Out of the legal range of punishments, the prosecution proposes that sentence which it considers the most appropriate.[18] In cases, where a death sentence can be handed down, the main criteria, based upon which the prosecution chooses and proposes a sentence, are the number of victims and the accused's previous convictions. Motive, obstinacy, cruelty of the method, behaviour after the crime, age, character, background, education of the culprit and feelings of the victim's relatives are difficult to evaluate. Also, the prosecution must take precedents into consideration.[19] This proposal by the prosecution, however, does not bind the court. One of the fundamental elements of Japanese penal law is the judges' discretion, but naturally they are bound to the legal range of sentences and also have the prosecutor's demand in front of them.[20] Still, in the history of modern Japanese penal law, there has not been a single case where a judgment exceeded the prosecution's demand, handing down a death sentence. If, however, the prosecution regards a sentence as too far below its demands, it can appeal for inappropriateness of the sentence.

Where exactly is the line drawn between capital punishment and penal servitude for life, between life and death? Are there rational grounds for this choice? Or is it a matter of fate whether a court hands down a death sentence in one case and a life sentence in another?

If the law provides death as punishment for a certain crime, the court must decide whether it can or must choose this punishment. The Penal Code does not give any criteria for this decision. Neither has the judiciary created any general foundations. Many past decisions take into account motive, how the weapon was obtained, treatment of the corpse, other planning, cruelty of the crime, age and

---

17 A mandatory death sentence is only provided for in Art. 81 Penal Code, for the inducement of external war.

18 E.g. Art. 199 Penal Code provides as punishment for homicide between penal servitude for three years and death. Art. 240 allows the court to choose between imprisonment for life and death in case of robbery causing death.

19 In detail see e.g. KINOSHITA HIROSHI, *Nagayama saikô saiban-ketsu no igi (The Meaning of the Supreme Court Judgment in the Nagayama Case*), in 36-10 Hôritsu no hiroba pp. 12, 15 (1983)

20 MURANO part A note 14 p.67. On the personal difficulties of many judges in dealing with the death penalty, see SCHMIDT, Part A note 29 pp. 583 et seq

previous convictions of the criminal as well as the influence of the crime on the victim's relatives and the public.

As has been stated above, mostly murders and robbery-murders are avenged with capital punishment. Among these precedents, multiple homicides and robbery-murders frequently are found, cases marked by extreme cruelty and cold-bloodedness. Often as additional aggravating elements there were rape, arson, hiding of corpses, access to life insurance payments as motive, cannibalism and so on.[21] Occasionally, death sentences have been handed down in cases of a single murder or robbery-murder, due to the despicability of the motive, for example, to take life to gain property. In cases of single murder, too, rape and killing for the purpose of gaining life insurance payments, are aggravating factors.[22] Moreover, a death sentence is more likely, if the victim is a woman

---

[21] 1. Sapporo High Court 12 September 1952: Quadruple homicide, 18 Kôkei-toku 92
2. Tokyo District Court 20 November 1956: Double robbery-murder, 97 Hanji p. 5
3. Sendai District Court 20 March 1957: Double robbery-murder, 107 Hanji p. 3
4. Tokyo District Court 20 December 1963: Double murder, 5-11 Ge-keishû = 12 p. 1176
5. Urawa District Court 17 July 1972: Murder, abuse of the corpse, cannibalism, 4-7 Keisai geppô p. 1315
6. Maebashi District Court 22 February 1973: Octuple murder, 708 Hanji p. 109
7. Yokohama District Court Osawara Branch 20 October 1975: Murder of a women and three children, 8-1 Keisai geppô 2 p. 454
8. Supreme Court 28 November 1978: Eightfold robbery-murder, 918 Hanji p. 133
9. Supreme Court 27 April 1984: Double murder, 1115 Hanji p. 134
10. Fukuoka High Court 4 September 1986: Murder of a woman and three children to gain life insurance payment, 1131 Hanji p. 27
11. Tokyo High Court 26 September 1986: Red Army Fraction case, 17-fold murder, 1218 Hanji p. 3
12. Tafu District Court 6 July 1967: Double murder, 1249 Hanji p. 132
13. Toyama District Court 9 February 1988: Double murder, 1288 Hanji p. 3
14. Osaka High Court 25 October 1988: Double robbery-murder, 1304 Hanji p. 55
15. Supreme Court 20 November 1989: Triple sword-murder, incl. patricide, 1349 Hanji p. 24

[22] 1. Tokyo District Court 15 December 1956: Robbery-murder, 101 Hanji p. 17
2. Tokyo District Court 27 December 1956: Robbery–murder and robbery -rape, 100 Hanji p. 10
3. Supreme Court 17 July 1987: Robbery-murder, 1248 Hanji p. 138
4. Supreme Court 15 April 1988: Robbery-murder, 667 Hanta P. 103
5. Supreme Court 28 March 1989: Murder for insurance payment, 1344 Hanji p. 23

or a child.[23] Since the Second World War, there have been only few death sentences for crimes other than homicide or robbery-murder. The number further decreased since the mid-1950s and today constitutes an absolute exception.[24]

Art. 51 of the Youth Law states that a criminal who at the time of the crime was 18 years of age or younger, and whose crime under the Penal Code would otherwise be punished by death, instead is to be sentenced to penal servitude for life. This provision must also be taken into consideration in the case of culprits between the age of 18 and 20. The reason for this regulation is the personal immaturity and easy outward influencability of a youth. Also, it is easier to correct youths by punishment.[25] Thus, there have only been few death sentences against youths of 18 or 19 years of age in the past half-century.[26] Although the courts here took into consideration the culprits' youth, due to planning, severity and cruelty of the crime and difficulty of correction and so on, they chose the most severe

---

23 1. Tokyo District Court 24 March 1956: Kyoko-chan-case, 3-6 Kôkei-toku p. 275
2. Niigata District Court 28 February 1966: Kiko-san-case, 8-2 Ge-keishû p. 305
3. Tokyo District Court 17 March 1966: Yoshiya-chan-case, 179 Hanta p. 188
4. Tokyo High Court 9 July 1987: Sayuri-chan-case, 1242 Hanta p. 131

24 1. Supreme Court 22 June 1955: Mitaka-case, derailment of train, causing death, 9-8 Keishû p. 1190
2. Yokohama District Court 20 March 1969: Derailment of train, causing death, one victim, 1-3 Keisai geppô p. 258
3. Supreme Court 24 March 1987: Company bomb series case, two victims, 81 injured, 1228 Hanji p. 22; punished under Arts. 1, 2 Explosives Control Law
4. Sapporo High Court 21 January 1988: Explosives attack, two victims, 95 injured, 1281 Hanji p. 22; Art. 1 Explosives Control Law

25 YOKOMIZO HIDEKI, *Jûyô hanrei gaido – shikei (Important Judicial Decisions – Capital Punishment)*, in Shikei no genzai (Capital Punishment Today) p. 277 (Ibaraki Rieko et.al. eds., Tokyo 1990)

26 1. Sapporo High Court 17 August 1956: Double murder, 85 Hanji p. 27
2. Supreme Court 17 August 1961: Double murder by high school pupil, 15-5 Keishû p. 1244
3. Kumamoto District Court 28 September 1961: Double robbery-murder, 3-9 Ge-keishû = 10 p. 916
4. Nagasaki District Court 16 December 1961: Robbery-murder, 3-11 Ge-keishû = 12 p. 1206
5. Tokyo High Court 12 November 1968: Robbery-murder, 22-1 Kagetsu p. 153
6. Supreme Court 20 December 1977: Murder of a little boy, 876 Hanji p. 127
7. Tokyo District Court 10 July 1979: Nagayama-case
8. Nagoya District Court 28 June 1989: Murder of a couple, 711 Hanta p. 266

punishment.[27] There were also cases where the courts saw death as the only appropriate punishment, but mitigated the penalty into imprisonment for life due to the youth of the culprit (Art. 51 Youth Law).[28]

So there are certain criteria for the death penalty, but in many cases the impression that such a sentence depends solely on 'fate' is forced upon one in the form of different opinions by different judges and thus different verdicts. A death sentence of a court of original jurisdiction can be revoked by the court of appeal, and the Supreme Court once again can quash the second judgment. A life sentence throughout the instances can become one of death. Even a finalised death sentence can be turned into an acquittal in a retrial.

The uncertainty of the foundations of sentences and the differences of the respective views of judges and courts become evident in cases where various courts in the same cases first handed down a sentence of death, then of life in prison. Such 'verdict reversals' (*gyakuten hanketsu*) exemplify the problem of the criteria for sentencing. In several cases where the court of original jurisdiction had sentenced the accused to penal servitude for life, and the court of appeal handed down a death sentence,[29] it is difficult to

---

27 E.g. in case 5. (Tokyo High Court 12 November 1968), a murder of a police officer by an 18-year-old, the court elaborated that the culprit's lack of socialisation could not be corrected, and one must exclude the possibility of a resocialisation. Since furthermore the character of the crime which had been committed in cold blood and cruelly, exceeded the level of a youth, there was no other choice but the death penalty.
Case No. 8 (Nagoya District Court 28 June 1989) was the first death sentence against a youth since the Nagayama decision (10 July 1979). In this case, six youths in sequence had attacked three couples, raped one woman and then strangled her together with her boyfriend. One 19- and one 17-year-old were sentenced to death. The sentence of the latter was mitigated to penal servitude for life, based on Art. 51 Youth Law. The other culprits were sentenced to penal servitude of various terms.

28 Shizuoka District Court 16 May 1969: Robbery–murder of a police officer, committed by a 16 year old, 22-4 Kagetsu p. 119
Chiba District Court Matsudo Branch 9. September 1971: Triple robbery-murder, committed by a 16-year-old, 24-2 Kagetsu p. 174

29 1. Takamatsu High Court 7 June 1951: Robbery-murder by a former police officer, 17 Kôkei-toku p. 19
2. Sapporo High Court 10 April 1953: Robbery-murder of two infants, 32 Kôkei-toku p. 13
3. Tokyo High Court 30 August 1956: Murder of a woman, 7-9 Kôkei-toku p. 358
4. Tokyo High Court 29 January 1969: Double robbery-murder, 20-1 Kôkei-toku p. 12

find the common points of the decisions. Decisive factor for the sentences in all cases were objective facts such as qualified results, commission of the crime, social impact and the aspect of general prevention.[30] In numerous other cases, a death sentence by a court of original jurisdiction was mitigated into a life sentence by a court of appeal.[31]

In the cases adjudged after the 1983 Supreme Court decision in the Nagayama case, the criteria put up by the highest court were applied. In particular, in cases where there was no planning of the crime or accidental elements such as passion or anger, the courts would hand down more lenient sentences. Overall, in contrast to the examples of multiple homicide, subjective points were instead taken into consideration: character and background of the culprit, mental condition at the time of the crime, repentance and so on. While the former judgments often chose the death penalty in light of general prevention, in the latter, emphasis was placed on special prevention,

---

5. Fukuoka High Court 17 March 1983: Homicide, 501 Hanta p. 241
6. Fukuoka High Court 18 October 1985: Triple robbery-murder, 588 Hanta p. 108
7. Takamatsu High Court 28 November 1989: Triple homicide, 721 Hanta p. 237

30 In decision 5. (Fukuoka High Court 17 March 1983), especially the unusual and explosive character of the accused as well as the unlikelihood of correction were decisive for the choice of the death sentence. Also, the crime had been committed only three months after the completion of a prison term for a similar crime, leaving the court no choice.

Despite a favourable background of the accused, in decision 6. (Fukuoka High Court 18 October 1985) due to the cold-bloodedness of the crime, a death sentence was handed down by the Fukuoka District Court.

Decision 7. (Takamatsu High Court 28 November 1989) chose death because of the accused's intelligence, who had carefully planned his crime.

31 1. Nagoya High Court 12 June 1950: Murder of own aunt and two other persons, 11 Kôkei-toku p. 57
2. Tokyo High Court 31 October 1974: Robbery-murder of a girl, 27 Kôkei-shû p. 474; the Supreme Court upheld this decision: 9 August 1977, 352 Hanta p. 138
3. Osaka High Court 25 March 1981: Robbery-murder, 1030 Hanji p. 136; the Supreme Court mitigated the decision of the district court, since a possibility for correction was acknowledged.
4. Osaka High Court 29 September 1982: Robbery-murder of a pensioner, 486 Hanta p. 172; the first two courts came to contradictory decisions on the mental state of the accused at the time of the crime as well as on her repentance and self-criticism
5. Tokyo High Court 20 March 1985: Murder, 1159 Hanji p. 170
6. Fukuoka High Court Naha Branch 1 February 1990: Murder, 1347 Hanji p. 147
7. Tokyo High Court 13 March 1990: Murder of two infants, 1347 Hanji p. 154
8. Takamatsu High Court 22 July 1993: Murder of a girl, injury of four persons by explosion, Japan Times 24 July 1993

that is, the correction of the culprit, which caused the courts to choose penal servitude for life.[32]

Thus, after decades of disagreement over the criteria for sentences, the judgments in the Nagayama case formed a turnabout in the jurisdiction over life and death. In the course of twenty years, seven courts handed down several groundbreaking, almost revolutionary judgments.[33]

Nagayama Fumio was born in June 1949 as the fourth son of the dysfunctional and extremely poor family of an apple farmer. Taking only two of the children with her, the mother in 1954 left the family. The father deserted the remaining children, including Fumio, who had to fend for themselves. Fumio only sporadically attended school, before starting to work as a day labourer in Tokyo from 1965. His first run-in with the law occurred that same year, when he attempted to leave Japan as a stowaway on a foreign ship. During the following two years, he frequently changed jobs and residence, and repeatedly committed petty crimes such as theft or trespassing. He was prosecuted a number of times, but always escaped with probation. His attempts to get accepted into the Self-Defence Forces failed, and he did not complete a middle school course. In late 1967, he sneaked onto the U.S. Yokosuka base, where he stole a pistol, ammunition, and a folding knife.

On the morning of 9 October 1968 he went to Ikebukuro in Tokyo, taking with him the knife and loaded pistol. After amusing himself for a day, he wandered around town and in the evening of 10 October, entered the Prince Hotel through a rear entrance. When

---

32 Other cases:
1. Supreme Court 4 June 1953: Robbery-murder. The court of original jurisdiction sentenced the culprit to 15 years in prison, the court of appeal to death. The Supreme Court revoked he death sentence, 7-6 Keishû p. 1251
2. Supreme Court 15 June 1972: Quintuple homicide. The first instance acquitted the accused, the second and third sentenced him to death, 669 Hanji p. 101
3. Tokyo District Court 26 May 1998, Aum sarin gas attack et.al. The defendant's confession, clear repentance and assistance in the investigation of other accused had the court choose a life prison term instead of the death penalty. Japan Times 27 May 1998 pp. 1, 2
On the application of the 'Nagayama critieria' by the courts, see e.g. IWAI MASAKO, *Shikei no tekiyô kijun (The Foundations of the Application of the Death Penalty)*, in 35-1 KEIHÔ ZASSHI pp. 91, 96 et seq (1995)

33 See Tokyo High Court 10 July 1979, 37-6 Keishû p. 690

spotted and stopped by security guard Nakamura, Nagayama worried that his pistol and thus the first crime would be discovered. From very close range, he shot the guard twice in the face and neck. Nakamura died shortly thereafter.

Fearing arrest, Nagayama travelled to Kyoto. Wandering around town one night, he reached the mountain gate of Yasaka Shrine and resolved to spend the night there. Around 1.35 a.m., he was discovered by guard Katsumi Ryûjirô, who, after a short argument, threatened to call police. Nagayama feared the discovery of his previous crimes and shot the guard four times in face and head. Katsumi died a few hours later.

Distressed about the killings, Nagayama decided to return to his home on Hokkaidô and commit suicide. On 10 October 1968 he asked one of his brothers to help him finance this trip. The brother advised him to deliver himelf to the police, but Nagayama refused. With ¥ 8,000 from the brother, and, with pistol and ammunition in his bag, two weeks later he arrived in Hokkaido. While doing sightseeing in Sapporo, he lost interest in suicide. When a few days later he had run out of money, he decided to shoot and rob a taxi driver. Late at night, with the loaded pistol, he entered a taxi and told driver Saitô Tetsusan, to drive him to the port. After half an hour he had the taxi stop, and suddenly and without warning shot Saitô twice in face and head from the back seat. Nagayama stole ¥ 7,000 in taxi fares and another ¥ 200 from Saitô's purse. Saitô died the following morning.

After returning to Tokyo, Nagayama worked as a port labourer for about one week, before he went to Nagoya. After playing around for some days, he decided to look for work in the harbour. Walking in that direction in the deep of night, a taxi driver offered him a lift. When the driver commented on Nagayama's Tokyo accent, he feared discovery. He had the cab stop, shot the driver four times in the head and stole about ¥ 7,000. Itô died the same morning.

Nagayama returned to Yokohama, buried the pistol and worked in odd jobs. After about five months, he retrieved the pistol. In the deep of night he broke into Hitotsubashi University, Harajuku Ward, searching for valuables, when he was discovered by security guard Nakatani Toshiyoshi. Since Nagayama feared that in case of arrest his former crimes would be discovered, he resolved to shoot the guard. He shot, but missed him.

The Tokyo District Court on 10 July 1979 sentenced Nagayama to death. Aggravating factors were the repetition of the crime, killing without a motive but with the object of stealing money or evading arrest. He furthermore had caused anxiety and fear throughout a wide region of the nation. Nagayama, the court explained, took the irreplaceable lives of four respectable, impeccable and good citizens. The four people killed were not victims of one and the same crime, but within one month four separate crimes were committed. If one included the attempted robbery and murder in Harajuku, there were five crimes.

The two homicides occurred rather accidentally, and were not planned. Nagayama committed the murders out of fear that previous crimes could be discovered. His motive was to evade arrest, and spontaneously he resolved to kill the guards using his pistol. The two robbery-murder cases had the motive, in Hakodate, to obtain money, and in Nagoya, to prevent the discovery of previous crimes and also to obtain money. He shot both taxi drivers with the pistol. In the attempted robbery-murder, he entered the office with the intent of theft, and was discovered by the guard when searching for valuables. To evade arrest, as in the previous crimes, he planned to shoot the guard and flee.

In all cases, a very dangerous weapon had been used. The weapon had been loaded previously, and it thus was prepared and could be shot at any time. In the Hakodate case, the robbery had been premeditated. In the Nagoya case, Nagayama planned the crime after he had boarded the taxi. As in the previous case, he had the taxi drive to an appropriate place and here, too, used the already loaded pistol. In both cases, he shot the defenceless victims from behind and killed them. In all murder and robbery-murder cases he shot the victims several times in head and face from a very close range, causing cruel wounds and applying a very accurate and cruel method of killing. In the final case of the attempted robbery-murder, he also shot from a very close range at the victim, but missed him.

The court took into account Nagayama's tragic childhood. However, when apprehended, and before the court, he showed no self-criticism or repentance. And although later on he donated the revenue of the books authored by him in prison to the bereaved families of the Hakodate case and showed remorse, he placed the cause for the crimes not with himself, but blamed society - which had left him poor and ignorant - capitalism, and the lack of motherly love.

At the time of the crimes, Nagayama was a minor, but not a so-called young minor: at 19 years and three to nine months a young adult. Detention was long, but the reasons for this lay mainly with Nagayama, who repeatedly appointed and dismissed his defence counsel.

Much to the surprise of legal circles and the public, in the appeal trial, the Second Criminal Bench of the Tokyo High Court mitigated the sentence into penal servitude for life. In its reasoning, the court pointed out the uncertainty and variations in the selection of death sentences in past cases, and admonished that with such a severe penalty coincidences must be excluded. Also, a death sentence should only be handed down upon unanimous decision of all judges. The court also had concerns regarding the facts of the case. Although Nagayama at the time of the crime was already 19, and therefore it was legally possible to sentence him to death, the spirit of the Youth Law, which prohibits the death penalty for minors, includes a decision on whether capital punishment should be applied in the case of a youth between the age of 19 and 20. Bearing in mind the poverty and instability of Nagayama's early life, as well as the fact that the social welfare net failed to catch him, he should be considered as a minor. Moreover, the court in sentencing took into consideration the improvement in Nagayama's behaviour since apprehension, the fact that he got married to a pen friend in 1980, and that he wrote and published books of poetry and prose, the revenues of which he donated to the families of his victims. For these reasons, the court chose a life sentence.

After the prosecution filed for appeal on grounds of inappropriateness of the sentence, the Japanese Supreme Court quashed the judgment of the Tokyo High Court,[34] pointing out the constitutionality of the death penalty and the absence of an alternative sentence in cases of extremely severe guilt. The despicable motives and brutal methods of Nagayama's crimes, the court said, left no choice but the death penalty, despite the

---

34 506 Hanta p. 73

favourable development of Nagayama after his apprehension. An application of the Youth Law was ruled out.[35]

---

35 In this trial, Nagayama appointed several counsellors. Renewed investigations were conducted in December 1984. In January 1986, Nagayama's attorneys demanded a psychological examination, claiming that the accused suffered from mental disturbances and hallucinations. This caused quarrels between Nagayama and his counsel. Nagayama withdrew the mandate of the main counsellor, the others quit. In July 1986 the court appointed counsel, and investigations were continued. Mrs. I, whom Nagayama married in prison, divorced him during this trial.
From the judgment (634 Hanta p. 105):
'... the four homicides and robbery-murders with a pistol occurred within less than one month in Tokyo, Kyoto, Hakodate and Nagoya. In this wide area, four patrolling guards and taxi drivers on duty one after the other were shot in cold blood. Fortunately the victim in the attempted robbery-murder five months later, was not killed; but this, too, was a crime, which through the use of a pistol caused serious danger [for the life of the guard]. The circumstances of all crimes were extremely brutal, and the repetition of the crimes, motive, number of victims, the severity of the damage and the general fear caused by the cases, had great influence on Japanese society. Under consideration of all these points, one must call it a very grave case, and the severity of the guilt of the accused, who had taken the life of four innocent citizens, cannot be measured.'
Minority opinion:
'It must be considered that the accused was a minor at the time of the crimes. The negative influence during the growth period of the accused prevented his healthy upbringing. His mental maturity therefore was very low, and some hold that he can be viewed like a youth of under 19 years of age. In the surrounding of the accused in his childhood, there are pitiable points, and as an infant, the accused had to suffer great hardships. All these problems in his life influenced the formation of his character. Therefore the appeal court decided to regard him like a youth of under 19 and consider this in the sentence.
Also, the crimes of the accused resulted from the special circumstances of the growth period. Initially, correction was not to be expected, but the accused [in prison] showed a strong will to learn. It furthermore must be considered that in prison he demonstrated various activities, such as the publication of his own literary products.
Furthermore, the accused had given the whole revenue of his books [to the bereaved families of his victims] or at least had offered to do so, thus showing the will to comfort the bereaved families. Before court, too, he showed repentance for having killed persons from his own social class ...
He married in prison, but this marriage later was divorced. In the appeal trial the accused was in an abnormal condition, disturbed with words and actions the proceedings of the trial, and violated the authority of the court. After the judgment of the appeal court, his condition improved ...
From the childhood of the accused until the crimes and the situation after the judgment of the appeals court, all circumstances have been thoroughly examined. In

In this judgment, the Supreme Court set up as criteria for choosing the death penalty the overall evaluation of nature, method and circumstances of the crime, cruelty, severity of the result, number of victims, previous convictions, and behaviour after the crime.

The court failed to clearly demonstrate where the line is drawn between a death sentence and one of imprisonment for life. Is it destiny whether an accused is sent to the gallows or his life is spared? Probably the best example of this 'fate' is the Nagayama case: after a death sentence before the court of original jurisdiction, imprisonment for life in the first appeal, the judgment being quashed by the Supreme Court and referred back for retrial, and another death sentence finally confirmed by the Supreme Court, Nagayama's fate was subjected to a constant change between life imprisonment and the threat of death.

Both the first High Court and Supreme Court decisions were met with criticism from Japan's legal scholars. The former was dismissed as a de facto abolition of the death penalty, since its stipulation that a death sentence be handed down only in a case where every court would do the same is practically impossible to achieve.[36] On the other hand, the Supreme Court's 'clear criteria' for sentencing remain extremely ambiguous in their concrete application. A case in which, also from the view of general prevention, the death penalty can be regarded as unavoidable is equally difficult to determine, as is unanimity of all Japanese judges. Similarly, all other enumerated criteria are of a highly subjective nature, and the difficulties of 'general deterrence' have already been demonstrated.[37]

In practice, 'planning', 'motive/circumstances' and 'comparison with similar cases' continue to be difficult to assess, despite the

light of the forementioned criminal demerit of the crimes, the circumstances, severity etc., the appeals court chose penal servitude for life. This is inappropriate.' The High Court on 18 March 1987 sentenced Nagayama to death. The judgement was upheld by the Supreme Court on 17 April 1990. The sentence was finalised and Nagayama was executed on 2 August 1997.

36 See e.g. KIKUTA KÔICHI, Shikei (Capital Punishment) p. 209 (Tokyo 1988), NATSUME FUMIO, *Renzoku pisutoru shasatsu ma jiken jôkoku-shin hanketsu (Judgment of the Court in the Second Appeal Trial in the Serial Pistol Murder Case*), in 1114 Hanrei jihô pp. 204, 206 (1984)

37 See e.g. Suzuki Shinji, quoted in KIKUTA note 36 p. 210

Supreme Court's guidelines. The difficulties of evaluating 'planning' can, for example, be demonstrated with the following example:[38]

The accused Y had lost all his possessions in horse race gambling, and resolved to commit a robbery. On 11 September 1951, he intruded into the home of 54-year-old housewife M. When he threatened her with a kitchen knife, demanding money, she pretended to give in. He let her go and put the knife on the floor. M grabbed the knife and yelled for help. To avoid discovery and arrest, Y resolved to kill M, dragged her into a corner and stabbed her twice in the neck. M bled to death. Y stole 121 Yen 50 Sen in cash from the purse of the deceased.

The court of original jurisdiction viewed the crime as not planned and without murderous intent. Rather, the woman's cries for help and the fear of discovery and arrest had caused a sudden and incidental resolve to kill. Y was sentenced to 15 years in prison.

The court of appeal handed down a death sentence: 'There are no understandable points in the motive, the crime was carried out upon planning. Further, the way in which the victim M was killed, was extremely brutal.'

Y's counsel applied for a second appeal: 'On the morning in question, Y opened the door to the victim's home, which he had just happened to pass. The crime at this place was an instantaneous, impulsive act, and initially there was no resolution to kill.'

On 4 June 1953, the Supreme Court, First Petty Bench, ruled: The homicide was not planned. Rather, the accused could not prevent it, since the victim with a loud voice called for help.' The court quashed the judgment of the appeal court and handed down a prison term for life.

One of the other criteria for choosing a sentence, that is, motive or circumstances, has similarly proven to be of a very subjective nature:

In the case described above, the court of original jurisdiction had found that the accused had been in a mentally disturbed condition for several days prior to the crime, culminating in an abnormal condition on the day of the crime. The appeal court, however, elaborated: '[The crime] resulted from the fact that the family [of the accused] lived in debt and poverty, that he had lost his work ...' The Supreme

38 In detail see KIKUTA note 36 pp. 214-215

Court, on the other hand, took up the elaborations of the district court about the abnormal mental condition of the accused.

The appeal court in addition had taken into consideration that prior to the crime the accused had wasted the revenue from the sale of the family home and without her permission had sold his wife's car; the court evaluated these points as aggravating. However, the court of original jurisdiction had acknowledged it as favourable for Y that at the time of the crime he had held a steady job. Regarding other circumstances, the appeal court found there were no mitigating circumstances, and the Supreme Court elaborated: 'Except that he gambled at horse races, he conscientiously did his work, and he repented his crime.'

The comparison with other cases, as suggested by the Supreme Court in the Nagayama case, is even more difficult.[39]

In the so-called Yasukuni-chan case, the accused Kajiwara in summer 1980 in Yamanashi Prefecture kidnapped five-year-old Ôkatsu Tsukasa and demanded from the parents ¥ 10 million in ransom. Two days later, he strangled the child and buried the corpse in a forest. The Kôfu District Court sentenced him to death. Three years later, in March 1985, the Tokyo High Court quashed this judgment and sentenced Kajiwara to life in prison, since 'the court of original jurisdiction ... neglected details.' The judgment was finalised.

While Kajima had just escaped death, the investigations in another kidnapping-murder case, the so-called Tsukasa-chan case made progress within the Hiroshima District Court Fukuyama Branch.

47 year old Tsuda Akira was accused to have kidnapped the nine-year-old son of the mayor of Fukuyama in February 1984. When the boy started to cry, Tsuda strangled him with a necktie. After hiding the corpse in a forest, he called the mayor and demanded a credit card as well as ¥ 150,000 in cash.

Although the court of original jurisdiction found: 'One can see repentance ... Killing was not planned ... The accused had no previous convictions', it chose the death penalty.

---

39 Cases cited in *Shikei to muki no wakareme wa...* (The Difference between the Death Penalty and Imprisonment for Life), in Asahi Shinbun (evening edition) 16 February 1987:

Two similar cases, two very different sentences. Kajiwara's motive, 'failure at work', had been regarded more favourable by the court than Tsuda's heavy gambling debts. On the other hand, Tsuda's crime had not been planned as carefully as Kajiwara's. However, even after having killed the child, Tsuda in cold blood demanded ransom from the family. The families of both victims demanded the death of the culprits. It remains unclear what exactly led to the different decisions.

There are a great number of cases where similar concerns have arisen. The courts continue to struggle with the criteria to be applied in sentencing violent crime. Legal scholars in Japan, such as Maesaka Toshiyuki[40] or Maeda Toshiro,[41] have so far produced a number of proposals for a standardisation of sentencing. None of these drafts, however, is convincing.

3. *The Execution*

Once a death sentence has been handed down and finalised, the next and final step is the execution of the sentence. Naturally, the convict is not led directly from the courtroom to the gallows; rather, several complicated procedures are necessary before a death sentence can be executed. By law, it is the task of the justice minister to give the signal for an execution by his signature and seal. What happens between the judgment and the minister's execution order?

Capital sentences handed down by a court of original jurisdiction or court of first appeal are in most cases appealed by the accused. If the Supreme Court turns down the second appeal, after a lapse of ten days, the judgment is finalised. The prosecution drafts an execution report, which is submitted to the Ministry of Justice and thereafter sent to the Department of Criminal Affairs (*Keiji-kyoku*), which is in charge of the execution of punishment. After the examination to ensure the completeness of the documents by the office of the Department of Criminal Affairs, an official is assigned to study the contents. When this task is completed, the official delivers the documents to the office of the Minister of Justice. There, the

40 MAESAKA part A note 12 pp. 34 et seq

41 MAEDA TOSHIRÔ, *Shikei tekiyô no senrei-teki kijun (Precedences on the Application of Capital Punishment*), in 23-10 Hôritsu no hiroba pp. 35 et seq (197)

documents are examined for several days to determine whether there are reasons for a stay of execution, retrial or pardon which had been overlooked in the trial. If no reasons for a stay of execution, retrial or pardon are found, an 'execution preparation document' (*Shikei shikkô kian-sho*) is drafted. The *Kian-sho* is submitted, in this order, to the Department for Criminal Affairs within the Ministry of Justice, the Department for Rehabilitation, and the Department for Parole for further examination.

Once all departments have agreed, the order is returned to the Department of Criminal Affairs, and finally forwarded to the Justice Minister's office. After a final examination, the convict's life now depends on the minister's signature. Once the Minister of Justice has signed, and a renewed examination of the physical and mental condition has been completed, an execution order (*Shikei shikkô meirei-sho*) is drafted and signed by the minister. The order is immediately forwarded to the prosecution, which now drafts the final order (*Shikei shikkô shiki-sho*). Once all formalities have been completed, the order is forwarded to the prison, where the execution is carried out.[42]

How is the timing of an execution decided? In Art. 475.2, the Code of Criminal Procedure provides that an execution order shall be issued within six months from the finalisation of the sentence. Also there is the custom to halt this period until the completion of a procedure of request for retrial, pardon, or until the finalisation of a judgment against an accomplice. Strictly legally speaking, however, an execution is possible while a request for pardon or retrial is pending, if the physical and mental condition of the convict permits it. A stay of execution is granted only after a decision to reopen a case or after pardon has been granted.[43]

---

42 SATÔ SHÛZÔ, HÔMU, Kensatsu ura no ura (Behind the Scenes of the Justice Ministry and the Prosecution) pp. 51-53 (Tokyo 1983); MURANO part A note 14 pp. 95-96. On the wardens' duty to execute, see e.g. SHIMIZU HANZÔ, *Shikei shikkô o kyôsei sareru keimu-kan (Wardens Who are Forced to Exectue the Death Penalty)*, in Shikei no gendai (Capital Punishment Today) pp. 122, 125 et seq (Ibaraki Rieko et.al. eds., Tokyo 1990)

43 Since almost all convicts on death row repeatedly request pardon or retrial, there virtually never is an execution within the prescribed period. Furthermore, the extensive examinations often cannot be completed within six months.
When looking at the figures of executions since the war, it is striking that between 1957 and 1961, the average period between the finalisation of a death sentence and the execution was two years and ten months, in 39 cases it was more than three and-

How are the individual convicts for execution determined? As will be explained in further detail below, from about the mid-1950s there have allegedly been efforts within the Ministry of Justice to reduce the number of inmates on death row to a limit of sixty. However, due to numerous death sentences, the number of death row convicts in Japanese prisons quickly rose, in turn leading to more executions. Besides, it allegedly was the attitude of the ministry to execute a certain number of convicts every year. In practice, there is the custom not to execute on *o-bon*, the Buddhist festival for the dead, and during the New Year holidays. Dangerous times for the convicts are dissolutions of parliament, cabinet reshuffles and other occasions, which cause a change in the position of the Minister of Justice.[44]

How is it decided which of several convicts is executed? The first criterion seems to be the number of days in prison. If several convicts fulfil the same objective requirements, then usually the one with an earlier finalisation date will be preferred.[45] Another issue is 'mental stability'. In this context it is of interest to study why after a moratorium of three years, in 1993, the convicts Kawanaka, Tachikawa, Kondô, Deguchi, Sakaguchi, Seki and Kojima were executed. For Kawanaka, Tachikawa and Kondô, all executed on 26 March 1993, it seems to be impossible to find objective reasons. All three had been without outside support, were isolated. The number three was explained at the time by opponents of the death penalty with the fact that there had been no executions in the previous three years, in this way keeping the previous average of one execution per year.[46] However, this contains the problem that, assuming that there had been 55 convicts on death row in mid-1993, it would take 55 years to 'clean out' the prisons, if no further death sentences were finalised. Since the life span of the individual is uncertain and no objective criteria for selection are discernible, the selection and earlier execution of a single convict would violate the principle of

---

a-half years. This tendency to postpone executions becomes more evident in recent years, where there has been a quantitative decrease of death sentences and executions. Between 1982 and 1989, for example, there were 13 executions. The average period between finalisation and execution was seven years and seven months, with the minimum period being six years and four months.

44 See e.g. MURANO part A note 14 p. 96

45 SATÔ note 42 p. 73; MURANO part A note 14 p. 106

46 Interpretation by KIKUTA note 6 p. 23

equality before the law. Already it has been shown that the criteria for sentencing are unclear, and often it appears that nothing but fate or an unlucky constellation are reasons for being sentenced to death. It seems that mere 'coincidence' or 'bad luck' determines the timing of an execution.[47]

4. *The Government*

The Government rarely expresses its position on the issue. Death sentences are not commented on, neither are executions, which are carried out under a veil of secrecy. The Ministry of Justice refuses to provide any information on the matter, other than – only since November 1998 – announcing that a certain number of executions have taken place on a certain date. Hardly a Justice Minister so far has spoken about his view on capital punishment.

One of the few forums, where the Japanese Government could not avoid making a statement, is the United Nations. Before the sixth UN General Assembly in 1980 on the prevention of crime and the treatment of criminals, the Japanese representative declared:[48]

> There is wide agreement within the Japanese population that the safe and secure environment we live in is mostly based on the deterrent effect of capital punishment and not only on the effective execution of political and economic measures for social justice as well as an effective and flawless legal system.

In November 1982, the Japanese representative before the third committee of the UN General Assembly stated: 'The majority of the Japanese people support the retention of the death penalty for criminals who have committed especially abominable crimes, and approve of it as an effective deterrent against such criminals.'[49]

In 1979, Japan ratified the International Covenant on Civil and Political Rights. In 1991, the UN General Assembly adopted the Second Optional Protocol to the International Covenant on Civil and Political Rights Aiming at the Abolition of the Death Penalty, which

---

47 JUDY WAKABAYASHI (*The Death Penalty in Japan*, in 6-2 Japan Forum pp. 189, 199 (1994)) suggests that the direct trigger for the March 1993 executions may have been the Justice Ministry's attempt to divert public attention from the Ministry's heavily criticised position in the Kanemaru affair.

48 AMNESTY INTERNATIONAL part A note 21 p.18

49 A.I. note 48 p. 18

provides: 'No one within the jurisdiction of a State party to the present Optional Protocol shall be executed. Each State party shall take all necessary measures to abolish the death penalty within its jurisdiction.' Only two industrialised nations voted against it: the USA and Japan.

Why did Japan oppose? In the Diet, the following reasons were presented:

(1) The problem of the abolition of capital punishment by a state has to be examined in light of popular sentiment and the crime situation.
(2) International public opinion on the abolition of capital punishment is not necessarily always unanimous.
(3) The Convention had not been discussed sufficiently in the UNHRC.

Japan thus clearly expressed that an abolition of the death penalty is not planned, outside interference not desired and comparison with 'international trends' and 'international public opinion' not regarded as expedient.

5. *The Justice Minister*

The final signature on the execution order and thus the last decision on the fate of a death row convict lie in the hands of the minister of justice. Such an order by the minister himself is provided for only in the case of capital punishment. It concludes the judgments and examinations by the judiciary and administration and in this way represents the threefold partition of the powers. This duty of the minister has become a core issue in the debate of the death penalty.[50] Among Japan's postwar justice ministers there were both proponents and opponents of the death penalty and varying ways to deal with the issue.

---

50 Unsurprisingly, the proponents of capital punishment insist that it is the minister's duty to sign execution orders, while the opponents of this punishment believe he should refuse to do so. E.g. JOSÉ LLOMPART, Keihô no shichi fushigi (The Seven Mysteries of Criminal Law) p. 247 (Tokyo 1987): 'The execution [of capital punishment] is a right of the state, but not a duty.' However, SATÔ (note 42 pp. 68-69) holds, independent from the personal conviction of a minister, the signing of an execution order is his duty. To neglect this duty for personal emotions is disregard for official duties. In such case the minister would have to resign.

After the executions of March 1993, then Justice Minister Gotôda Masaharu declared that he would respect the law: if a justice minister does not sign an execution order for personal convictions, although the death penalty is provided for by law and death sentences are handed down, the order of the state cannot be protected and the foundations of the state's legal order will be shattered. After all, a justice minister is merely the top of a bureaucratic organisation. If his underlings submit a document, including an execution order, he has the duty to sign.[51]

Not all previous ministers fulfilled their duty easily, however some even refused to sign. For whether a minister signs or not can depend on his character and personal attitude. Three groups of justice ministers can be distinguished so far, according to their attitude towards signing execution orders: the hawks, the doves and the in-betweens.

The Doves

Over the past half-century, many of Japan's justice ministers proved to be reluctant to sign execution orders. Some publicly declared to never sign, others, as can be concluded from the statistics, did not sign for unknown reasons.

During the period of office of Akama Bunzô, minister of justice from November 1967 until November 1968, no death sentences were executed. It is reported that the minister, when for the first time confronted by his administrative vice minister with an execution order and the request to sign it, acted almost hysterically, and categorically refused to sign at all during his term of office.[52]

---

51 Asahi Evening News 28 November 1993. In general on this issue in the 1993 context see also FUKUDA MASAAKI, *Hômu daijin ni shikei shikkô no gimu wa aru ka* (*Does the Justice Minister have the Duty to Executive Death Sentences?*), in 35-1 Keihô zasshi p. 112 (1995); FUKUDA MASAAKI, Shikei shikkô: hômu daijin no gimu ka? (Execution of Death Sentences: The Justice Minister's Duty?) (Tokyo 1994)

52 Allegedly, when presented with an execution order for the first time, Akama said: 'What? Show this to me' - saw that it was an execution order, jumped up from his chair and yelled at the vice minister: 'You idiot! I won't do something like that!' The vice minister calmly explained: 'Mr. Minister, since executions lately have stagnated, you definitely must sign.' Akama: 'What have the other justice ministers done?' Reply: 'They all have signed. One apparently 23 times.' Akama: 'I don't care, what the others do, but I won't do this.' – 'You must!' – 'If I do this, I will be

The issue of the minister's official duty became clear in the period between November 1989 and March 1993, where no death sentences were executed in Japan. The reasons for this, among others, included the refusal of former Justice Minister Satô Megumu, a Buddhist priest, to sign execution orders.[53] Satô was one of the few LDP members of the 'Forum 90, Demanding the Ratification of the International Convention on the Abolition of Capital Punishment' (*Shikei haishi kokusai jôyaku no hijun o motomeru fooramu 90*; Forum 90).[54] In a note to the second Forum 90 symposium he declared that as head priest of a Jôdô Shinjû sect temple he had refused to sign execution orders, for as a religious person he felt that human life is of greatest importance.[55] Dandô Shigemitsu believes that Satô's statement was not the real reason for his refusal, but that he had merely attempted to express his attitude in simple words. His real opinion was rather that Satô in expectation of a ratification of the aforementioned Second Optional Protocol to the ICCPR had viewed further executions as unjust.[56]

---

the next one to get caught.' The vice minister had to quit the minister's office without having achieved anything. Ten days later, he is said to have tried his luck again, but still Akama was not willing to sign. The minister's attitude remained unchanged three weeks later: 'No matter how often you come, it is decided. I won't do something like that. or 'Mr. Vice Minister, do not enter my office again!' Akama's rejection, even fear of signing an execution order, allegedly went so far that even if the vice minister entered his office in a different matter, he seemed to be wanting to escape. (SATÔ note 42 pp. 66-68) Another, who also did not sign, plagued by the same doubts as Akama, reports: 'I have not signed for the following two reasons: firstly I hesitated to do what so many ministers before me have not done, and secondly for the practical reason that my employees never brought me such documents. During my period in office, death row convicts Menda and Taniguchi were acquitted in retrials, and public opinion had doubts about the death penalty. If I had requested Hirasawa's files for signing, I would have made the headlines the next day.' see AMNESTY INTERNATIONAL, Japan. Debating Abolition of the Death Penalty (London 1992) a.i. document ASA 22/04/92

53 CAROL HUI, *An Amoeba Called Japanese Justice*, in 33-15 Japan Times Weekly p. 7 (1993)

54 JAPAN TIMES 29 March 1993. The Forum 90 has over 5,000 members, including some 200 lawmakers and well over 500 lawyers.

55 AMNESTY INTERNATIONAL, Japan. Death Penalty p. 2 (London 1992) a.i. document ASA 22/01/92; A.I. note 52 p. 1

56 DANDÔ Part A note 13 p. 49

The Hawks

Others had no personal scruples. Many postwar Japanese justice ministers proved to be 'hawks', freely signing all execution orders presented to them by their ministry.

Kobayashi was a man who had heads roll like no other Japanese justice minister after the war. When he was submitted an execution order for the first time, he allegedly was deeply shocked and offended by the brutal details of the crime. During his term of office in 1970, there were 26 executions.[57]

The Relecutantly Dutiful

Most ministers so far have attempted to separate their personal views and emotions from their office duties, signing the execution orders submitted to them, because the law provides it. Even within this group of ministers there are differences in the reasons causing the respective minister to sign. While one fought an inner struggle every time, another was convinced about the correctness of his behaviour.

So far the best example for the latter type was Justice Minister Inukai (October 1952 - April 1954). Inukai, repeatedly praised by the media for his humane convictions, and about whom it even had been reported that he never had signed a single execution order, in fact ordered at least 24 executions.[58]

Former Justice Minister Tanaka Isôji (December 1966 – November 1967; December 1972- November 1973) believed that the minister has the duty to sign execution orders, as long as the law provides for it. A view, which made him some kind of 'Super-Kobayashi',[59] when, in October 1967, he called an informal press

57 He reinforced his intention to sign a lot a few weeks later, when he happened to meet the head of the Department at a function: 'I have run out of [execution orders]. Bring it to me when another one is ready.'

58 In 1953, where there had been no change in the office of justice minister, 24 convicts were executed. 24 execution orders which no one but Inukai could have signed. For the periods between 30 October and 31 December 1952 and between 1 January and 22 April 1954, it is not possible to give information about orders signed by Inukai, for the statistics merely give total figures for one calendar year and the executions of 1952 and 1954 could have been ordered by Inukai's predecessor and successor.

59 SATÔ note 42 p. 74

conference to announce the completed signing of 23 execution orders.[60] Tanaka, too, made it clear that he saw this as his duty. However, he made no secret of his loathing for the convicts and the sympathy he felt for the victims, for whom he prayed.[61]

While Tanaka apparently had no scruples against fulfilling his official duties, but rather had been convinced of the correctness and necessity of executions, other ministers did not sign devoid of doubts, and often were even plagued by pangs of conscience. Katô Kanagorô[62] (April 1954 – June 1954) for example, likened his emotions at the time to those of doctor who knows that he cannot help his patient, but will give injections until the very last moment.[63]

Justifying his actions as 'for the good of the convict', former Justice Minister Oshima Tetsuzô[64] (July – December 1960) stressed that signing executions orders can not be a joyful act for anyone. Nevertheless, it is the minister's duty.[65]

While Katô and Oshima practiced a strict separation of their official duties and personal feelings, or at least ostensibly did so, Karasawa Toshiki[66] (July 1957- June 1958) confessed that this duty threw him into an emotional conflict for the fear that he might be confronted with the signing of execution orders. He signed, but afterwards sought comfort in prayer.[67]

---

60 The opinions of the reporters on how to deal with this were divided in 'We must ignore this' and 'This has to be published.' Most, including Satô, believed that it would only stir up unrest if we write this; the people would think that the minister had lost control.' Only one reporter from the Sankei newspaper held: 'We must write about this to prevent it in future'. Only the Sankei wrote about it. SATÔ note 42 p. 75

61 MURANO part A note 14 p. 107. Tanaka's 'great interest' in the death penalty was also shown upon a different occassion. Two days before the described above announcement of 23 execution orders, Tanaka proposed during a press conference that he himself and the reporters should witness an execution. The reporters thought that Tanaka spoke nonsense. The minister, however, contacted the Department of Criminal Affairs, but department head Itô Eisaku rejected the minister's request. However, he and the reporters were allowed to visit the then newly built execution site in Tokyo prison. SATÔ note 42 p. 76

62 Number of executions unclear

63 Sandee mainichi 16 December 1962

64 Five executions

65 Sandee mainichi 16 December 1962

66 10 executions

67 MURANO part A note 14 p. 107; Sandee mainichi 16 December 1962

Also not free of doubts was Ueki Kanerô[68] (December 1960 – July 1963; February– July 1971), who admittedly struggled with the anger felt over the crime and doubts whether, for example, a confession had been obtained properly.[69]

As can be seen from these few examples, the majority of Japan's postwar justice ministers regarded it as their duty to sign execution orders, uninfluenced by private emotions or convictions. There have hardly been any, however, who did not have any scruples.

The Detached and Dutiful

When executions were resumed in 1993, the Japanese media rediscovered the issue of capital punishment and the opponents of this penalty vehemently protested, causing Gotôda and his successor Mikazuki to publicly justify their acts. Three days after the executions of 26 March, Gotôda stated that

> it is obvious and natural that the government executes convicts sentenced to death, to keep law and order in society. Also, the time for abolition has not come yet in Japan. If a justice minister does not execute the judgments of the courts, this undermines the law and the foundations of the state.

Gotôda also said that the executive would not fulfil its duties under the principle of separation of powers, if it neglects the execution of judicial decisions. 'Under the current provisions, judges hand down death sentences, and it is wrong if a justice minister does not execute these judgments for political considerations.' Gotôda furthermore stated that his predecessors should not have assumed their posts as justice minister if they felt unable to agree to executions for personal beliefs. 'If they were not aware of their responsibility, they should

---

68 17 executions or number unknown

69 Sandee mainichi 16 December 1962. Ueki's approach seems to have been not to sign in case of doubt. According to some reports, the mother of death row convict Saitô Sachio had heard rumours about the imminent execution of her son. She went to Tokyo to meet Ueki: 'My son is innocent. Don't execute him. Leave me my child!' Allegedly the minister was impressed by the mother's energy and promised her not to execute Sachio during his term of office. Whether Ueki had really been generous cannot be confirmed, since it is not known how far the preparatory proceedings in Saitô's case had progressed at the time or whether there had anyway been no danger of execution for a pending retrial request. Saitô was found not guilty in the retrial of his case. KIKUTA note 6 p. 24

have resigned once they had learned about it.'[70] He added that the people could freely discuss the subject of an abolition of capital punishment, since this is a different question than that of the execution of existing laws.[71]

Gotôda, promoted out of office in mid-1993, was called 'razor blade' for signing three execution orders. Had he not, however, merely fulfilled his official duties, while his predecessor Satô failed to do so by not signing? Even if Gotôda was criticised by the opponents of capital punishment for having executed three convicts at a time, to state a political example, is it not really Satô who ignored the Japanese laws and made decisions based only on his personal convictions?[72]

Eight months after the executions under Gotôda, on 26 November 1993, four convicts were executed in one day, ordered by Mikazuki Akira, the justice minister of Prime Minister Hosokawa's anti-LDP coalition government. Prior to his appointment, Mikazuki had been an attorney and law professor. This 'handicap' may have contributed to especially careful decisions. Mikazuki clarified his attitude already upon assumption of office in August 1993, when he

---

70 Asahi Evening News 28 November 1993; Nikhon Keizai Shinbun 27 November 1993

71 Japan Times 30 March 1993. That the signing of execution orders is not regarded by everyone as a duty of the justice minister is shown in reports, according to which there were movements to prevent the execution of Kawanaka on 26 March 1993. Shiga Setsu, an LDP representative who advocates the abolition of capital punishment and who knew about the plans by Kawanaka-attorney Nakamichi, reported to Gotôda that there were movements to sue the Justice Minister in case of the execution of Kawanaka. Gotôda's reaction was simple: 'Whether they sue me or not, is only their problem.' Shiga also remembers Gotôda's criticism: 'Why do jurists say that it is okay not to execute a finalised judgment? I cannot understand this.' On the afternoon of the 29th, Gotôda stated before the Diet: 'Theory and practical tasks of the justice minister are fundamentally different.' Asahi Shinbun 20 November 1993. Also see FUKUDA note 51 p. 116

72 Kikuta, too, traces the fact that Gotôda's four predecessors did not sign any orders, to the increasing international trend of abolition, as well as the then seemingly imminent ratification of the Second Optional Protocol to the ICCPR. But unlike Hui, who strives for an objective description of the issue, Kikuta, a zealous proponent of abolition, interprets the ministers' behaviour completely different: the ministers did not neglect their duty, when refusing to sign, but rather were very brave. A.I., too, called the attitude of Gotôda's predecessors respecting of a 'de facto moratorium'. KIKUTA note 6 p. 24; AMNESTY INTERNATIONAL, Japan. Resumption of Executions and Ill-Treatment of Prisoners on Death Row p. 1 (London 1993) a.i. document ASA 22/09/93

stated that he would respect judgments made by the courts. He also declared regarding capital punishment that somebody who wants to abolish this punishment must not accept an appointment as justice minister. It would contradict the spirit of the Code of Criminal Procedure if penalties were not executed. This also applies when the execution of the penalty is as painful as the signing of an execution order. He also admitted the existence of a discussion on this issue, and declared that he supported an eventual abolition of capital punishment. When exercising the duties of a justice minister, there is no room for personal feelings. After all, public opinion demands the retention of capital punishment. The Human Rights Committee's demand that the Japanese Government abolish capital punishment was commented on by Mikazuki on 9 November: 'Japan has recently shown restraint [in executions], and it is not so that cruel punishment is increasing.'[73] Immediately after the executions of November, Mikazuki refused any comment.[74]

His successors all have adopted the same line of having to sign as part of their position, regardless of their personal views.

Most ministers refrained from commenting on the issue. Since there is no other way to determine exactly who and when can be held responsible for how many and whose executions, the only opportunity is thus taken away to gain clarity. To find out which minister has ordered how many executions, besides rather coincidental leaks of information from the ministry or information from the families of executed, the only way is to compare the yearly statistics with the ministers' terms of office. Akama, for example, who declared that he had not signed a single order, was in office during the second Satô Cabinet, from 25 November 1967 until 30 November 1968. There were no executions in 1968, but 32 in 1967. Akama's predecessor was Tanaka. In some cases, however, the statistics cannot provide clarity. In 1964, for example, there were no executions. In July 1963, Takahashi Hitoshi had taken office. In 1963 there had been 12 and in 1965 four executions. Whether some of these had been ordered by Takahashi cannot be said, unless the exact dates of the executions are known.

---

73 Kôbe Shinbun 27 November 1993

74 Asahi Shinbun evening edition 27 November 1994

A statement before journalists, as given by Tanaka, is the great exception. Many other former ministers showed forbearance with their views, and only vaguely commented on media questions. For example, Okuno Masaaki merely stated: 'Neither in 1980 nor in 1981 was I in office for the whole year from January through to December. Please decide for yourself.' Like Okuno, most ministers even after the end of their term do not want to disclose if and how many executions they have ordered.

How many a minister attempted to avoid such a topic is illustrated by this example: Okuno replied to a question raised in the Upper House Legal Affairs Committee by representative Nakayama about what he thought about the death penalty, that principally he believed it would be good to create a society without capital punishment.[75] Nakayama's question about the reason why Japan, unlike most other industrialised nations, retain the death penalty, was answered:

> There may be states which have abolished [the death penalty] and such which consider doing so, as well as some which contemplate a reintroduction after abolition. Since a life is taken forever, it is an important problem which has to be considered carefully. Also there are some, who roll up the abolition of capital punishment as an international movement... Naturally, violent crime won't disappear, but does not [capital punishment] have a controlling effect in the sense that one is punished for what he has done? Violent crime does not disappear, and also an abolition of capital punishment does not have the support of the public.

Nakayama asked: 'If a person was erroneously sent to the gallows, whose responsibility would that be?' Okuno: 'There is the system of retrial and various other mechanisms to prevent such errors.' Nakayama continued to grill the minister: 'But what if?' Okuno did not react: 'I do not think that this would ever happen.'

Nakayama:	'Do you think that the public wants an abolition of capital punishment?'
Okuno:	'Violent crimes remain, and if one only strives for the abolition of the death penalty, I fear that this would be insufficient.'
Nakayama:	'Do you believe in a preventive effect of the death penalty against violent crime?'

75 Quoted in MIHARA part A note 5 p. 306

Okuno: 'As long as there is such crime, must one not do everything to prevent it? Must we not first of all take care of the abolition of such things?'

Table B-5: Terms of Office of Postwar Japan's Justice Ministers/Executions per Year

Year	**Exe.**	**Minister**	**Term of Office**	**Year**	**Exe.**	**Minister**	**Term of Office**
1945	9	Iwata	08/45-05/46			Ueki	02/71-07/71
				1972	7	Maeo	07/71-07/72
1946	11	Kimura	05/46-05/47			Sato	07/72-12/72
				1973	3	Tanaka	12/72-11/73
1947	12	Katayama	05/47-06/47	**1974**	4	Nakamura	11/73-11/74
1948	33	Suzuki (Yoshio)	06/47-10/48	**1977**	4	Setoyama	10/76-12/77
		Yoshida	10/48-11/48	**1978**	3	Furui	12/77-11/79
1949	33	Ueda	11/48-06/50				
1950	31	Ôhashi	06/50-12/51	**1979**	1	Kuraishi	11/79-07/80
1951	24	Kimura	12/51-10/52	**1980**	1	Okuno	7/80-11/81
1952	18	Inukai	10/52-04/54	**1981**	1	Sakada	11/81-11/82
1953	24			**1982**	1		
1954	30	Katô	04/54-06/54	**1983**	1	Hatano	11/82-12/83
		Ohara	06/54-12/54	**1984**	1	Sumi	12/83-11/84
1955	32	Hanamura	12/54-11/55				
1956	11	Makino	11/55-12/56	**1985**	3	Karasaki	11/84-12/85
1957	39	Nakamura	12/56-07/57	**1986**	2	Suzuki (Seigo)	12/85-07/86
1958	7	Karasawa	07/57-06/58	**1987**	2	Endô	07/86-11/87
1959	30	Aichi	06/58-06/59	**1988**	2	Hayashida	11/87-12/88
1960	39	Ino	06/59-07/60			Hasegawa (Takashi)	12/88
				1989	1	Takatsuji	12/88-06/89
						Tanigawa	06/89-08/89
		Koshima	07/60-12/60	**1990**	0	Gotô	08/89-02/90
1961	6	Ueki	12/60-07/62				
1962	26	Nakakaki	07/62-07/63			Hasegawa	02/90-09/90
						(Shin)	09/90-12/90
				1991	0	Kajiyama	12/90-11/91
						Satô	
1963	12	Kaya	07/63-07/64	**1992**	0	Tawara	11/91-12/92
1964	0	Takahashi	07/64-06/65	**1993**	7	Gotôda	12/92-08/93
1965	4	Ishii	06/65-12/66	**1994**	2	Mikazuki	08/93-04/94
						Nakano	04/94-05/94
						Nakai	05/94-06/94

1966	4			**1995**	3	Maeda	6/94-08/95
						Takigawa	08/95-10/95
						Miyazawa	10/95-01/96
1967	23	Tanaka	12/66-11/67	**1996**	7	Matsuura	11/96-09/97
1968	0	Akama	11/67-11/68	**1997**	4	Shimoinaba	09/97-07/98
1969	18	Saigô	11/68-01/70	**1998**	5	Nakamura	07/98-03/99
1970	26	Kobayashi	01/70-02/71	**1999**	3	Jinnouchi	03/99-10/99
						Usui	10/99-06/00
1971	17	Akita	02/71	**2000**	3	Yasuoka	06/00-
		Hamano	11/74-12/74			Komura	
1975	17	Inaba	12/74-12/75				
1976	12	Fukuda	12/75-10/76			Moriyama	04/01-

Nakayama later quizzed Okuno's successor, Sakada, before the Upper House Legal Affairs Committee.[76] Sakada stated – after being requested not to refer to a disputed opinion poll conducted by the Prime Minister's Office:

> Surely there is the opinion of the individual Sakada, but I am here now as minister of justice. Among the scholars and in various states, recently a tendency for the abolition of the death penalty can be observed. I myself, too, think that a world without capital punishment is desirable, but the time has not come yet. It seems better not to quote the statistics of the Prime Minister's Office. But the opinion of the majority of the people as sovereign is an aspect which must not be ignored. In 1980, 62.4% believed that principally there is no need to abolish capital punishment. 4.3% held that it would be better to abolish. These are data. Especially recently, the social situation has become increasingly complicated, science and technology progress, drugs and stimulants are abused, there is serious crime such as hijacking etc. ... which are all threatened with the death penalty. Even though some say that [capital punishment] does not have a preventive effect, I think it does. This has also become evident in the Prime Minister's Office's poll.

That one minister signs and another does not undoubtedly contradicts equality before the law. Either all have to be executed or none. Either all ministers fulfil their duties or all must refuse to sign. There must not be disagreement. Which of the two options should be chosen is not only a legal and political question, but is foremostly a moral question to be decided by the Japanese legislator. Must not the justice minister fulfill his duties, as long as there is no different

---

76 Quoted in MIHARA note 66 pp. 308-310

decision by the legislator? How would it be if the transport minister because of personal feelings prohibited all bikers from wearing safety helmets? Or if the health minister prohibited the treatment of the seriously ill, since it would constitute an intrusion in the course of nature, fate, the work of god or whatever? Nobody would excuse such a violation of official duties. Is it not just the same in the case of the justice minister? Gotôda repeatedly declared that he had to suppress personal feelings when signing execution orders. It is said that Gotôda personally opposed the death penalty. If that is so then he succeeded in strictly separating the 'official' and the 'private'. He fulfilled his official duties. This must be considered independently from the issue of capital punishment itself.

The opponents of capital punishment point out the necessity of a question of life and death, such as capital punishment, being decided upon conscience and moral feeling of the individual representatives in parliament, as for example, had been the case in Great Britain when this punishment was abolished in 1969. This can undoubtedly be supported. Once again it must be stressed that a vote, alteration, amendment or abolition of laws on the one hand, and the execution of current laws on the other must not be mixed up. It is not enough to criticise the justice minister, even if one views his acts as reprehensible. Rather, those who want to realise an abolition must aim at a reform of the laws.[77]

6. *The Ministry of Justice*

Japan's politics since the war has at no time been marked by personal continuity. This also applies to the ministers of justice, who hardly stay in office for more than one year on the average. In

---

77 Gotôda and Mikazuki are history. Their short-lived successor Nakano after only a few weeks catapulted himself out of office without having even touched upon the issue of capital punishment. The next minister, Nakai Hiroshi, made no statements on his attitude during his short period in office. In May 1994, shortly after having taken office, four representatives approached him, asking him not to sign execution orders. Nakai refused to talk to them. Asahi Evening News 18 May 1994 The first minister of the LDP-SDP coalition, Maeda Isao (LDP) declared upon assumption of his office in June 1994 that he would approach the matter upon the basis of the law. Maeda signed three execution orders on 1 December 1994 and three on 26 May 1995. Nihon Keizai Shinbun 2 December 1994, Asahi Shinbun 27 May 1995. None of his successors has made an official statement on the issue.

the 1990s, they belonged to several parties and political denominations, and most of all held different attitudes on the duty to sign execution orders. The bureaucracy, however, showed continuity. Work within the Justice Ministry continues unaffected by changes in government or the person of its minister. Here the decisions are made who is executed when. Therefore it is most of all of importance to find out which policy or strategies the ministry follows regarding capital punishment. One of the ministry's strategies, opponents of the death penalty believe, is to keep the number of convicts on death row below a certain limit. Since in the 1960s there were at times more than 80 convicts on death row, the ministry has occasionally striven to 'clean out'. For this reason, 'mass executions' such as those under Tanaka took place. This manoeuvre also should 'make up' for ministers who signed few orders or none at all.[78]

There also seem to be political motives. If possible, years without executions should be avoided, to show the public that capital punishment exists, that sentences are executed, and that the ministry does not intend to alter this situation.[79]

It remains questionable, however, how the Justice Ministry wants to inform the public about the existence of the death penalty, when the circumstances of executions are kept an absolute secret. As has already been shown, there have been no public executions since the *Meiji* Period. That today almost everywhere in the world executions are carried out behind high walls inaccessible to the general public, is the consequence of the excesses which until the middle of the 20th century had frequently turned executions into public fairs and led to a degeneracy of the people. Also, a direct confrontation with executions could appear cruel to the public and shock it. Some believe that the often martyr-like and hero-worshipping depiction of the convict by the media even provides some sort of incentive for further crime.[80]

In the United States, where executions are also carried out behind prison walls, the media can inform the public until the very end of the procedure. It is known who, when, where and how execution

---

78 MURANO part A note 14 p. 102

79 YASUDA YOSHIHIRO, *Naze ima shikei shikkô na no ka* (*Why Death Penalty Executions Now?*), in 80 Impakushon pp. 6, 13 (1993)

80 KIMURA KAMEJI, Shin-kenpô to keiji-hô (The New Constitution and Criminal Law) 175 (Tokyo 1950)

takes place. In Japan, however, a veil of absolute secrecy covers all executions and the Justice Ministry releases no official information. It is only since November 1998 that the number and date of executions are made public. Executions of death row inmates are neither announced prior to the fact nor are any other details confirmed afterwards. It is almost as if capital punishment does not exist. The media report sensationally about every murder case, stressing the culprit's brutality and the pain of the victims. Media interest generally ceases once the trial starts. A death sentence is mentioned, if at all, at best as a small notice on the society pages. Acquittals are rarely reported. Nobody learns how the inmates fare in prison. This has the consequence that although most Japanese know about the existence of capital punishment, many have no knowledge about its practical execution.[81]

The policy of secrecy starts even earlier, with the restrictions on the convict's contacts with the outside world. According to the Prison Law, they ought to be treated the same way as prisoners awaiting trial. Until 1963, there were no practical differences. A convict on death row could receive up to ten visitors a day in a room without partition windows, and in writing could communicate with anybody. In 1964, the convicts' contact with the outside world was restricted upon a decree by the head of the Department for Rehabilitation within the Ministry of Justice.[82]

Today, visits and written communications are permitted only with close relatives.[83] There are reports that even meetings or written

---

81 KIKUCHI SAYOKO, *Himitsu shugi o tsuranuku hômu-shô no [shikei-ron] (The Justice Ministry's Theory on Capital Punishment: Secret Executions), in* Shikei no genzai (Capital Punishment Today) p. 115 (Ibaraki Rieko et.al. eds., Tokyo 1990)

82 15 March 1963 Kyôsei-kyoku-chô tsûtatsu: Shikei kakutei-sha no sekken oyobi shinsho no hatsuji ni tsuite. Initially, restrictions were limited to the case that there were concerns about danger to the detention of the convict and general social insecurity. Also, if the mental stability of the convict was threatened, or when damages were caused to the operation of prison. (TSUJIMOTO YOSHIO, *Shikei-shû no shogû, jiyû na gaibu kôtsû o mitomeru beki (The Treatment of Convicts on Death Row*), in Shikei no genzai (Capital Punishment Today) p. 246 (Ibaraki Rieko et.al. eds., Tokyo 1990). In 1990, the 'Draft Bill on Penal Institutions' (*Keiji shisetsu-hô-an*) was drafted, aiming at the securing of the convicts' mental stability by ensuring detention and creating a condition of mental stability'. The draft in detail regulated, with whom, when and how a convict could have written or personal contact. In detail see TSUJIMOTO up.cit. p. 247

83 At times, even adopted family members are excluded. For a more detailed study of the treatment of death row inmates see e.g. SAKAMOTO TOSHIO, *Shikei shikkô*

communications with the counsel or family members for the preparation of a request for retrial or pardon have been obstructed.[84] Some critics in Japan suspect that by isolating a convict, the Justice Ministry attempts to suppress all hope for survival, and have him prepare for death.[85] Also, the public should learn as little as possible about the existence of capital punishment, so as to have no interest arise in the subject. The existence of the death penalty and convicts on death row should be forgotten. As regards the fate and daily life of the convicts in prison, however, at least their families and attorneys know the facts, and can inform the public. The Japanese Ministry of Justice covers itself in silence about executions. Even the convicts' nearest family members are not informed about the imminent death, but normally are informed of the convict's 'demise' a few days after an execution. Only the number of executions is publicised. Since there is no official announcement regarding who was executed when and where, apart from 'leaks' in the ministry or prison or announcements by the convict's family, the identity of an executed convict can only be confirmed by checking whether he his name has been erased from the family registers.[86]

---

to shikei-in no shogû (The Execution of the Death Penalty and the Treatment of Convicts on Death Row), in 69-10 Hôritsu jihô p. 18 (1997); KUZUNO HIROYUKI, *Shikei haishi – tomoni ikiru shakai no tame ni (Abolition of Capital Punishment – For a Society in Which We can All Live Together)*, in 502 Hôgaku seminaa pp. 73, 74 (1996)

84 KIKUCHI note 81 pp. 119-120. Many convicts, such as Nagayama, put their energy in the writing of poetry, prose or diaries, which they published. Their works moved many and sometimes also became commercial successes, which helped to pay the costs for retrial requests etc. This possibility of publishing own literary products today is no longer permitted.
On 5 November 1993, the UNHRC demanded that the Japanese Government abolish the death penalty and criticised this inappropriate restrictions on communicaton. ASAHI SHINBUN 2 December 1993. In the Third Periodic Report on the ICCPR of December 1991, the Japanese Government stated that the Prison Law provides that a prison warden has to decide depending on the case, whether a convict can receive visitors (Art. 45 para. 1). In practice, death row convicts are permitted to meet family members or their attorney in the presence of guards. This is not the case, if there is the danger of an obstruction of the aim of detention. A.I. note 52 p. 4

85 See e.g. KIKUCHI note 81 p. 119

86 Nihon Keizai Shinbun 27 November 1993. Kawanaka, executed in March 1993, was erased from his register one week after the execution. The wife of Kondô, executed the same day, was informed by being told that she should pick up his belongings. Japan Times 28 and 29 March 1993

As in all execution cases in the past, the Justice Ministry after the executions of 1993 refused all comment. On 29 March 1993, three days after a set of executions, the head of the Department of Criminal Affairs, Hama Kunihisa, stated before the Upper House Legal Affairs Committee that the purpose of secrecy lies in the prevention of negative influences on the convicts' families and other persons concerned, of damage to their honour and mental condition. Furthermore, secrecy is necessary for the mental stability of other convicts.[87]

The Justice Ministry's almost absurd strategy of secrecy is best exemplified by the story that Nakamichi, counsel of Kawanaka who was executed in March 1993, in his communications with the ministry for weeks after the execution had to refer to a living Kawanaka, since he had not received any official confirmation of his client's death. This kafkaesque regulation is seen as part of an official policy of secrecy, whose logic is not even understood by most proponents of capital punishment, for it ruins any deterrent effect. One year after the fact, the convicts appear as numbers in the statistical yearbooks. In Japan, as in most nations of the world, executions originally were public, for they aimed at general prevention. In the endeavour to become a 'civilised nation' by Western measures, however, from the middle of the *Meiji* Period executions were transferred behind the impregnable walls of prisons.[88]

As mentioned, the Justice Ministry today cites two reasons for the executions' 'veil of secrecy'. Firstly, it aims at concealing the identity of the families, sparing them the shame of being publicly known as relatives of a death row convict or an executed criminal. Secondly, the Justice Minister is protected from counter-reaction or protests, for executions are carried out upon his order.

Japanese abolitionists believe that if the public knew everything about the circumstances and proceedings of executions, it would be horrified and demand an abolition.[89] The illusion of general prevention, however, can be kept by non-announcement. Also, even if an execution should quench the bereaved families' thirst for

---

87 Asahi Shinbun 28 November 1993

88 CAROL HUI, *Gagged in Silence or Killed by Publicity?*, in 33-15 Japan Times Weekly p. 6 (1993)

89 See e.g. KIKUTA note 36 pp. 22-23

revenge, if the details are not made public, the victims due to a lack of information cannot enjoy an easing of their pain.[90]

As Camus had already seen, the logic of non-publicity lies in avoiding a spectacle, which would nourish the sadistic feelings of the people. Surely, today it does conform with the sentiment of the people to turn one's eyes from such barbarity. Historically, the mutilating punishments of antiquity and the middle ages have been rejected in the age of humanism and eventually abolished almost everywhere in the world. Also, the elaborate execution methods, which aimed at killing a convict as slowly and painfully as possible, to keep the people from crime, have been gradually eased. Today all states, which provide for and execute the death penalty, attempt to let the convict die as quickly and painlessly as possible.

It speaks for changes in the future that in recent years information on executions has repeatedly leaked from within the ministry. There seem to be opponents of capital punishment even there, which shows that the system once believed to be solid is eroding.

7. *Parties and Politicians*

As has been demonstrated above, the minister of justice usually is not led by personal emotions or party programs when deciding about signing an execution order, but by his official duties. It does not make a difference whether the minister is a member of the conservative LDP, which supports the death penalty, the Social Democratic Party, which demands the abolition of capital punishment in its party program, or any other political party. For abolition or legal reform and the execution of current norms are two different issues.

How did other politicians, Diet members and ministers of state react to the executions of 1993, which clearly ended all changes for abolishing the death penalty in Japan? Naturally, there were no official comments on these executions. The opponents of capital punishment were furious and called for protest demonstrations, and the media, too, reported in an unusually intensive way. Politicians of all persuasions, however, hardly commented. The representatives of the ruling LDP made no comments at all and even the opposition

90 KIKUCHI note 81 p. 188

members did not seem to be excessively moved by the executions of March 1993. This decades-old pattern for the first time changed dramatically after the executions of 26 November 1993. Members of government who belonged to political parties, which for years had fought for an abolition, now could not avoid commenting. It was this contradiction which in all corners of parliament, in the media and among the general public, caused an outcry and put the issue for two weeks in the limelight as never before or since.

In recent years, the movement for an abolition of capital punishment seems to increasingly have found support in the Japanese Diet. In an opinion poll conducted in December 1989 by the 'Committee to Stop of the Execution of Capital Punishment', 81 representatives had responded that they opposed the death penalty. However, in March 1992, 136 members of parliament openly supported the activities of Forum 90, which promoted the ratification of the Second Optional Protocol to the ICCPR on the Abolition of Capital Punishment.[91] In March 1993, a total of 183 representatives, mainly from the SDP, belonged to the Forum 90.[92] Most political parties, however, have no official program on the death penalty.

In their '17 Articles on Human Rights' (*Jinken ni kansuru 17 jô sengen*), upon the 200th anniversary of the French Revolution the Social Democrats took a position against capital punishment. Chairwoman Doi Takako said: 'We can understand the feelings of the victims, who call for 'an eye for an eye, a tooth for a tooth'. But there is danger of totalitarianism when the state attempts to suppress crime by applying the death penalty.' The Communist Party in its 1946 draft for a new Japanese constitution had included a provision on the abolition of capital punishment, and then-chairman Kijima Hideo affirmed this attitude of the party in a letter to Amnesty International in 1990. In other Japanese political parties, too, there are members who oppose the death penalty. After the executions of 26 March 1993, LDP member Shiga Setsu set out to form an association of representatives for the abolition of capital punishment.[93]

---

91 A.I. note 52 p. 9

92 Japan Times 29 March 1993

93 Japan Times 29 March 1993. Already in June 1990, Shiga had criticised the government's policy of secrecy before the Lower House Legal Affairs Committee. The then-chairman of the Justice Ministry's Execution Committee, Imaoka, commented that the principle of secrecy is observed according to instruction.

After the executions of November 1993, all eyes turned to the new government, of which many had expected an abolition or at least a non-application of capital punishment. The reason for these expectations had been the participation of the Social Democrats in the coalition government. The evening edition of the *Mainichi Shinbun* newspaper on 27 November 1993 quoted attorney Nakamichi Takemi as follows:[94]

> In the cabinet there are nine opponents of the death penalty. Are not [before this background] the executions of great meaning for the Justice Ministry? Furthermore, the fact that these had been the second executions since March, leads to the conclusion that capital punishment is to be firmly established. We fear that the sentiments of the people are to be paralysed and conformed.

Three days later, the Daily Yomiuri quoted an attorney of the Tokyo Bar Association: 'Four executions in one day have two meanings for the Justice Ministry.' For one it should be shown that executions were to continue even after the change in government, and also the executions were an answer to the United Nation's Human Rights Committee's demand to abolish the death penalty.

It is of interest that the Social-Democratic Vice Minister of Justice, Sasagi Hidetsune, claimed to have learned about the executions only the day after the fact, on 26 November 1993.[95] Sasagi, a former attorney, openly supported the activities of 'Forum

---

Shiga's question why in Japan capital punishment is not abolished, although most Western and an increasing number of Asian nations have done so, was answered by then-Justice Minister Hasegawa: 'The preservation of justice as the foundation of state and society as well as the trends in public opinion must be considered and carefully evaluated. As I see it, the majority of the people currently regard the death penalty as appropriate for persons who have committed violent crime, and therefore the death penalty must be retained.' The director of the Department of Criminal Affairs answered the question after the general preventive effect of capital punishment with the reply that it could not objectively been proven. KIKUCHI note 81 pp. 117-118

94 The Yomiuri Shinbun also reported in its evening edition of 27 November 1993 the following statement of Nakamichi: 'These had been political executions, to demonstrate the state's intention to retain capital punishment.'

95 On the occasion of an SDP study group meeting, Sasagi had spent the day in Tochigi. During discussion on 27 November, he was called by a newspaper, which informed him about the executions. From the side of the ministry the media were later requested not to harass the vice minister.

90'. Asked about his view on the executions, he merely replied that 'one could talk about this.'[96]

Politicians of whom citizens' movements had hoped for, had even expected a commitment to the abolition of capital punishment, were thrown into a dilemma. Social Democrat and MITI Minister Itô Shigeru for example stated:[97]

> As a member of cabinet I cannot comment. Personally, I definitely regard the death penalty as a serious problem, about which I do not think categorically. There is the view that life weighs more than the whole world. Even viewed from the feelings of the victims, it is necessary. I do not join a 'Society for the Abolition of Capital Punishment', but I would join in a 'Society which Contemplates an Abolition of Capital Punishment.'

Eda Satsuki, Minister for Science and Technology under Hosokawa, on 27 November commented that 'the executions are a bad thing; very regrettable.' Eda, who had had experience as a junior lawyer at the Tokyo and Yokohama District Courts, is an outspoken opponent of the death penalty and as vice-chairman of the amnesty group in the Japanese Diet has led several campaigns for the abolition of capital punishment: 'I believe that even the Minister of Justice has to make a decision based on his official duties and his personal opinion. I think it is time to consider what the legislator in the future has to do about an abolition of the death penalty.'

In an interview he stated: 'Capital punishment exists, and the Minister has acted. There are no different attitudes. As a single politician, however, one has to strive for an abolition.'[98] In this way, Eda separated the 'personal, individual opinion' from the 'current

96 Asahi Shinbun 2 December 1993

97 Asahi Shinbun (evening edition) 27 November 1993

98 Mainichi Shinbun 28 November 1993. The Yomiuri Shinbun quoted Eda in its evening edition on 27 November: 'As a concerned representative I find it terribly regrettable. I feel helpless ... As a member of Cabinet I cannot comment on acts done by the Justice Minister in office... In Japan there was the expectation that the death penalty would no longer be executed in practice. But this had not been clearly decided on the political level. Since the death penalty still is provided for by law, it is applied even under the current cabinet.' The Japan Times quoted Eda as saying that the Justice Minister had acted in his own responsibility, and that it is not an act where the cabinet would intervene. But although the death penalty is provided for by law, the law changes. Eda also pointed at the worldwide trend towards abolition and commented that it is inappropriate if the state determies a life as ended, for all men are equal in that they have to live their own life.

view'. Eda did not stand alone with this differentiation. The other members of cabinet, too, who previously had supported an abolition of the death penalty, acted similarly. For example, the Minister for Local Self-Government, Satô, said: 'Among the industrialised nations, there are many, which have abolished [the death penalty]. I think that Japan, too, has reached a time to think about abolishing [capital punishment].' The Director of the Economic Planning Agency, Kubota, stated: 'I am convinced that in Japan, too, at some stage capital punishment will be abolished.' Labour Minister Sakaguchi, Construction Minister Uehara, Yamahana, Minister for Political Reform and Chairman of the SDP, Transport Minister Itô and Health Minister refused to comment at all. Open criticism on the executions thus could not be heard from among the government. All persons mentioned, except Sakaguchi, are SDP members. This statement by the vice-minister of justice was exemplary of the conflict of the former opposition party (which all of a sudden became the ruling party), and thus was confronted with a situation not compatible with its previous political goals. He stated that 'the worldwide trend goes towards abolition. But as long as [in Japan] the people do not agree, an immediate abolition is impossible ... It is hard to be a member of government.' Chief Cabinet Secretary Takemura Masayoshi on 29 November 1993 confirmed the executions of 26 November 1993 and stated that executions must be conducted as long as the law provides for the death penalty. Before a press conference, he declared: 'If someone who has been sentenced to a fine or imprisonment does not pay or complete his sentence, it would be regarded as strange. The same applies to the death penalty. Most people would not support it if a death sentence was finalised but the convict not executed.' To answer the question of whether the death penalty should be retained or not, he replied: 'It should be freely discussed whether it is good that man can take life under a certain legal system. To obey an existing law is one thing, to question it, another.'[99]

Like Eda, many cabinet members of the Hosokawa Government supported an abolition of the death penalty. But with the sudden end of the 'post-LDP' era in 1994, and the re-capturing of rule in Japan by the LDP - supported by the SDP, which by now had betrayed all

99 Mainichi Shinbun 30 November 1993

principles they had ever stood for - the discussion ceased. Capital punishment is firmly established in Japan.

PART C:
DISCUSSING CAPITAL PUNISHMENT IN JAPAN

PART C

DISCUSSING CAPITAL PUNISHMENT IN JAPAN

In Europe, capital punishment became the topic of discussions as early as the 16th century. In 1516 Thomas More ('Utopia') for the first time expressed opposition to the death penalty on religious grounds. On the other hand, a prominent supporter of this punishment was no other than Martin Luther. Other convinced proponents of the death penalty were Dutch enlightener Hugo Grotius (1583-1645), Britain Thomas Hobbes (1588-1679), French enlightener Montesquieu (1689-1755) and Rousseau (1712-1778). From about the mid-18th century, capital punishment preoccupied thinkers and philosophers as a social phenomenon. The ideas of enlightenment provided the incentive for a discussion, ignited by Italian criminal jurist Beccaria. His treatise for the first time brought the issue of capital punishment into the eye of a wider public.[1] At around the same time, Tomaso Natale from Palermo, influenced by the thoughts of French enlightenment, also protested against autocratic procedure, the death penalty and torture, and demanded a more humane criminal law.[2] Thereafter, numerous treatises were

---

1 Cesare Bonesana Marchese di Beccaria, born in 1738 in Milano. In Dei delitti e delle pene (1746), the representative work on penal law in the period of enlightenment, he asserted that capital punishment was neither appropriate nor necessary. He vehemently criticised the penal system of the time, which was based on autocratic state power. Furthermore, he rejected the notion that the death penalty was supported by the social contract, since man could not delegate the right to life to the state. Beccaria also denied that capital punishment has a deterrent effect. Moreover, the execution of a death sentence was a cruel act, damaging society. He saw the essence of punishment not in retaliation, but in prevention of future crimes. A penalty in excess of this necessary limitation is cruel and inappropriate, he held. Thus the death penalty had to be abolished.

2 'The prevention and extinction of crimes by capital punishment is insufficient ... Capital punishment is equally painful for third parties, and more than fear, it causes curiosity. Compassionate persons might be deterred for a while, but they are mostly the parents, friends and acquaintances of the convict. Even if the death penalty should have a deterrent effect, it is merely superficial and not sufficient to prevent violent crime until a distant future.' See L. GÜNTHER, *Thomaso Natale, Marchese di Monterosato, ein in Deutschland vergessener*

written on this matter, by Mittermaier[3] and Pestalozzi, among others.[4] Great philosophers like Kant (1724-1804) and Hegel (1770-1831) recognised no other punishment than death in case of homicide.[5] Feuerbach (1775-1833), who had been strongly influenced by Kant, opposed an abolition in his critcism on the 'Kleinradischen Entwurf zu einem peinlichen Gesetzbuche für die Chur-Pfalz Bayrischen Staaten' (Kleinrad Draft on a Penal Code for the Palatine-Bavarian States). As a relatively moderate proponent of the death penalty, Professor Wilhelm Kahl (1849-1932) of Berlin needs to be mentioned.[6]

In Japan, the thought of abolishing capital punishment was unimaginable until the end of the *Tokugawa* Period. With the opening of the country and the influx of Western thought since the *Meiji* Period, gradually the arguments of the Western discussion on capital punishment became known. As early as 1868, Kanda Kôhei, a Holland-Scholar, introduced the debate in his article 'Criminal Procedure in the West' (*Seiyô shokoku kôji saiban no koto*).[7] Tsuda Mamichi, who at the end of the *Tokugawa* Period had studied in the Netherlands and brought his knowledge on Western legal science back to Japan, was the first Japanese who, based on Beccaria's ideas, openly demanded that the death penalty be replaced with penal servitude. Although Tsuda found a weighty supporter in Nishi Amane (1829-1897), the *Meiji* Period's representative philosopher and enlightener, the thought of an abolition did not even cross the minds of early *Meiji* legislators.[8] It was only from the second decade of that period that a substantial debate on capital punishment materialised among practitioners and scholars in the magazine

---

Vorläufer Beccarias (Thomaso Natale, Marchese di Monterosato, a Predecessor of Beccaria's, Forgotten in Germany), in 48 Archiv für Strafrecht und Strafprozeß (1901)

3 Die Todesstrafe nach dem neuesten Stand der Ansichten in England, Nordamerika, Frankreich, Belgien, Dänemark, Schweden, Rußland, Italien und Deutschland, über die Abschaffung dieser Strafart (1840)

4 Über Gesetzgebung und Kindermord (1873)

5 Kant especially criticised Beccaria's demand for an abolition of capital punishment as 'sophistry and perversion' and held that 'a person who has killed another, must die. This is a prerequisite of justice.'

6 Before the jurists' conventions 1910 in Danzig and 1912 in Vienna he explained capital punishment as an important structural element of punishment. See e.g. LEDER note 107 pp. 275-300

7 DANDÔ Part A note 13 p. 167

8 MURANO Part A note 14 pp. 42-43

Kangoku Kyôkai Zasshi[9] of the 'Japanese Prison Association'. This slowly developing discussion culminated, when Ogawa Shigejirô, then editor of the magazine, in 1907 published a special issue as well as a number of articles in regular issues on 'prison', in which forty prison officials presented their – overwhelmingly negative - views on capital punishment. This early Japanese discussion on the death penalty already included most aspects of the current debate. The arguments pro and con can be summarised as follows:

A. Arguments for capital punishment

- Under the social contract, the state has the right to take life in case of violations of the provisions of this contract.
- A person who kills another must be killed.
- The death penalty is indispensable to satisfy the feelings of retaliation of the victims and their bereaved families.
- The death penalty has a deterrent effect and prevents violent crime.
- Public safety can only be protected by the complete removal of a criminal from society.
- As long as public opinion supports capital punishment, the people's legal consciousness makes the death penalty necessary.
- As long as there is violent crime, an abolition is premature.

B. Arguments against the death penalty

- The social contract does not contain the right to take life.
- Capital punishment is disregard for human life.
- Even if a criminal is killed, his victims do not return, and the feelings of victims and bereaved families are not satisfied.
- The death penalty does neither deter nor prevent violent crime.
- The death penalty is incompatible with the concept of correctional and educational punishment.
- The death penalty is not applied objectively and is unjust.
- The death penalty cannot be undone; in the case of an execution after an erroneous judgment, no rescue is possible.
- Public opinion is irrelevant, for the people neither have sufficient information nor the awareness and expertise to make a decision.

Since the beginning of the discussion, these arguments have hardly changed, although their contents have undergone some major alterations. For example, during the past two centuries, torture has been abolished, and thieves are no longer hanged. Thorsten Sellin

9 Magazine of the Prison Association. The Kangoku Kyôkai Zasshi was the predecessor of today's Keisei. Nihon Kangoku Kyôkai was the predecessor of today's Kyûsei Kyôkai.

noted in his 1959 report[10] on the death penalty that the preventive effect of fear of the death penalty was disproved by the historic trend to substitute capital with other punishments and to execute as quickly and painlessly as possible. Prevention has been further diminished by the removal of executions from the public eye. Thus, although a sense of justice and morality is constantly present in man and necessary in social life, the conceptions of what is just and moral have undergone tremendous changes. Therefore the death penalty, too, does not depend on some unalterable principle, but like all policy, on changes in views and convictions, which are influenced by the situation and circumstances of social life.

1. *Capital Punishment and the Japanese Constitution*

According to the currently dominating theory, capital punishment is constitutional.[11] One of the main representatives of the opposing view, Kimura Kameji, argued the unconstitutionality of capital punishment from the principles of pacifism, democracy, respect for the individual, common weal and the prohibition of cruel punishment.[12] More recent abolitionist theory especially studies the question of violations of human rights by a possible contravention of the death penalty against the constitutional principles of individual dignity and respect for life.[13]

---

10 THORSTEN SELLIN, The Death Penalty – A Report for the Model Penal Code Project of the American Law Institute p. 20 (Phildalphia 1959)

11 In detail see PETRA SCHMIDT, *Die Todesstrafe in Japan: Einige verfassungsrechtliche Aspekte (Capital Punishment in Japan: Some Aspects of Constitutional Law)*, in 4 Zeitschrift für Japanisches Recht p. 91 (1997); HIRAKAWA MUNENOBU, *Shikei seido to kenpô riron, jô: kenpô-teki shikei-ron no kôsô* (*Capital Punishment and Constitutional Theory I: Structure of the Constitutional Theory of Capital Punishment*), in 1100 Jurisuto p. 63 (1996)

12 KIMURA Part B note 80 pp. 177 et seq

13 DANDÔ Part A note 13 pp. 90, 146; JOSÉ LLOMPART, Ningen no sonchô to kokka no kenryoku (Human Dignity and State Authority) p. 245 (Tokyo 1990) also asserted an abolition of the death penalty for individual dignity and respect for life.

1.1 *Prohibition of Cruel Punishment (Art.36* Kenpô*)*

Art. 36 *Kenpô* reads: 'The infliction of torture by any public officer and cruel punishments are absolutely forbidden.' In a precedent decision of 12 March 1948, the Supreme Court expressed its opinion on the effect of this provision on the death penalty:[14]

> The death penalty ... is an extreme and severe punishment, but one cannot consider the death penalty ... a cruel punishment in the meaning of Art. 36 *Kenpô*. Although it is called 'capital punishment', its form of execution, like that of any other penalty, is judged from a humanist point of view according to time and situation. If in the future, laws should be enacted which provide for execution methods such as burning, gibbetting, crucifixion or boiling, this would have to be called unconstitutional. Currently, [this is not the case].

A minority opinion of four justices showed that this must not be a definitive or final interpretation: 'The constitution reflects the public sentiment at the time of its enforcement, and in this way has created provisions such as the aforementioned one; still, one cannot think that the death penalty will be recognised forever. The decision whether a punishment is cruel or not is a question which is decided by public sentiment. Since this public sentiment can change with time, at one time it can regard the death penalty as not cruel, but as cruel at a different time ... In such a case, the interpretation of Art. 36 *Kenpô* will automatically be restricted and capital punishment as a cruel punishment regarded as unconstitutional. But currently such a time has not come yet...'[15] This opinion was supported by one justice in a minority opinion to a Supreme Court decision of 21 September 1993.[16]

---

14 2-3 Keishû p. 191

15 Further Supreme Court decisions on the cruelty of capital punishment: 30 June 1948 in 2-7 Keishû p. 777 and 06.04.1955 in Keishû.

16 Unpublished decision, cited in Asahi Shinbun evening edition 21 September 1993 p. 1; Daily Yomiuri 22 September 1993 p. 1. Justice Ono, however, pointed at the possibility of a change of the social and legal circumstances of a retention of the death penalty, at acquittals of convicts on death row in retrials, as well as at the international tendency of abolition and the acceptance of the Second Protocol to the ICCPR on the abolition of capital punishment. This minority opinion caused a stir, since Justice Ono proposed an experimental stay of execution to study eventual effects on the development of crime. He furthermore proposed to guarantee a balance of crime and punishment by introducing two kinds of penal servitude for life, i.e. with and without the possibility of parole.

The Supreme Court was especially criticised for failing to examine the cruelty of capital punishment itself, and instead investigating the currently applied execution method of hanging. Critics also found fault in the court's assessment of the cruelty of hanging in comparison with execution methods of the distant past and within the limits of the pain caused in the moment of execution.[17] For the issue at stake is not a quantitative reduction of the pain caused to the convict in the instant of execution, critics say, but rather how much suffering the currently used method causes, that is, whether it is cruel.[18] The Supreme Court also failed to define, when and how exactly physical and psychological torment is 'unnecessary' and thus cruel.[19]

The passionate fighter for an abolition of the death penalty in Japan, law professor Kikuta Kôichi, holds it impossible to execute a convict without causing mental anguish.[20] Therefore the death penalty is, regardless of the method of execution, always cruel. Dandô Shigemitsu, éminence grise in the field of Japanese criminal law, believes that the discussion is not about the cruelty of the execution. The convict dies anyway. The cruelty of capital punishment lies in the time before execution, the psychological torment, which the convict suffers while waiting for death.[21]

Thus, neither the Supreme Court nor Japanese legal science have succeeded in ascertaining whether the death penalty is cruel in the meaning of Art. 36 *Kenpô*. Even attempts to define 'suffering' fail to convince. It remains unclear at what stage of capital punishment and from whose view cruelty should be examined.

---

17 SCHMIDT Part A note 29 p. 177 et seq; NAKAYAMA ISAO, *Shikei goken-ron hihan (Criticism on the Theory of the Constitutionality of Capital Punishment)*, in 61 Handai hôgaku p. 57 et seq

18 SCHMIDT Part A note 29 p. 178; NAKAYAMA note 17 p. 58

19 In detail see SCHMIDT Part A note 29 pp. 178 et seq; KIKUTA Part B note 36 p. 174

20 KIKUTA Part B note 36 p. 176

21 DANDÔ SHIGEMITSU, *Ajia ni okeru shikei haishi no jitsugen o mokushi shite (Aiming at the Realisation of an Abolition of the Death Penalty in Asia)*, in 38-10 Hôgaku seminaa p. 32 (1993). Another variety in the search for an explanation of the cruelty of capital punishment is provided for by MASAKI (Part A note 9 pp. 87-92) who points out another weakness in the argumentation of the Supreme Court, i.e. its seeming focus on the point of view of a third part when judging cruelty.

1.2 *Protection of Lawful Procedure (Art.31* Kenpô*)*

Art. 31 *Kenpô* reads: 'No person shall be deprived of life or liberty, nor shall any other criminal penalty be imposed, except according to procedure established by law.' Criminal procedure must be just. 'Lawful procedure' must not only be regulated by law, but needs to guarantee a certain minimum of justice. The aim of this provision is what in U.S. law is called due process of law.[22]

The current Japanese Penal Code (*Keihô*) states in Art. 9 that the death penalty is one applicable punishment. Art. 11 *Keihô* states as place of execution 'in prison' and as execution method 'hanging'. Nowhere is it said how exactly this is to be done.[23] The Supreme Court on this issue cited the law-like force of *Dajôkan* (Great Council of State) Edict No. 65 of 1872. The court dispelled all doubts about a loss of the edict's validity under the 1947 Law concerning the Force of Provisions which were in Force at the Time of Enactment of the Japanese Constitution (*Nihon koku-kenpô shikô no sai gen ni kôryoku o yûsuru meirei no kitei no kôryoku-tô ni kansuru hôritsu*). Later studies, which raised doubts whether the decree had ever gained independent force or at least had been abolished in 1872 through enforcement of the *Kaitei Ritsurei*, have neither been developed by the judiciary nor by legal scientists.[24]

Even if the edict should continue to have legal force, critics hold, doubts remain as to the lawfulness of the death penalty, since Arts. 11 *Keihô*, 475 Code of Criminal Procedure and 71, 72 Prison Law merely mention 'hanging', 'place of execution', 'rope', and Edict No. 65 contains no concrete provisions on form and method of execution. Also, the latter provides for an aboveground method of hanging, while the currently used method is an underground form of strangling.[25] The Tokyo High Court in a decision on 28 September 1960[26] elaborated that it suffices that the law determines 'hanging' as

---

22 MIYAZAWA TOSHITOSHI, Verfassungsrecht (Constitutional Law) pp. 105 et seq (Köln... 1986)

23 In detail see SCHMIDT Part A note 29 p. 186

24 In detail see SCHMIDT Part note 29 pp. 194 et seq; TETSUKA YUTAKA, *Meiji rokunen dajôkan fukoku dai-roku-go-go no kôryoku (The Validity of Dajôkan Decree No. 65 of 1872)*, in 37-1 Hôgaku kenkyû p. 3 (1958)

25 On the differentiation, especially from a forensic point of view, see SCHMIDT Part A note 29 pp. 198 et seq.

26 238 Hanrei jihô pp. 17 et seq. The Supreme Court rejected the second appeal in this case on 6 December 1961, since it had to be dealt with in a criminal trial. 285 Hanrei jihô p. 7

execution method and thus clearly distinguishes it from other forms such as beheading. All other issues brought up by critics were rejected by the court as unessential. In a decision handed down on 19 July 1961, the Supreme Court stated:[27]

> [Even if] the current method of execution of the death penalty ... is not carried out according to the provisions of Edict [No. 65], [the current method] does not contravene the basic details of the method regulated in Edict [No. 65] and thus does not violate Art. 31 of the Japanese Constitution.

1.3 *Interaction between Arts. 31 and 36* Kenpô

As early as 1950, Kimura Kameji[28] pointed out problems regarding the meaning of 'lawfulness', i.e. the definition of 'law'. He repeatedly insisted that an interpretation which sees in Art. 31 *Kenpô* a confirmation of the death penalty is not permissible, due to the contradiction between Arts. 31 and 36. As has been shown above, Kimura sees a clear prohibition of capital punishment as cruel punishment in Art. 36 *Kenpô*. If one follows this line of argument, then the death penalty inevitably must be regarded as unconstitutional and all provisions providing for it as invalid. But in such a case no laws could exist which under Art. 31 *Kenpô* justify the existence of capital punishment.[29]

The issue demands a closer look at Kimura's train of thought: the central meaning of Art. 31 is, he holds, to discuss the principle of lawful punishment from a historic and comparative aspect. Based on the spirit of pacifism, the respect for the individual and the prohibition of cruel punishment is essentially restricting Art. 31 *Kenpô*; but even a legal limitation of capital punishment violated the constitution. For with the principle of lawful punishment, Art. 31 *Kenpô* does not order the provision of a certain punishment but states that punishment must be carried out by lawful procedure. Thus one cannot automatically conclude that the death penalty is unconstitutional, because there are laws on capital punishment.[30]

---

27 15-7 Keishû p. 1106

28 KIMURA Part B note 80 pp. 139-141, 189-192; SCHMIDT Part A note 29 p. 192

29 Irrespective of the question whether this treatment of the relation between capital punishment and Art. 31 is still acute, if one already regards the death penalty as unconstitutional due to its violation of Art. 36.

30 KIMURA Part B note 80 ibid.

Kimura further holds that Art. 31 is an administrative provision and therefore could not provide the authoritative basis for the state to take life. A restriction of authority must be based on Arts. 11, 12, 36 *Kenpô*.[31] It is these provisions, upon which people who contravene the 'common weal' are punished in practice. But the real meaning of Art. 31 *Kenpô* to Kimura[32] lies in the fact that the procedure for the execution of this punishment is provided for by law. But even if such laws on the application of the death penalty are justified by Art. 31, this interpretation contradicts Arts. 11 and 13 *Kenpô*, which are the fundamental principles of the Japanese Constitution. For 'life' which under Art. 31 can be taken, is the 'right to life', guaranteed in Art. 13 *Kenpô*. Kimura's elaborate train of thought has so far failed to convince the judiciary.[33]

Some representatives of Japanese legal science today again point at the insufficiency of applying the principle of due process of law indiscriminately. In this context it is important to point out how the various procedural provisions on the protection of procedural rights relate to one another. Literally, Art. 31 merely protects the

---

31 Art.11 Japanese Constitution: 'The people shall not be prevented from enjoying any of the fundamental human rights. These fundamental human rights guarantee to the people by this Constitution shall be conferred upon the people of this and future generations as eternal and inviolate rights.'
Art.12: 'The freedoms and rights guaranteed to the people by this Constitution shall be maintained by the constant endeavour of the people, who shall refrain from any abuse of these freedoms and rights and shall always be responsible for utilizing them for the public welfare.'
Art.13: 'All of the people shall be respected as individuals. Their right to life, liberty, and the pursuit of happiness shall, to the extent that it does not interfere with the public welfare, be the supreme consideration in legislation and in other government affairs.'

32 KIMURA Part B note 80 pp. 39 et seq

33 SCHMIDT Part A note 29 p. 193; in one of its few precedent decisions on the constitutionality of capital punishment, the Supreme Court on12 March 1948 (2-3 Keishû p. 191) elaborated on the relation between the death penalty and Art. 31: 'According to Art. 31 Japanese Constitution, the respect for the life of the individual must be guaranteed in case of punishment by lawful procedure. This also applies to a punishment taking life. For, as it is the case in the constitutions of most modern and civilised states, the death penalty must be regarded as acknowledged by the constitution. Although there is no general prevention by the deterrence of capital punishment, through the execution of this penalty, the foundations of special social evil are removed and society is protected. Here, the humanistic view of the whole takes precedence over that of the individual. The retention of capital punishment is acknowledged as necessary for the common weal.'

lawfulness of procedure. Miyazawa Kôichi sees Art. 36 *Kenpô* as the special norm, guaranteeing that 'cruel punishment' will not be inflicted.[34] This elaborates on the nature of penalties, which are guaranteed due process under Art. 31. Thus, Miyazawa says, Art. 36 has precedence over Art. 31 and this refutes the arguments of proponents of capital punishment who derive its constitutionality merely from Art. 31. For one of the fundamental elements of due process of law is the guarantee of non-punishment of innocent persons. Viewed in this way, a punishment of innocent persons is cruel and therefore unconstitutional.[35] The acquittals of four death row convicts in retrials in the 1980s are seen as evidence for the possibility of erroneous judgments in death penalty cases and thus for the cruelty of this punishment.

Further doubts are raised from the uncertainty of the criteria of sentencing. Japanese penal law does not contain any provisions regarding this issue, and criteria put up by the Supreme Court in 1983 in the so-called Nagayama case did not really provide an improvement. The danger of inadequate verdicts and judicial arbitrariness can be seen as in contradiction to the principle of due process of law and as cruel - and therefore the death penalty in violation of Art.36 *Kenpô*.[36] The same applies to the uncertainty of criteria for the execution of finalised sentences.[37]

1.4 *Capital Punishment and the 'Right to Life', 'Individual Dignity' and the 'Common Weal' (Art. 13* Kenpô*)*

Art.13 *Kenpô* reads: 'All of the people shall be respected as individuals. Their right to life, liberty, and the pursuit of happiness shall, to the extent that it does not interfere with the public welfare,

---

34 HIRAKAWA note 11 p. 68

35 HIRAKAWA note 11 p. 73. DANDÔ Part A note 13 p. 16, who, however, views capital punishment as cruel in any case.

36 HIRAKAWA note 11 p. 74 fn. 35; KOYAMA, *Shikei no shii-teki sabetsu-teki tekiyô* (*The Arbitrary amd Discriminatory Application of Capital Punishment*), in 20-2 Seinan Gakuin Daigaku Hôgaku Ronshû p. 69 (1987). Also see on criteria for sentencing e.g. IWAI YASUHIRO, *Shikei no tekiyô kijun* (*Criteria for the Application of Capital Punishment*), in 35-1 Keihô zasshi p. 91 (1995); ONOSAKA HIDEO, *Shikei to kenpô chitsujo* (*Capital Punishment and Constitutional Order*), in 35-1 Keihô zasshi p. 71 (1995), who points out that Art. 31 Japanese Constitution does not merely relate to the 'if', but also to the 'how' of punishment.

37 See SCHMIDT Part A note 29 pp. 524 et seq; also see e.g. FUKUDA TAIRA, Keihô sôron (Criminal Law, General Part) p. 122 (Tokyo 1995)

be the supreme consideration in legislation and in other governmental affairs.'

In the Supreme Court's most famous decision on the constitutionality of capital punishment, the court on 12 March 1948 stated that the individual's right to life is restricted under Art. 13 *Kenpô* in favour of the common weal. Since Art. 31 *Kenpô* also acknowledges that human life can be taken by punishment, as long as this is conducted by lawful procedure, the death penalty cannot be called a cruel punishment.

The court's view did not remain uncriticised. Art. 13 *Kenpô*, Kimura[38] states, states that citizens are respected as individuals, and thus manifests the principle of individual dignity; it furthermore declares that 'life, liberty and other rights of the people for the pursuit of happiness demand greatest respect in legislation and other policy of the state'. In this way, Art. 13 *Kenpô,* based on the concept of human rights, protects the people's rights as individuals; this respect is not guaranteed by punishment with death and therefore capital punishment is incompatible with Art. 13 *Kenpô*. The core of the problem lies in the second half-sentence of Art. 13, which permits laws to restrict this right in the name of the common weal. As long as the common weal is not harmed, it says, the people's right to life will be protected as much as possible. Therefore this right is formally not protected in the case of a violation of the common weal, and it is possible to restrict or withdraw it, although the Constitution in Arts. 11, 97[39] protects the fundamental rights as eternal, and inviolate. This is the interpretation of the Supreme Court.[40] Kimura,[41] however, holds that, viewed from the nature of human rights, their withdrawal is impermissible in any case. If the Constitution approves of a withdrawal of these rights in the case of a collision with the principle of the common weal, they therefore cannot be eternally protected rights.

38 KIMURA Part B note 80 pp. 55 et seq

39 Art. 97: 'The fundamental human rights by this Constitution guaranteed to the people of Japan are fruits of the age-old struggle of man to be free; they have survived the many exacting tests for durability and are conferred upon this and future generations in trust, to be held for all time inviolate.'

40 Other Supreme Court decisions, too, confirm that the guarantee of fundamental rights must not contradict the common weal. E.g. Supreme Court 18 May 1949, 3-6 Keishû p. 830

41 KIMURA Part B note 80 pp. 59-60

This raises the question about the definition of the 'common weal', which is stronger than human rights. The Supreme Court in its 'common weal'-based 1948 decision failed to provide such a definition. To approach a definition of the essential contents of the common weal, first of all it should be made clear what it is not. As a passive definition it is generally recognised that the common weal is not advantage, happiness or well-being of the individual. From this it can be concluded in reverse that it must be advantage, happiness or well-being of the community and all of its members. It is not the sum of the well-being of all individuals in society, but the immanent well-being of all its members. If this immanent well-being is not the sum of the well-being of all individuals, who form the entirety of society, then it must be a well-being surpassing them.[42] Kimura[43] comments that the common weal at the same time is a well-being immanently surpassing all members of society. This, Kikuta explains, has the meaning of a well-being formed in the reciprocal relation of all members of society. There, the common weal is the 'joint well-being of all members of society', is 'social solidarity'.

If one thus reconsiders the death penalty within the scope of Art. 13, which contains such a common weal, then the right to life as the right that life not be taken, that is, the right not to be killed, is withdrawn based upon the common weal. But Kimura[44] believes that capital punishment cannot be justified by Art.13 *Kenpô*. For, he argues, in the common weal of Art. 13 the well-being of criminals as members of society must also be included. Therefore the withdrawal of the right to life of a criminal by capital punishment is a contradiction against the principle of individual well-being. If furthermore the common weal is the basis of individual well-being, and if the basis of individual well-being is the life of the individual, which cannot be taken, then the death penalty is a violation of the common weal and the life of the individual.

What is striking in this discussion, is that the content of the 'right to life' has at no point been made clear. This 'right to life', according to the majority opinion, is the right to enjoy life. The enjoyment of fundamental rights, stated in Art. 11 *Kenpô*, thus

---

42 MIYAZAWA note 22 p. 83; also see HIRAKAWA note 11 p. 76

43 KIMURA Part B note 80 p. 133 et seq

44 KIMURA Part B note 80 p. 163

contains the 'right to enjoy life' according to Art. 13, but not a right to the subject, life itself.[45]

Kimura,[46] on the other hand, sees in the 'right to life' not only a necessary right for the positive protection of life, but also a right that life is not taken, that it is not killed. The right that life is not taken cannot be permitted from the point of view of the common weal. The problem is that it contradicts the common weal to damage liberty or property of another for the protection of one's own life. Within this limitation, he says,[47] restriction and withdrawal of the right are permissible, but only comprise the means necessary for the protection of the right to life, not the right that life is not taken. Nonetheless, the death penalty, whose contents is the taking of life, is not permitted. It cannot be justified that the majority is damaged in order to realise the postulation of life, liberty and happiness of the individual. For by causing damage for the protection of individual rights, the meaning of the protection of human rights is undermined. Here, the protection of human rights as well as of the common weal are equally to be understood as the joint well-being of the majority of the people. If this joint well-being contains 'killing', this cannot automatically give the state the authority to take the life of that person. Undoubtedly, the state has the duty to take measures against persons who have violated the fundamental rights of others. But its responsibility in no case goes so far as to extinguish the life of the person concerned.[48]

Again, the Supreme Court on 12 March 1948 commented on the issue. The decision became famous mostly for its emphasis that 'human life weighs more than the whole world'. The basis of this idea is the individualistic value concept that the life of the individual cannot be sacrificed for the good of the majority. Nevertheless, the Supreme Court accepted without objection that sacrifices are possible for a complete protection of the common weal.

The Supreme Court further approved of capital punishment for its effect of special prevention and removal of social ills for the protection of the common weal. Independent from doubts about the

45 KIKUTA Part B note 36 p. 169 explains this interpretation saying that this thought had been taken directly from the U.S. Virginia Bill of Rights of 1776, which guaranteed the 'enjoyment of life'.

46 KIMURA Part B note 80 p. 164

47 Ibid.

48 KIMURA Part B note 80 p. 167

deterrent effect and the talionic principle of retaliation based on conflicting, equally ranked human rights of several individuals, the question is raised about the ignorance of human dignity. Also, the protection of individual life by execution of another, regarded as a social ill, is an extreme discrimination and contradicts the commandment of the respect for human dignity. Irrespective of other problematic aspects of special and general prevention, capital punishment as the threat of death a violation of human dignity.[49]

By the late 1950s, the highest Japanese court had thus commented on all major constitutional issues related to capital punishment and in this way hampered a further development by Japan's judiciary and legal science, who principally accept Supreme Court judgments as final and unalterable decisions on any legal matter.

2. *Capital Punishment and Social Contract*

The idea that all men are born free and equal, and that for the protection of these rights a reciprocal contract is necessary, which bestows certain rights on the state, formed during the bourgeois revolution in the 17th and 18th century.[50] The citizens delegate all rights, including the right to life, to the state. If, by killing a person, a citizen violates the contract's provision not to harm another, the state is authorised to take the culprit's life. First criticism on this theory came from Beccaria, who principally supported the idea of the social contract, but rejected the notion of a citizen delegating all rights to the state, including his right to life.[51]

In Japan, especially Takeda Naohira advocates the death penalty due to the social contract, based on the nature of punishment: Since man is innately inclined to act egotistically and selfishly, no one can protect his own life, liberty and well-being without a guaranteed promise of non-damage. To gain such a promise, first of all one has

---

49 In detail see HIRAKAWA note 11 pp. 77 et seq. Hirakawa himself in this context doubts the state's authority to punish. His elaborations on the social contract as a possible basis for this authority and the ignorance of the human dignity by the execution of punishment, however, seem irrational.

50 Rousseau elaborated his thoughts in the treatise Du Contrât Social (1762).

51 While Rousseau saw each member of society delegating all his rights to the community, Beccaria held that because of simple necessity, man had delegated a part of his freedom to the community. But that had merely been the smallest part and only as much as inevitable.

to vow oneself not to damage life, liberty and well-being of others, and to offer an effective method to keep this promise. A mutual promise of all members of society is needed to recognise such reciprocity before the law and to secure for every individual as much liberty as possible and the prerequisites of a peaceful, joint well-being. The naturalist school of law calls this mutual promise '*Contrât Social*', social contract. The contract is observed by the individual's reason and conscience, which, however, tends to be weak. To protect the citizens from the egoism of others, a 'contract to tolerate disadvantages, damage and privations' needs to be concluded for the protection of the aforementioned promise and as restitution for the advantages gained by violations of the promise of non-damage. If the contract is broken, its provisions must be immediately executed, i.e. the state and legal system must prevent the violator from successfully avoiding discovery and execution. This vow to tolerate disadvantages forms the basis of the social contract as a 'sanctional law'. Does it stipulate that man offers his highest value, life, as a just and effective remedy for damage of life? Or does a 'substitute' of a lesser value suffice? Those who oppose the death penalty interpret the social contract as stipulating: 'I have promised not to kill you. Even if I unilaterally break this contract and kill you, you must promise not to kill me'. Does not a law which places the life of an egotistic criminal above that of his law-abiding victim misjudge modern law's principle of equality and dignity of life and the recognition of human rights?[52]

However, Takeda seems to be the sole defender of this theory in present-day Japan, and has met with widespread criticism of his theories.[53] Another representative for many other death penalty opponents, Tsujimoto Yoshio[54] believes that the argument of the social contract could be just as well used against the death penalty, for it has contributed to overcoming absolutism and as the

52 TAKEDA NAOHIRA, *Shikei (Capital Punishment)*, in Kaisei keihô junbi sôan (Preparatory Draft for a Criminal Law Reform) pp. 39-40 (Tokyo 1961)

53 See e.g. ÔNO SADAYOSHI, *Shikei seido no rekishi 1* (*The History of Capital Punishment I*), in 2 Handai Hôgaku p. 31; NAGAOKA RYÛICHI, Hanzai-gaku I (Criminology) p. 313; MIYAZAWA KÔICHI, *Shikei haishi-ron no isshikô (Some Thoughts on the Abolition of Capital Punishment*), in Kyôsei ronshû pp. 276 et seq (Ogawa Tarô ed., Tokyo 1968)

54 TSUJIMOTO YOSHIO, *Shikei e no apuroochi (An Approach towards the Death Penalty*), in Hô no riron (Legal Theory) pp. 170-171 (Hara Hideo et.al. eds., Tokyo 1985); also see YOSHIOKA KAZUO, Keiji-gaku (Criminal Law) p. 168 (Tokyo 1980)

foundation of all rights has created freedom of conscience and human rights.

3. *Deterrent Effect*

Deterrence means that through the execution of punishment, the occurrence of further, similar crimes can be prevented in the future. First of all, two kinds of deterrence must be distinguished:

1. deterrence aimed at the future action of the person being punished as individual prevention (special prevention);
2. deterrence aimed at the future action of other persons as general prevention. Undoubtedly, the death penalty is effective in the former case.

Primarily, deterrence requires that man regards life as his most precious good, which he wants to protect more than anything else, especially from the threat of capital punishment. Furthermore, it calls for a consciousness of this threat. If the death penalty constitutes such a threat, then the greater the threat the more the fear would have to increase. So far, no one has been able to calculate how high the probability of execution has to be to make the death penalty an adequate threat.[55]

In Japan, as in most parts of the world, the general preventative effect of the death penalty – the deterrent - is the core of argumentation in the debate for and against. The proponents of the death penalty acknowledge that crime is caused by social and natural causes, but still insist on the deterrent effect of this punishment. The expression 'human life weighs more than the whole world' is born from man's desire to live. As long as this wish exists, they say, the preventive effect of the threat of capital punishment cannot be negated. For once life is lost, there is no way to regain it. Therefore, the threat of capital punishment keeps potential criminals from committing a crime.[56]

---

55 See SELLIN note 10 pp. 19-20

56 MIHARA KENZÔ, Shikei sonpai-ron no kenkyû (Genealogy of the Discussion on Capital Punishment) pp. 44-45 (Tokyo 1991). MOTOJI ARAKUMA (Nihon keihô-ron (Japanese Criminal Law) p. 775 (Tokyo 1939)) cannot accept any other punishment than death for asocial, violent criminals and believes that capital punishment is necessary for the maintanence of the social order. One of the first

One of the leaders of the Japanese movement for the abolition of capital punishment, Kikuta Kôichi,[57] regards its deterrent effect as mere fiction. He insists that all subjective criteria such as humanism or views on life must be ignored and instead actual facts be examined to be as utilitarian as possible. He admits that a scientific experiment on the preventive effect of capital punishment is practically impossible. Most of all it is regularly pointed out that even if there is a deterrent effect of capital punishment, it would be ineffective for a certain kind of violent criminal and in case of political crimes.[58]

Although it is generally accepted that a deterrent effect of the death penalty can neither been proved nor disproved, it still forms the core of all discussion. Uematsu Tadashi,[59] one of the main proponents of capital punishment in Japan, regards the deterrent effect of the death penalty as necessary to hold up the social order. It is argued that in Japan, unlike in some other countries, the existence of the death penalty's deterrent effect is obvious, and therefore capital punishment must be retained. Even among the proponents of capital punishment some, like Fujigi Hideo,[60] doubt such an effect and wish for a future abolition of the death penalty, for 'it is a fact that the deterrent effect of capital punishment has become very small ... It seems to be a logical solution to retain the death penalty as an abstract last punishment, but to apply it only very carefully in practice.'

---

proponents of this theory was Italian doctor Cesare Lombroso (1835-1909). He conducted anthropological studies on the skulls of criminals and develped the concept of 'atavism', i.e. of the 'born criminal'. Most of all he reasoned for the idea of articifial selection of criminals through the death penalty for the protection of society. Lombroso's disciple Enrico Ferri (1856-1929) further developed this concept in that artificial selection is not only a right of society, but also coincides with the natural law of evolution.

57 KIKUTA Part B note 36 p. 11

58 MIHARA Part A note 5 p. 142; MOTOE TAKEYOSHI, *Shikei no keiji seisaku-teki igi no tsuite (On the Criminal-Policy Meaning of Capital Punishment)*, in 35-1 Keihô zasshi pp. 81,86 et seq (1995)

59 UEMATSU TADASHI, Keihô sôron (Criminal Law, General Part) p. 316 (Tokyo 1958). For a very similar argumentation see e.g. ONO SEIICHIRÔ, Shinchô – keihô kôgi sôron (Lectures on Criminal Law, General Part) p. 129 (Tokyo 1956)

60 FUJIGI HIDEO, Keihô kôgi – sôron (Lectures on Criminal Law – General Part) p. 31 (Tokyo 1976). Also see MATSU HIROSHI, in Asahi Shinbun (Evening edition) 23 May 1974

When discussing the retention or abolition of the death penalty on the grounds of deterrence, it always was and still is focused on the person of the criminal. But is there a 'standard' type of a criminal, who can be deterred by capital punishment?
Uematsu Tadashi explains in his textbook on criminal law:[61]

> There are innumerable examples that man cannot let go of life ... It is impermissible to deny the death penalty's deterrent effect for an exceptional phenomenon. The statistics presented by the opponents of capital punishment show that even in case of an abolition violent crime did not rise. But this is not enough to negate the death penalty. For there are also examples of an increase in crime rates after an abolition. If capital punishment is abolished in a secure, stable and peaceful society, there will be no rise in crime. It is like giving no more medicine to a sick person, whose illness is in a natural process of recovery. This couldn't be called a negative influence under these conditions. It cannot prove the ineffectiveness of the medicine ... If society is unstable, it does not surprise anyone that crime cannot be prevented, even with the use of capital punishment. But this does not lead to a negation of the death penalty. For if the illness is stronger, no medicine can keep the patient alive.

Those who think like Uematsu believe that a seasoned criminal does think about the penalty before the commission of his crime and will weigh the advantages of his crime and the damage in the case of discovery, whereas a young criminal might not act in this way, which in many cases leads to a simple theft turning into robbery or another serious crime. Thus, while punishment for one type of criminal might mean nothing but can keep away another from crime, clearly the existence of a punishment, which takes away man's highest good exerts a great preventive effect on the criminal. Therefore, one cannot simply conclude that capital punishment is not deterrent from the fact that a criminal did not think about the penalty before committing a crime. For if there is such an effect, this person will not become a criminal, an object to study.

---

61 UEMATSU TADASHI, Keihô gairon I – sôron (Criminal Law - General Part) pp. 348-349 (1974 Tokyo). Also see for statements UEMATSU note 208 p. 316. AOYAGI FUMIO supports Uematsu's opinion. 'The number of persons who think about death as the possible punishment for a planned crime and give up their crime, is not known and cannot be measured.' In Asahi Shinbun (Evening edition) 13 July 1982

There are other, more complex aspects to the issue. Psychologist Ogi Sadayoshi explains in a 1974 essay on 'The Psyche of Convicts Sentenced to Death or to Penal Servitude for Life':[62]

> It is rare that murderers are unusual. If one meets and examines them, the first peculiarity is that they are normal people. This is even more evident when compared with other criminals, such as thieves, where there are many listless, strange persons, persons who are unable to look after themselves. As a young psychologist in Tokyo Prison I had had the opportunity to meet many murderers. Even after I had given up this work, I continued to visit prisons and talk to [murderers]. I can say with conviction that most murderers are normal people. It is a terrible thought that murderers are as normal as we are; we are in no way different from them. There is the possibility that we may become murderers.

Of a completely different opinion is psychiatrist Takemura Nobuyoshi.[63] He holds, supported by others such as Saeki Chihiro,[64] that among violent criminals there are many who, due to their retarded mental condition, cannot be kept from committing crime by the threat of capital punishment. To them, the death penalty is meaningless. Jurist and anti-death penalty activist Maesaka Toshiyuki[65] does not want to go quite as far as declaring the average violent criminal as mentally ill, but he certainly regards them as somehow 'different' from 'normal' people. For social ignorance, poverty, hatred, jealousy and anger are at work and create a 'murderous passion'; here, the thought that in case of arrest the punishment would be death is secondary.[66]

---

62 OGI SADAYOSHI, Shikei-shû to muki-shû no shinri (The Psyche of Convicts on Death Row and Convicts Sentenced to Life) p. 232 (Tokyo 1974)

63 TAKEMURA NOBUYOSHI, *Shikei seido o megutte – seishin igaku-sha no tachiba kara (On the System of Capital Punishment – Seen from the Viewpoint of a Psychiatrist)*, in 33-12 Jiyû to seigi pp. 38, 40 (1982)

64 SAEKI Part A note 4 p. 401. Also see KIMURA Part B note 80 p. 173

65 MAESAKA Part A note 12 p. 84

66 Criminals like serial murderers Kurita Genzô, a disturbed man, who had been sentenced to death for octuple robbery and murder, or Furutani Fusayoshi, who as a child had been abused and grown up in extreme poverty and later committed ten murders, for which in 1978 he was sentenced to death, are examples of such criminals. On these cases see e.g. MAESAKA Part A note 12 pp. 74, 77.
In Japan, only a relatively small number of criminals seems to suffer from mental defects: among 1,991 homicides committed in 1971, only 37 of the culprits were officially found to be mentally abnormal. In another 87 cases, mental weakness was suspected. In 1982, 1,684 murders were committed. Here, 52 of the culprits were

What influence does the existence of the death penalty have on criminals or persons who are about to commit a crime? Can, as the proponents of capital punishment hold, the thought of the death penalty keep a potential criminal away from his planned act, out of fear for his life?

Kimura[67] believes that there is at least no direct force in the death penalty that keeps people from committing crimes due to its omnipresence in human conscience. Rather, there may be an indirect preventive force at work, for the threat of death creates disgust for certain crimes and thus effectively influences the psyche of man. But this effect does not stem from the severity of punishment, but from the certainty of prosecution. Those for whom this kind of deterrence is effective, are the weakest elements of society: women, children, the elderly, people with phobias, those who fear death, and who believe that others, too, must fear death. Legal scholar Mihara Kenzô[68] is of the opinion that individuals, who commit capital crimes such as murder, are usually guided by the desire to complete the crime and avoid discovery. They do not think about the penalty imposed the in case of discovery. Like Mihara, Ogawa Tarô[69] insists that it would be illusionary to assume that a criminal would give up his plan for a crime because of the existence of the death penalty. Takigawa Yukitoshi[70] as early as 1928 wrote in support of this opinion:

> Crimes avenged with death are mostly those against life as well as political crimes. In the case of murder, often sudden passion is at work or the crime is well considered and planned. The criminal is overwhelmed by the stimulus of the crime and does not think about anything else, or has already considered everything. The death penalty has no deterrence.

---

acknowledged as mentally ill, another 110 were suspected as such. Between 1968 and 1972, a total of 439 mentally ill or retarded had committed homicides, between 1979 and 1982, 756, between 1988 and 1992 the number further increased to 767. Hanzai Hakusho 1973 pp. 48, 52; 1983 pp. 81, 84; 1993 pp. 203

67 Part B note 80 p. 174

68 Part A note 5 pp. 142-143

69 OGAWA TARÔ, Keiji seisaku no suii to mondai (Changes and Problems of Criminal Policy) p. 45 (Tokyo 1970); OGAWA TARÔ, *Shikei ni okeru seisaku to wa nani ka – hô seishin wa shikei sonzoku o kimeta ga (What is the Policy Regarding Capital Punishment?*), in 48-9 Economisuto pp. 68, 71 (1970)

70 Part B note 80 p. 123

There are doubts whether all who commit a crime threatened with death are mentally disturbed, whether all commit crimes for passion and whether all are convinced that they will not get caught. Capital crimes in fact are committed. Every year in Japan about ten people are sentenced to death. If one insists that this produces no deterrence, especially not for criminals, proof is needed. It is inappropriate to assume a certain type and insist that capital punishment has no deterrent effect.

Kimura Kameji,[71] Miyazawa Kôichi[72] and many other opponents of the death penalty believe that it is not the death penalty that prevents crime, but the likelihood of detection and the surety of prosecution. On the other hand, Ogi, due to his long experience and many conversations with death row inmates, regards this argument as ineffective. He found that most criminals simply lack self-restraint; therefore capital punishment cannot be an effective deterrent:[73]

> We have asked the convicts the following question: 'Did you prior to or while committing the crime consider that it could be punished with death?' Not a single one had thought about this before the crime. A few during the act briefly had done so. Out of these, three were sentenced to death, one to imprisonment for life. When, after the crime, psychological excitement waned, 20% were convinced that they would be punished with death. Seen from this perspective, the death penalty has no deterrent effect, which protects society from violent crime. For all questioned convicts had known about the existence of the death penalty before committing the crime. But due to the impulsiveness of the act and the inability to see the consequences of their actions, they could not foresee the death sentence and exercise self-restraint.

---

71 KIMURA Part B note 80 pp. 145, 47. KIMURA (id. p. 174) gives the example of Great Britain, where in 1940, 97 out of 295 murderers (32%) committed suicide immediately after the crime. In detail also see ARTHUR KOESTLER, *Die Rache ist Mein (Revenge is Mine)*, in: Die Rache ist Mein – Theorie und Praxis der Todesstrafe (Revenge is Mine – Theory and Practice of Capital Punishment) pp. 7, 31 (Arthur Koestler et.al. eds., Stuttgart 1961)

72 MIYAZAWA KÔICHI, *Shikei haishi no tachiba (From the Standpoint of Abolishing the Death penalty)*, in 37-1 Hôgaku kenkyû p. 85 (1958). UEMATSU TADASHI (*Shikei no sonzai igi (The Meaning of Retaining the Death Penalty)*, in 376 Kenshû pp. 3, 19 (1979)), a proponent of the death penalty, agrees with the view that certain prosecution more effective in the prevention of crime than the threat of severe punishment. A 100 percent detection, however, is impossible.

73 OGI note 62 p. 72

Ueki,[74] too, focuses on the psyche of the criminal. In the case of an abolition of the death penalty, he believes, homicides would decrease. For a criminal is normally aware that he might be punished. If his crime is threatened with a severe penalty such as death, the criminal will commit further crimes to prevent arrest. Thus an increase in crime occurs for other reasons. Any deterrent effect of the death penalty must therefore be counteracted. Kimura[75] even goes so far as to compare the well-publicised confrontation between the convict and the state, with the gladiators of ancient Rome fighting wild beasts; like the brave gladiators, the men on death row become the object of compassion and sometimes they are even seen as heroes. This effective suggestion causes people with mental defects to commit further murders. Based on some isolated instances – none of which have occurred in Japan - Kikuta[76] warns of 'extended suicide', a reaction against society, where those who lack the strength to commit suicide beg for the death penalty by killing others. Nagayama Fumio, sentenced to death and executed in 1997 for quadruple homicide and robbery-murder wrote in his *Muchi no namida* ('Tears of Ignorance'):

> For violent criminals, the death penalty is necessary. But to prevent such crimes, it would be better if it did not exist. For in my opinion it is difficult to control this criminal impulse. At least in my case, the last two crimes might have been prevented had there not been capital punishment.

74 See Shakai kagaku ronshû No. 42 p. 7

75 Part B note 80 pp. 79, 80

76 One example is the case of Umeda Terumi, culprit in the Mitsubishi Bank-Kitabatake Robbery Murder Case: 'If I am arrested, I will be sentenced to death, no matter whether I kill one or ten.' It doesn't play a role any more how many people one kills - the culprit will be punished with death anyway. The death penalty even causes murder. KIKUTA (Part B note 36 p. 18) thinks the same applied to Japan's most famous postwar serial murders, Kohira, Kurita and Ôkubo. On 'extended suicide' also see SELLIN note 10 pp. 65-68. Another possible example is that of Takuma Mamoru, who in June 2001 killed eight primary school students in Osaka, in the hope of being sentenced to death and executed after he had failed several attempts to take his own life. Japan Times online, 12 June 2001 <http://www.japantimes.co.jp/cgi-bin/getarticle.pl5?nn20010612a2.htm>

Legal scholar Sumitani Mamoru[77] denies the deterrent effect of capital punishment, for crime occurs for natural causes as a phenomenon caused by economic or instinctive reasons. Attempting to suppress this with punishment is meaningless. In the same line, Masaki Akira,[78] one of the most passionate fighters for an abolition of the death penalty in postwar Japan, regards the prevention of crime by eliminating social ills as more essential than deterrence:

> Punishment as a means of suppressing crime provides only a once-off relief. Punished or not, crime has deeper causes. Food, housing, clothing, alcohol or poverty must not be disregarded or even underestimated. Severe sentences and the prevention of crime are based on the state seeking to escape its responsibility. [The state] rather has to see its duty in removing all social factors causing crime.

The proponents of capital punishment have always argued that the death penalty's deterrent effect is so big that in the case of an abolition, violent crime would increase. The opponents of capital punishment assert the opposite, that is, that neither abolition nor retention has any influence on crime statistics. Neither camp so far has succeeded in proving its point of view.

The seminal work in empirical research on capital punishment is undoubtedly Torsten Sellin's *The Death Penalty* (1959). Sellin[79] examined the crime statistics of a few selected states of the U.S. with similar socio-economic conditions, some of which apply capital punishment, others having abolished it. In the result of his study, Sellin could not find any differences in the crime rates, i.e. he believed that he had proved that the death penalty does not have a greater deterrent effect than other penalties. The counter-thesis against Sellin's theory was published by Isaac Ehrlich in 1975 and 1977. Criticising the fact that no representative of the opposition against the death penalty, from Beccaria to Sellin, has ever analytically studied the general value of deterrence, but has merely examined the question whether the death penalty has a greater deterrent effect than other punishments, Ehrlich again studied empirical data and theories to examine the relationship between the

---

77 SUMITANI MAMORU, *Shikei no hanzai gokushi-ryoku ni tsuite no giron (On the Preventive Force of Capital Punishment)*, in Gendai no keiji-hô-gaku (ge) (Contemporary Criminal Law Pt. 2) p. 319 (Hiraba Yasuji et.al. eds., Tokyo 1977)

78 MASAKI Part A note 9 p. 157

79 Note 10 pp. 21 et seq

deterrent effect of capital punishment and homicide. This investigation produced exactly the opposite results to that of Sellin's study.[80] However, even Ehrlich himself did not consider his results as absolute evidence, for other elements such as employment rate or income have a greater preventive force than the death penalty. He demonstrated only one thing: the existence of a deterrent effect can neither be proven nor refuted.[81]

Since in Japan neither the exact dates of executions nor the identity and crime of an executed convict are made public, the extent to which the execution of a death sentence can directly influence the actions of potential criminals cannot be confirmed. The statistics do not provide any clues. Since the end of the Second World War, both the number of finalised death sentences as well as that of executions has continuously decreased. According to the theory of deterrence, this reduced threat of capital punishment for homicide should have led to an increase of violent crime. But on the contrary, since the late 1940s, the number of murders has decreased. The non-influence of death sentences and executions on criminals is further shown in that in years with especially many death sentences or executions, no increase in murder rates could be observed in the same or following year.

Since no empirical studies on the effect of capital punishment on violent crime have been or could possibly be conducted in Japan, Sellin's and Ehrlich's studies continue to provide the material for discussion.[82] The proponents of capital punishment in Japan criticise Sellin, arguing that his findings cannot be applied on Japan, since Japanese circumstances cannot be compared to those of the U.S. Kikuta, in his 1988 treatise *Shikei* (Capital Punishment) counters this argument:[83]

> Among all states where so far the death penalty has been abolished, there are agrarian and industrialised nations, wealthy and poor, Roman

---

80 ISAAC EHRLICH, *The Deterrent Effect of Capital Punishment, A Question of Life and Death*, in 65-3 American Economic Review pp. 397, 415 (1975)

81 Also see Sellin's studies on this issue: note 10 pp. 39 et seq

82 DANDÔ SHIGEMITSU, The Criminal Law of Japan: The General Part p. 290 note 21 (Littleton 1997) similarly bases his assumption that there exists no deterrent effect of the death penalty on a study conducted by American criminologist Edwin Sutherland (EDWIN H. SUTHERLAND & DONALD R. CRESSEY, Principles of Criminology pp. 292 et seq (7th ed. 1966)

83 Part B note 36 pp. 32-33

and Germanic, quiet and temperamental ones. There are countries, such as Germany and Italy, who experienced defeat in the war, but there are also victors of the war. All these nations have in common that after the abolition of capital punishment, violent crime has not increased ... Uematsu's argument that violent crime has not risen because the abolition had taken place in peaceful times fails to convince.

Table C-1: Relation between Death Sentences, Executions and Murder in Japan[84]

Year	Murd.	DST	DSM	EX	Year	Murd.	DST	DSM	EX
1947	1,938	105	14	11	**1974**	1,912	6	3	4
1948	2,495	116	60	33	**1975**	2,098	5	2	17
1949	2,716	55	17	33	**1976**	2,111	4	3	7
1950	2,892	62	15	31	**1977**	2,031	9	5	3
1951	2,865	44	12	24	**1978**	1,862	6	4	3
1952	2,871	37	6	18	**1979**	1,853	7	0	1
1953	2,944	22	3	24	**1980**	1,684	9	4	1
1954	3,081	20	3	30	**1981**	1,754	2	1	1
1955	3,066	34	12	32	**1982**	1,764	11	5	1
1956	2,617	24	2	11	**1983**	1,745	5	2	1
1957	2,524	35	4	39	**1984**	1,726	6	3	1
1958	2,683	25	3	7	**1985**	1,780	9	4	3
1959	2,683	28	6	30	**1986**	1,676	5	2	2
1960	2,648	12	0	39	**1987**	1,584	6	3	2
1961	2,619	29	5	6	**1988**	1,441	10	7	2
1962	2,348	12	3	26	**1989**	1,308	2	2	2
1963	2,283	12	7	12	**1990**	1,238	2	0	0
1964	2,366	12	3	0	**1991**	1,215	3	1	0
1965	2,288	16	6	4	**1992**	1,227	1	0	0
1966	2,198	14	6	4	**1993**	1,233	4	2	7
1967	2,111	6	1	23	**1994**	1,279	8	2	3
1968	2,195	15	4	0	**1995**	1,281	11	0	3
1969	2,098	9	3	18	**1996**	1,218	1	0	7
1970	1,986	9	2	26	**1997**	1.282	3	2	4
1971	1,941	4	0	17	**1998**	1,388			6
1972	2,060	4	3	7	**1999**				5
1973	2,048	4	4	3					

DST: All death sentences; DSM: DS for murder; EX: executions; Murd.: Murder

84 Death sentences before courts of original jurisdiction. Hanzai Hakusho 1963 pp. 20-21; 1973 p. 2; 1983 pp. 5-6, 102; 1993 pp. 3, 65, 344-346; 1997 pp. 212, 408. TSUJIMOTO YOSHIO, *Shikei seido o kangaeru (Thoughts on Capital Punishment)*, in 27 Jccd (1983)

Both sides overlook in this discussion that Japan, too, is in a peaceful state; its constitution renounces war, and for the foreseeable future, tensions are not expected. Would it not be appropriate here to propose an abolition of capital punishment for times of peace and, as in many other countries, provide for the death penalty only for times of crisis and war?

Or should it be completely replaced by another penalty? To secure the social order, jurist Makino Hideichi[85] principally supports the death penalty, but only as an exceptional penalty. Based on the theory of correctional punishment, Makino[86] believes in a strong deterrent against certain crimes, and therefore believes that capital punishment should be retained as an 'exceptional penalty'.

That a possible deterrent effect of capital punishment in no case exceeds that of imprisonment for life is another oft-cited argument of the opponents of the death penalty. Maeda Shinjirô rejects the deterrent effect of capital punishment, but neither does he believe in imprisonment for life as an appropriate substitute:[87]

> To explain the existence of capital punishment as 'deterrence' means to aim for a general preventive effect by causing strongest fear in man through the unpredictable punishment called 'death'. Undeniably, a punishment which in an instant takes away life forever means a threat to the average person and causes fear. But this effect evaporates after a while ... Our minds become deadened at reports on severe punishment, and the death penalty for the worst criminals draws the rude curiosity of the people ... Imprisonment for life, too, is a punishment that creates pale and thin prisoners without hope and freedom. It is a punishment to which one cannot agree, since it is humanely complicated and makes state responsibility meaningless.

A different issue from so-called general deterrence of third persons is that of the special deterrence of the culprit. Through execution, further crimes by the same person are absolutely and infallibly prevented. But it is doubtful whether there are not other methods, such as the complete isolation of the criminal from society, which

---

85 MORISHITA TADASHI, Keiji seisaku daikô I (Criminal Policy Pt. I) pp. 39-40 (Tokyo 1985). In support of this view also see KAGAWA TATSU, Keihô kôza – sôron (Criminal Law, General Part) p. 433 (Tokyo 1980).

86 MAKINO HIDEIICHI, Nihon keihô (Japanese Criminal Law) pp. 489-490 (Tokyo 1939)

87 MAEDA SHINJIRÔ, Keiji-gaku genron (Criminal Law) pp. 234, 249 (Kyoto 1954)

could have the same result. Indeed, the vast majority of those who demand that capital punishment be abolished suggest that it be replaced with imprisonment for life. Such a 'replacement' is met with a number of concerns. For example, the imprisonment of a murderer endangers other inmates as well as prison guards. Moreover, a prison sentence cannot sufficiently protect society, since even in case of imprisonment for life the possibility of pardon or parole exists, enabling the murderer to repeat his crime after release. Although in Japan, parole for a life sentence is generally granted comparatively late, on the average after 25 to 30 years, there is no 'absolute' life sentence until natural death. It is unpredictable what would happen if those imprisoned for life were deprived of all hope to regain their freedom one day.

One of the main arguments of the pro capital punishment group against its substitution by lifetime imprisonment is, however, the possibility of parole. Data on this issue are rare, but Sellin found that capital criminals who had been released on parole, in general behaved far better than other released criminals.[88] In Japan, too, the proponents of capital punishment consider its substitution by another penalty as impossible, since in the case of violent crime there is no chance for correction. Also, 'life' means a burden for the state budget. The opposition vehemently rejects this argument, since an assertion on the impossibility of correction constitutes a selective idea, even a form of 'species selection'.[89] Instead there must be a different kind of punishment. If prison sentences in the previous form are not a useful substitute for the death penalty, then they are not effective. Instead, one must think about a more rational, i.e. more effective system. Kimura proposes an unspecified prison term.[90] This suggestion, however, merely gives a new name to the existing concept of imprisonment for life and seems unlikely to provide an effective contribution to solving the issue at stake.

4. *Retaliation*

Capital punishment is the oldest form of punishment, and in earliest times had equated with retaliation. Primitive society believed that as

---

88 Note 10 pp. 76-78

89 MURANO Part A note 14 pp. 148-149

90 KIMURA Part B note 80 pp. 187-188

reprisal for injuries, a victim had to inflict an even greater damage upon his foe. The judaic principle of 'an eye for an eye', the *lex talionis*, was re-retaliation from one generation to the next, and had blood call for blood. Satisfaction was done only when the enemy was ruined.[91]

The concept of retaliation latently is contained in the idea of revenge. If the idea of revenge is strong and society expects strict punishment for general prevention, penalties become more severe and execution methods more cruel. To achieve the greatest possible preventive effect, public execution of punishment is inevitable. For this reason, at any time and anywhere in the world, in times of unrest, cruel punishment, first of all the death penalty, was applied.[92]

In Japan, the retention of the death penalty to the present day is explained by the need for revenge. Capital punishment shall not be retaliation but a form of atonement, that is, one who has taken life, must pay with his own.[93] The opponents of capital punishment reject the idea of retaliation as the primitive *lex talionis,* for, as Kimura believes, these instincts have been overcome by culture, humanism and morality.[94]

Nevertheless, calls to respect the feelings of victims of violent crime and their families form a central point in the Japanese debate. Until the *Tokugawa* Period, a person whose parents had been killed, had the duty to find the culprit and take revenge. This form of self-justice has been abolished and today the state has the responsibility to protect life, limb and property of its people and regulate the damage in case of injury. Individual injuries are compensated and regulated by financial support from the state for the victims of crime ('Law on the Compensation of Victims of Crime', *Hanzai higai-sha hoshô-hô*). But money does not bring back the life of a homicide victim. Therefore, the proponents of the death penalty hold, a murderer must pay with his own life for the life he has taken.[95]

---

91 MIHARA Part A note 5 pp. 7, 8; KIMURA Part B note 80 p. 25

92 See e.g. MIHARA Part A note 5 pp. 10-11

93 See, for example, FUJIGI note 60 p. 31

94 Note 80 p. 55. Also see e.g. MURANO note 1 p. 146. TOKORO KAZUHIKO (*Hanzai no yokushi to shikei (Crime Control and Capital Punsihment)*, in 69-10 Hôritsu jihô p. 8 (1997)) admonished that the victim's or society's thirst for revenge can hardly be the basis for the application of the law, for it would grossly violate the stipulation of justice.

95 KIKUTA Part B note 36 p. 54. This desire to satisfy the feelings of the victims plays an important role at trial, as has been shown e.g. in the first Supreme Court

Even abolitionist Dandô Shigemitsu, from his experience as a judge, agrees that the courts must take into consideration the feelings of victims and relatives. He believes, however that the law and the courts do not uncritically acknowledge this. Kikuta, on the other hand, questions whether all the people really call for the death of a criminal to satisfy the victims' feelings. Both scholars agree that in no case must this be the foundation of judicial decisions. In the words of Dandô Shigemitsu:[96]

> Even if the murderer is sentenced to death, his victim cannot be brought back to life; a feeling of emptiness remains. Therefore many bereaved families do not want the death sentence for the culprit. This is truly moving and noble ... But generally speaking, man will not be satisfied with any penalty but death for the murderer of a close relative. Justice calls for the satisfaction of such human feelings. But when considering carefully, also from the point of justice, one should imagine an execution, the convict crying out 'I didn't do it'. I [Dandô] have heard that a long time ago. Psychiatrist Ogi says that among those sentenced to death, many suffer from 'illusions of innocence', but could there not really be an innocent person? Maybe some people believe something like this could not happen today. But nobody can guarantee that. Satisfaction of the victims' feelings does not contradict the demand for justice.

Surely one must not forget compassion and measures for the victims. But neither ought there be planned suffering caused to the family of the murderer.[97] That today punishments such as quartering are not in use does not mean that there is no pity for the victims. The legal proverb, 'One shall hate the crime and not the criminal' (*tsumi o nikunde hito o nikumazu*) does not mean that the problem is evaded. This attitude is not an exception, as is shown in an April 1984 *Asahi* newspaper report about a life sentence in a case of arson causing

---

decision in the Nagayama case. Here, the insufficient consideration of the victims' feelings was cited as a reason for the revocation of the previous life sentence. The endless pain of the bereaved family of murder victims demands retaliation: 'The man has killed three people. There is no room for compassion. Even his mother says she wishes for his early execution.' Quoted in Yomiuri Shinbun (Evening edition 4 September 1984).

96 Part A note 13 p. 183

97 Or, as Mitsui Akira, a former judge with the Tokyo High Court, bluntly put it: 'An over-evaluation of the victims' feelings is a mistake.' Asahi Shinbun 16 March 1987

death. The relatives of the victims said: 'Fear and the pain that the most precious thing has been taken cannot be removed.'[98]

Also, in each year between 1953 and 1960 in Japan about 2,000 persons were murdered, but on average only three of the culprits were sentenced to death. In the same period, out of 2,500 cases of robbery and murder per year, an average of 12 death sentences were handed down. Death sentences occupied less than 1% of all verdicts. How could the feelings of the remaining 99% of the victims be satisfied?

Not much has changed since, as the following figures show: in 1988, more than 1,600 persons were killed in criminal acts, but only twelve death sentences handed down (0.7%). In 1996, one death sentence was handed down in a year when about 1,400 people lost their lives through crime. Furthermore, Arai Akira[99] argues, one must not forget all those whose relatives died in traffic accidents, fire or natural disasters. In 1988, 2,553 people in Japan died in traffic accidents. This number had risen to almost 10,000 by 1996. Should a person who caused an accident be executed to satisfy the feelings of the bereaved?

Judicial practice in Japan has demonstrated that the feelings of the victims indeed can have considerable influence on the sentence and thus on the decision on life or death. This raises questions about a justice which has 'life or death' depend on the feelings of the bereaved. In a sensational case there is also the danger that public pressure causes the judges to hand down a death sentence, while on the other hand it is equally doubtful whether is can be permissible that, as happened in the Nagayama appeal trial, an accused buys himself out.

What would happen with the pain and sorrow of the culprit's family if he were punished with death to satisfy the feelings of the victims' relatives? Must they silently endure their grief? Surely

---

98 Asahi Shinbun (evening edition) 24 April 1984. Another, similar, case, was d in HIGUCHI SHIGEO, *Seimei (inochi) no omosa (The Weight of Life)*, in 36-10 Jiyû to seigi p. 47 (1985). On the complexity of the victims' feelings and the stereotype that they all want the murderer of a loved one to g, for it would calm their hearts, see e.g. HIRAKAWA MUNENOBU, *Shikei-ron no riron-teki wakugumi ni tsuite (On the Theoretical Framework of Capital Punishment)*, in 69-10 Hôritsu jihô pp. 13, 16 (1997)

99 ARAI AKIRA, *Higai-sha e no shazai to shikei haishi (Apology to the Victims and Abolition of Capital Punishment)*, in Shikei no genzai (Capital Punishment Today) pp. 98, 99 (Ibaraki Rieko et.al. eds., Tokyo 1990)

their suffering is no less than that of the victim's family? The sorrow of the victim's family is understandable, but this misfortune must not be extended.[100] The death penalty throws both the families of the victim and of the culprit into financial calamities, since it is often the provider who is killed or executed.[101]

Compensation for the victims of crime, however, is not a problem unique to the death penalty, but rather is one of the penal system as a whole.[102] Victims of crime do not receive appropriate compensation. For, unlike those of the Civil Code, the Penal Code's provisions do not solve the problems of the parties concerned, but rather relate to the upholding of social order and the security of social life. Nonetheless, causing financial difficulties to all concerned can hardly be the desired effect of crime prevention.[103] If this issue cannot be solved, the death penalty must be replaced by another punishment such as imprisonment for life, to compensate the families of the victims.

A - clearly insufficient - system for the financial compensation of crime victims has existed in Japan since 1981. Masaki Akira points out that the financial burden to the state budget could be eased by having a criminal contribute through prison labour. Even in the case of the worst criminals, imprisonment for life is more appropriate than the death penalty. Currently, all income from prison labour is property of the state. The amount of wages is calculated under a bonus system, that is, the state pays the inmates some kind of 'good will money'. This 'bonus' is calculated based on the kind of work, efficiency and work conditions, and principally is paid at the time of

---

100 KIKUTA Part B note 36 p. 55

101 MASAKI Part A note 9 p. 132. HANAI TAKUZÔ, Keihô zokuron (Criminal Law, Special Part) p. 188 (Tokyo 1922)) wrote: 'He was punished and died. His wife became a widow. His children orphans. The death penalty leaves behind widows and orphans. They have commited no crime, but they are punished. To live, the widow sells her honour. To eat, the children steal. The death penalty ought to prevent crime; instead it creates crime.' MIHARA (note 205 p. 178 fn. 12) reminds that this problem is not restricted to the families of convicts on death row.

102 YAMASHITA TOMOYOSHI, *Shikei no zehi ni kansuru ikkôsai* (*Some Thoughts about Pro and Con Capital Punishment*), in 16 Kansai Gaikokugo Daigaku Kenkyû p. 177. TAKEUCHI TADASHI (*Shikei mondai no ikkôsai (Some Thoughts on Capital Punishment*), in 376 Kenshû p. 35 (1979)), too, sees this point: 'Of course, the problem of a system for victim compensation by the state is a vast field, and if such a system is created, then the problem of how such wages should be treated must be consideredoblem of the livelihood of the family of the sentenced.'

103 MIHARA Part A note 5 p. 179

release. A price increase is included in yearly raises, although the payments remain very low. For example, the average monthly wages in 1988 stood at little more than U.S. $ 20.

Masaki proposes that the authorities in charge of the prison system and the Labour Ministry allot work to the inmates. From the wages, two thirds should be paid into a compensation fund. The rest is to be used for the livelihood of the inmate and his family. With the sum paid into the compensation fund, a system for the support of the victims could be created. In this way the financial damage caused by the crime and the livelihood of the bereaved could be balanced.

Saitô Yoshiyuki specifies the main points of such a system:

1. Strengthening the penal-political idea of social rehabilitation of the criminal;
2. a system of state compensation to mitigate the victims' feeling of retaliation and to support the rehabilitation of the criminal;
3. the state could obtain money from the criminal's prison labour, to be used for compensating the victims' financial damages.

Dandô points out, however, that the victims' anger would hardly be appeased by this.

Even if the culprit paid the money earned in prison as compensation to the victims, there are cases where the victims reject such payments. Although, Dandô believes, these people would not be satisfied even if the culprit were slowly tortured to death. For even though the murderer is executed, the slain victim does not return, and a feeling of emptiness will remain.

Uematsu opposes the introduction of a system of compensation through prison labour while abolishing capital punishment, for it could hardly be pleasant for the families of the victims to accept compensation from the culprit. Even the plan to pay this money into a state fund and then have the state pay compensation separately could provide only a limited contribution, since the number of sentenced serious offenders is too small.

Naturally, the small sum gained by prison labour constitutes a practical problem. Masaki defends his concept, since the meaning of such a system mostly lies in the mitigation of the victims' feelings and not merely in financial compensation. With this statement, however, he contradicts his own argument that the victims must be spared financial calamities to be able to forgive.

Whether such a new system will be introduced or the existing scheme improved, all that could possibly be achieved is an easing of the financial situation of the victims of crime. What could be done to appease their anger, their desire for revenge?

It has already been explained that the stance of the victims and their families can influence a court decision. Undisputedly, it is meaningful if the culprit attempts to gain his victims' forgiveness. But this must be assessed positively and must not depend on his financial means. How far can forgiveness then be decisive for the verdict?[104]

The Tokyo High Court in March 1990 revoked a death sentence, mitigating it to penal servitude for life, after the culprit had paid the proceeds of a real estate sale to the families of his two victims. There have also been a few cases where the will to pay compensation was acknowledged by the courts as good intention, leading to a milder penalty. Nevertheless, such a 'buy-out' causes a kind of 'family punishment', which can throw the culprit's family into financial misery, and discriminates against those who are unable to provide the required sums. There also is the problem of the evaluation of 'repentance' of a criminal: regret and self-criticism cannot be measured objectively.[105]

---

104 A system for the financial compensation of crime victims has existed in Japan since 1981: 'System of Financial Support of Crime Victims' (*Hanzai higai-sha kyûfu-kin seido*). The Japanese State pays persons who suffered damages to life or limb through crime or their bereaved families a kind of insurance (*kyûfu-kin*), distinguished in payments for damages and to bereaved families. It attempts to mitigate the psychological and economic damage suffered. Between 1981 and 1985, however, average payments amounted to merely ¥ 3.45 million, a small part of what is paid for example in case of a deadly traffic accident. According to the Keisatsu Hakusho of 1991, within ten years from the establishment of the sytem, a total of ¥ 4.962 billion were paid to 2,330 persons.
Yamaguchi Atsushi wrote: 'The lack of provisions for victim restitution does not mean that it has virtually no role to play in the Japanese justice system. Rather, victim restitution is considered to be one of the crucial factors affecting the decisions of prosecutors, the criminal courts and the parole boards...' ATSUSHI YAMAGUCHI, *Victim Restitution and the Japanese Criminal Justice System*, in Crime Prevention and Control in the United States and Japan P. 167 (V. Kusuda-Smith (ed.), New York 1990), cited in JOHN OWEN HALEY, The Spirit of Japanese Law p. 77 (1998)
For suggestions on how to improve the present system, see e.g. MASAKI Part A note 9 p. 584

105 In general on the issue of remorse, compensation and the victims' forgiveness, see HIROSHI WAGATSUMA & ARTHUR ROSETT, *The Implications of Apology: Law and Culture in Japan and the United States*, in 20 Law and Society

Frequently the question is raised whether criminals sentenced to death, like other offenders, are victims of society. Again, the Nagayama case serves as a good example.[106] After toing and froing between sentences of death and imprisonment for life, the Supreme Court on 17 April 1990 rejected the second revision, finalising Nagayama's death sentence. Nagayama, abandoned as a child by parents and society, at times starved, insulted for his poverty, almost beaten to death, had led an unusually poor life from birth until his arrest. His poverty-stricken and persecuted existence caused several other crimes before he eventually killed four people. Negligence by society in the first appeal trial was given as a reason for the mitigation into a life sentence.

5. *Miscarriages of Justice*

Before the International Seminar on the Protection of Human Rights in Asia (*Kokusai rengô Ajia chiku jinken yôgo seminaa*) held in Tokyo in May 1960, the Japanese side reported as follows: 'Since 1882, 2,792 persons have been executed in Japan among them, there was not a single case of erroneous judgment. The Japanese judges apply the death penalty very carefully. The execution is carried out upon order by the Justice Minister after a very careful procedure.'[107]

The opponents of capital punishment argue that even if the judicial route is exhausted, errors can occur, as long as judgments are

---

Review pp. 461-498 (1986); also see HALEY note 104 pp. 76 et seq; ARAI note 99 pp. 99 et seq

106 See above

107 MIHARA Part A note 5 p. 382. MUKAE TERUYOSHI, Shikei haishi-ron no kenkyû (Studies on the Abolition of Capital Punishment) p. 54 (Tokyo 1960)) comments: 'What surprises me is that the number executed is 2,792 persons, but that it is said that there was not a single case of false judgment. In short, since third parties do not know whether it was an erroneous judgment or not, the accused cries that he is innocent. Here innocence must be proven in collaboration with other evidence. There is the proverb 'the dead don't talk' (*shijin ni kuchi nashi*). One must call the idea that no miscarriage of justice can be uncovered after an execution irrational ... The Japanese court system ... is three-tiered, and furthermore there are various means of legal redress such as retrial, complaint etc. ... But whether in the end it is a false judgment, one cannot say for sure. In cases where the Japanese media have caused stir ... very zealous attorneys who do not care about interest or profit, as well as the activities of other parties concerned, have proven that judgments were erroneous.

made by man. Man can err; and if a false judgment is executed, there is no way back: the state has committed a terrible crime. This problem gained wide publicity when in the 1980s four convicts after decades on death row were acquitted in retrials of their cases.

Proponents of capital punishment, such as Takeda Naohira,[108] argue that miscarriages of justice are not an exclusive feature of capital crime, and that the issue must not be discussed in the context of the death penalty. It should merely be debated whether the death penalty should be retained or not. Anything else would lead to a confusion of arguments.

Kagawa Tatsuo principally agrees, but comments as follows on demands for an abolition of the death penalty because of the danger of miscarriages of justice:[109]

> As long as the trial is conducted by man, one cannot expect that no mistakes occur. But once a death sentence is executed on an innocent, reversal is impossible ... This is not a special characteristic of the death penalty ... Therefore, the discussion on the abolition [of the death penalty] is unrelated to the problem of erroneous judgments. The proponents of an abolition should instead say that capital punishment must be abolished and not that it must be abolished because of the danger of miscarriages of justice. Rather, in practice ... the application of the death penalty must proceed especially carefully.

One of the death penalty's main supporters, Uematsu Tadashi,[110] sees miscarriages of justice as a problem of the past:

> Under the present system there are fewer erroneous judgments resulting in the death penalty than in other cases. For prosecutors and judges must proceed carefully ... That miscarriages of justice in capital punishment cases presented an enormous problem in the period of enlightenment was due to the fact that at that time remnants of feudal law existed.

Dandô,[111] on the other hand, sees here the core reason for an abolition: 'If one considers that in each death sentence there is the possibility of executing an innocent, the death penalty becomes the

---

108 Note 52 p. 116-117
109 Note 85 p. 434
110 Note 61 pp. 343-344
111 Cited in in AMNESTY INTERNATIONAL, The Case against Capital Punishment p. 1 (London 1992) a.i. document ASA 22/05/92

epitome of inhumanity and cruelty.' Former prosecutor Yasuhira,[112] believing firmly in the infallibility of Japan's criminal justice system, disagrees:

> No one has ever heard of such a case in Japan; among those sentenced to death and executed since the *Meiji* period, there has not been a single case of an erroneous judgment. Almost all cases of capital punishment go through three instances, and even after finalisation, the documents are thoroughly examined within the Ministry of Justice; the Minister of Justice considers carefully before signing an execution order. There are almost always applications for retrial after a finalisation of a sentence that prevent an execution.

The core argument is the fallibility of man. Man can never exclude mistakes with absolute certainty. No matter how carefully and precisely a court proceeds, the possibility always remains that due to a combination of unfortunate circumstances, an innocent is sentenced to death and even executed.[113]

In this context, the pressure put on the judges by the importance of a case must be considered. Especially in cases sensationalised by the media, such as very brutal murder and other grave cases, the judges are subjected to a fundamentally different psychological effect than in hackneyed theft cases. Such cases exert an enormous social influence, making a lenient penalty virtually impossible. The weight of public expectation causes enormous inner pressure on judges and influences the evaluation of the evidence.[114]

Other parties to a trial, such as witnesses or the defendant himself, also provide a factor of uncertainty. If their statements are not backed up by other evidence, one must not simply trust in the credibility of testimony.[115] If a trial is believed to be flawless, the accused confesses, erroneous judgments can still occur. Despite the postwar abandonment of the doctrine that a conviction primarily be

---

112 YASUHIRA MASAYOSHI, Sekinin shugi no keihô riron (The Principle of Responsibility in Criminal Law) pp. 653-654 (Tokyo 1968)

113 See e.g. FUJIMOTO TETSUYA, Keiji seisaku gairon (Criminal Policy) p. 129 (Tokyo 1984)

114 MITSUI AKIRA, *Gohan to saiban-kan (Erroneous Judgments and Judges*), in 528 Hanrei taimuzu p. 16 (1984)

115 OTANI MAKOTO, rather unconvincingly, in *Shikei haishi-ron* (*On the Abolition of Capital Punishment*), in 11 Sendai Hôgaku Ronshû pp. 55-56; KAGAWA note 85 p. 434.

based on a confession as the ultimate evidence, Japan's court still tend to place great emphasis on confessions.

Even if a convict believes that justice has not been done, after a death sentence has been finalised there remains hope for a convict to find relief through retrial, pardon, amnesty or extraordinary appeal. From the early *Meiji* Period until the end of the Second World War, decisions about amnesties (*taisha*) and pardons (*tokusha*) were the prerogative of the Emperor, who decided upon application by the Justice Minister. Today, according to Art. 73 No. 7 of the Japanese Constitution, it is the task of the cabinet to decide on amnesties, paroles, mitigation, the exemption from punishment and rehabilitation.[116]

After the war, several general amnesties (*seirei onsha*) were granted for various reasons. The majority of those who profited from the amnesties were traffic violators and perpetrators of lesser crimes.[117] There have also been ten amnesties; convicts on death row profited only from the first three on the occasion of the end of the war, the proclamation of the new constitution and the enforcement of the peace treaty. The former two were conducted according to the prewar Pardon Law. Sixteen inmates on death row were granted a mitigation, another eight individual pardon. Thus, until 1954 a total of 24 convicts sentenced to death had their penalty mitigated into penal servitude for life under an amnesty. These mitigations must be seen as exceptions, a tribute paid to the turmoils

---

116 Pardon Law (*Onsha-hô*, of 28 March 1947) Art. 2 reads: 'Pardon is granted to certain convicts.' Art. 6 reads: 'In the case of mitigation of punishment, the kind of crime or punishment is laid down in ordinances or [the mitigation] carried out against certain convicted criminals.' Art. 8: 'An exemption from the execution of punishment is carried out against certain convicts, but not against convicts sentenced to or released on parole.' Art. 9: 'The rehabilitation is conducted against persons who fully or partially loose qualifications through judicial decision based on legal provisions, or [rehabilitation] is decided on or carried out against certain persons by government decree. This does not apply to persons whose execution of punishment is not yet completed or who have been exempted from the execution of punishment.' Art. 12: 'Pardon, mitigation of certain culprits, excemption from execution and rehabilitation of certain culprits are conducted against persons named by the Central Committee on Rehabilitation.'

117 Only convicts whose sentence has already become finalised are eligible. This can lead to consequential results: in the expectation of a mitigation upon an amnesty after the death of Shôwa Tennô, four culprits who had been sentenced to death before lower courts, retracted their appeals, causing the finalisation of their sentences. Their hopes were not fulfilled.

of the war and the postwar period.[118] Not a single death row convict has profited from an amnesty since.

Pardon, too, is a means which has so far brought rescue only to a very small number of prisoners on death row. Upon request by the convict or the prison management, the 'Central Committee on Rehabilitation' (*Chûô bensei hogo shingi-kai*), as the Justice Ministry's department in charge, examines the case. If the committee agrees to a pardon, the file is forwarded to the minister of justice. The prerequisites for a pardon are of a rather subjective nature: remorse of the culprit, forgiveness by the victims and their families, the attitude of the public in the concrete case. Mental defects or severe illness of the convict can be decisive factors.

After a draft bill on the alleviation of requirements for retrial in certain cases failed to pass parliament in 1968, then Justice Minister Saigô promised to grant more pardons.[119] The criteria are unknown. For example, on 17 June 1975, death row convict Ishii was granted pardon. The same day, his accomplice Nishi Sadao was executed.

Representative of the difficulty of a death row convict to be pardoned is the third pardon request in the so-called *Teigin* case:[120]

At around 3 p.m. on January 26, 1948, a middle-aged man entered a branch of the Teikoku-Bank (short: Teigin) in Tokyo's Toyoshima district. Wearing the armband of Tokyo's emergency services, the man stated that he had been sent by the public health department, since several cases of dysentery had occurred in the vicinity. As an alleged prophylactic he administered a fluid to all sixteen employees. This substance in fact was cyanide. The unsuspecting employees immediately suffered from tormenting pain, while the culprit stole cash and cheques totalling ¥ 10,000. Twelve employees died, the others suffered the severest injuries.

Seven months after the crime, police in Otaru on Hokkaido arrested scenic painter Hirasawa Sadamichi. He was interrogated until he confessed. Hirasawa was sentenced to death in all three instances. His sentence became finalised on 7 May 1955.

---

118 The cases mentioned above included e.g. such where all related documents had been lost during the war, and the death sentences could not have been executed anyway. In detail see MURANO Part A note 14 p. 126

119 MURANO Part A note 14 p. 129

120 In detail see MORIKAWA TETSURÔ, Teigin jiken (The Teigin Case) (Tokyo 1980)

Hirasawa submitted a total of 17 requests for retrial and four for pardon. In June 1980, the Kyôdô news agency announced the sensational news that 'Hirasawa's pardon is pending'. The result of the Central Committee on Rehabilitation's deliberations on Hirasawa's third request for pardon was announced on 19 December 1980: request overturned.

Even after Hirasawa's natural death in prison in 1987, doubts remain about his guilt. His attorneys repeatedly insisted that the real culprit was someone who during the war had worked for the Japanese Army's bacteriological research unit. The Allied headquarters had thought this plausible, and allegedly evidence existed. This trail, however, was not followed up. Rumour held that Hirasawa's arrest had served the purpose of somehow solving the case to the satisfaction of the public, while diverting attention from the U.S.' own interest in the acquisition of the results of Japanese Wartime research on bacteriological weapons. It did not help that the leader of Hirasawa's support group was tried for forging evidence to support Hirasawa. Nevertheless, the sentiment at the time of the third request for pardon was generally so that it was believed that 34 years after the arrest and 27 years after the finalisation of the sentence, by now 91 year old Hirasawa had sufficiently repented.

The Prosecution and the Department for Penal Affairs within the Justice Ministry, however, never wavered in their firm belief that in no case could a murderer of twelve be pardoned. Accusations that the committee's deliberations were influenced were rejected. Nevertheless, the Ministry stressed that Hirasawa was the worst of all death row inmates at the time, and thus a pardon would destroy the balance with 'lighter' cases, even if granted in consideration of Hirasawa's age. Allegedly, the prosecution's reluctance to grant a pardon went so far that the Department of Penal Affairs had informally decided to pre-empt a committee decision by executing Hirasawa. On the other hand, the execution of a man his age would hardly have been acceptable to the public. Whether the prosecution's firm decision to execute if a pardon was granted was reported to the committee is not known. Surely, the committee knew about the prosecution's aversion. This probably altered the mood within the commission, for Hirasawa's rescue by pardon could have meant his sure death on the gallows. Hirasawa's petition for pardon was denied on 19 December 1980, and thus the last chance for his execution was thwarted.

In the context of the *Teigin* case, the following is noteworthy. Art. 32.1 of the Penal Code sets forth the prescriptive period as follows: '(a) Thirty years with reference to the death penalty.'

7 May 1985 marked the 30th anniversary of the finalisation of Hirasawa's death sentence. On 5 April, his counsel took action for protection of human rights under the Habeas Corpus Act (*Jinshin hogo-hô*). The case was dismissed by the Tokyo District Court on 30 May 1985. An immediate complaint before the High Court was rejected on 20 July 1985. Attorney Endô insisted that 'execution of the death penalty' in Art. 32 Penal Code is to be understood as 'execution of a finalised death sentence'. This, he held, must be interpreted as both the execution of the death penalty in the narrow sense as well as that of imprisonment. He saw it as an extreme injustice that a fugitive of thirty years should fall under this provision but not one imprisoned for the same amount of time. Also, Hirasawa's execution after more than thirty years would constitute a cruel punishment. If the justice minister did not intend to execute Hirasawa, then the purpose of imprisonment to execute the death sentence lapses, what in turn contradicts Art. 11.2 of the Penal Code. Endô demanded Hirasawa's immediate release.[121] The court rejected this line of argument, because 'the reason that no execution order was issued for more than thirty years was due to Hirasawa's continuous requests for retrial or pardon. Even after thirty years, an execution of the death sentence would not constitute a cruel punishment. Since prescription had not run for a single day, the continuance of imprisonment was seen as lawful. The court's decision mirrored the view held by the Justice Ministry, which rejects a prescription of a death sentence, if the criminal escapes the execution, for example by escaping from prison. Also, 'execution' in the meaning of Art. 32 Penal Code is not only that of the death sentence, but that of the finalised sentence. Therefore the provision could not be applied to persons who are imprisoned for the purpose of executing a finalised sentence. Endô countered that, from a humanitarian point of view, it is unbalanced to exclude the

121 In detail see LLOMPART note 13 p. 247

possibility of prescription for prisoners, while admitting it to fugitives.[122]

Albeit not anchored in the law, indeed – as the court pointed out - legal practice holds that executions are not carried out while applications for retrial or pardon are pending. Repeated applications can in fact delay an execution for years. Hirasawa's case serves as a most extreme example. During the 32 years between the finalisation of his death sentence and his death, there was only a total of 82 days where neither a request for retrial, nor one for pardon was pending.[123] Also, the four death row convicts who in the 1980s were acquitted in retrials kept themselves alive by repeated requests for retrial. Out of 56 finalised death convicts at the turn of 1992/93, 26 had pending retrial applications or were preparing such.[124]

The Japanese courts, which are still regarded as extremely conservative, do their reputation honour by plastering the way to a retrial with obstacles, and for a long time completely closing it to death row convicts.

Criminal cases are adjudicated by either a single judge or a bench, depending on the gravity of a case. Lighter cases are usually dealt with in one hearing, in other cases, weeks, sometimes months lie between the hearings. A trial can take years. Judges can change during a trial, since they are usually transferred every three to five years. In an appeal, a defendant can attack the actual as well as the legal explanations of the court.[125] An appeal court can hear additional evidence. A second appeal to the Supreme Court is possible, among other reasons, for violations or misinterpretations of the constitution or Supreme Court precedents. It can furthermore quash a judgment for serious errors in and/or of the facts. Once a decision has been finalised, the convict can request a retrial for a number of reasons.

The possibility of retrial for the first time in Japan was legally provided for in an edict of January 1876. Only the Prosecutor-General upon instruction by the Justice Ministry was authorised to

122 See ENDÔ MAKOTO, Hômu-shô to no shôtatsu o osoreta chisai kettei (A District Court Judgment in Collission with the Ministry of Justice) p. 102 (n.y.)

123 DANDÔ Part A note 13 p. 265

124 DANIEL H. FOOTE, *'The Door that Never Opens?' Capital Punishment and Post-Conviction Rewview of Death Sentences in the United States and Japan*, in 19-2 Brooklyn Journal of International Law p. 415 fn. 238 (1993)

125 See FOOTE note 124 p. 480

request a retrial, and only if there were grounds to assume that the original trial had been faulty. The same authority was provided for in another edict of 1877 for civil and criminal cases. The parties for the first time received the right to request a retrial by the – French-influenced - Code of Criminal Procedure (*Chizai-hô*) of 1880.[126]

The Code of Criminal Procedure, promulgated in 1922 after the German model, altered the provisions on retrial in that mistakes or procedural errors no longer had to be proven, but a retrial now could be applied for by both the prosecution and the defendant. A newly introduced provision (Art. 485 No.6) stated that a retrial could be requested.[127]

> When in regard to the case new definite evidence has been discovered, such that a person pronounced guilty could be found not guilty or acquitted, or a person sentenced could be granted a remission of their sentence or a lesser charge than the one admitted in the original judgment should be recognised.

The Code of Criminal Procedure of 1948 has adopted this provision almost without changes. However, a retrial is now only permitted for the benefit of the convict. No longer can the prosecution request

---

126 The law stated that a retrial could only be requested in favour of a defendant, and the prosecution must not introduce further procedure after an acquittal. However, according to Art. 301, a retrial was tied to very strict prerequisites:
(1) Proof that the alleged victim is still alive or was already deceased before the crime;
(2) punishment of another person for the same crime;
(3) officially recognized alibi;
(4) punishment of a person who through fraud caused the punishment of the applicant;
(5) official proof that records of the trial were forged or false, or
(6) revocation of another judgment, on which the verdict was based.
ODANAKA TOSHIKI & ÔDE YOSHITOMO, *Saishin hôsei no enkaku to mondai jôkyô (History and Problems of Retrial)*, in Keiji saishin no kenkyû (Studies on Retrial in criminalCCases) pp. 63, 65-69 (Kamo Yoshisuke ed., Tokyo 1980)

127 Further reasons in Art. 485:
(1) Forgery or alteration of documents on which the finalised judgment had based;
(2) wrong testimony;
(3) false accusation by witnesses of the prosecution;
(4) alteration of a decision on which the sentence was based;
(5) in case of violations of patent rights, trade marks etc.,
(6) if the allegedly infringed right later became invalid or was repealed;
(7) when a judge, prosecutor or police official had committed an offence in relation with the treatment of the case.

a retrial of a person found not guilty.[128] Although the current code is different from its predecessor only in the wording, some commentators hold the view that due to the spirit of respect for human rights under the postwar constitution, a more liberal interpretation than that of the 1922 code is appropriate.[129] Daniel Foote[130] notes, however, that in the first few postwar years, the provisions were interpreted far more strictly than before the war.

Most requests for retrial are based on 'new definite evidence'. This provision is often characterised as necessary to find the balance between the respect for finalised decisions (and thus certainty) and the search for the truth.[131] In the first decades after the war, the courts changed to a more strict interpretation of this criterion[132] and placed more weight on the respect for finalised judicature. The Supreme Court's Grand Bench decided on 21 April 1950[133] that one could gather from Art. 39 of the Japanese Constitution the need to respect finalised decisions, and thus the prerequisites for a retrial must be interpreted clearly and strictly. According to the wording, Art. 39 prohibits double jeopardy in the case of acquittal, but not a retrial requested by the convict after a guilty verdict. The hurdles

---

128 See Art. 39 Japanese Constitution: 'No person shall be held criminally liable for an act which was lawful at the time it was committed, or of which he has been acquitted, nor shall he be placed in double jeopardy.'

129 See e.g. FUJINO HIDEICHI, *Saishin ni tsuite (On Retrial)*, in 374 Keisatsu kenkyû pp. 87, 90 (1961)

130 Note 124 p. 421

131 See Nagoya District Court 15 July 1959 in 1 Ka-keishû p. 1550; Supreme Court 27 May 1958 in 12 Keishû p. 1683. The most important prewar decision had rather stressed the latter point.
Imperial Court of Cassation (*Daishin'in*) decision of 6. September 1924 (3 Daihan Keishû p. 663). In a case of theft of fish by several persons, all accused were sentenced by the Hakodate District Court (*Hakodate Ku-saibansho*) after confession. One, however, appealed and was acquitted when the storehouse manager testified that the allegedly stolen fish had been given to the defendants as a gift and incentive. Based on this new and definite evidence, the others applied for retrial but both the District and High Courts dismissed the appeal. The Court of Cassation decided: 'The provision concerned does not contain any limitation on the kind or nature of new evidence, and therefore it is appropriate to assume that it is a basis for a new trial, when this evidence concerns the evaluation of facts in the original judgment.' Furthermore, a new trial was justified, since based upon the new evidence it could be assumed that the defendants received the fish and then sold it or the like. Thus, to the court, a possibility of innocence sufficed.

132 'New definite evidence'

133 4 Keishû p. 666

which now had to be overcome to reach a retrial were placed very high by the Supreme Court. The term 'new evidence', for example, was interpreted very narrowly. The evidence should not be new only to the court, but also to the accused. Had he or she known about this evidence at the time of the original trial, it was no longer 'new'. The Supreme Court's Third Petty Bench ruled on 19 October 1954:[134] 'If the accused knows about the evidence and does not present it to the court, and after finalisation of the sentence requests a retrial based on this evidence, then this evidence is not new evidence. This decision did not remain uncriticised by those who wanted more weight to be placed on the search for truth. It was held that evidence must be regarded as 'new', when presented for the first time to the court.[135] Legal science regarded evidence as not new when the accused knowingly and intentionally had withheld it from the court, but not if the evidence had not been presented even though the accused could have discovered it, but negligently failed to do so.[136]

Until about the mid-1960s, dissonance existed about whether recognised new evidence should be adjudged separately or in combination with previously presented evidence. Since then it has been decided in favour of an 'overall assessment' (*sôgô hyôka*).[137]

More difficult was the interpretation of the evidential value of new evidence. Whereas the Imperial Court of Cassation in 1924 had rather low requirements, the Supreme Court in 1958[138] demanded that 'definite evidence' must have both force of proof as well as of conviction. Although the Japanese have adopted the principle *in dubio pro reo* in their laws (*utagawashiki wa hikoku-nin no rieki ni*), their courts have interpreted it strictly, demanding evidence exceeding 'justified doubt', that is, a clear proof of innocence.[139]

This practice soon met with stern criticism, especially from among legal science.[140] First signs of a change in the Japanese

---

134 8 Keishû p. 1610

135 MITSUDÔ KAGEAKI, *Saishin shôkô-shô,* in 37-6 Hôritsu Jôhô p. 22

136 FOOTE note 124 pp. 426-427.

137 ODANAKA/ÔDE note 126 p. 113

138 27 May 1958, 12 Keishû p. 1683

139 Other courts defined: 'Force of evidence of high reliability' (Tokyo District Court 29 June 1954 (5 Hanrei jihô p. 311) or 'Evidence which is sufficient to assume a high probability to assume the applicant's innocence' (Nagoya District Court 15 July 1959 (1 Kô-keishû p. 1550). Also see Supreme Court decision 20 May 1975, 29 Keishû p. 177

140 Examplarily, e.g. ODANAKA/ÔDE note 126 pp. 77-80

judiciary could only be observed from about the mid-1970s. On 31 March 1975, the Tokyo District Court decided that the law does not require a positive proof of evidence, but rather a clear proof suffices which causes justified doubts on the guilt of the person convicted.[141]

It was only in 1979 that the hitherto 'closed door' of retrial was opened for convicts on death row: in June in the Saitagawa case, in September in the Menda case, and in November in the Matsuyama case. Slightly earlier, there had been several sensational retrial cases, where convicts originally found guilty of murder, robbery and murder or similarly grave crimes, were found not guilty and were acquitted.[142]

Have there indeed, as the Japanese Government assures, never since the *Meiji* Period been a single case of erroneous judgment in death penalty cases? Since the introduction of a Western legal system in the *Meiji* Period, there have been a number of doubtful cases.[143]

---

141 See FOOTE note 124 p. 430

142 SATÔ note 13 pp. 140-141

143 In the Tokyo-father-murder case, Udagawa, who was sentenced to death by the Tokyo District Court for patricide on 26 January 1904, was found not guilty by the Tokyo Court of Appeals (Kôso-in). In the original trial, the court had assumed that the motive for the crime had been to gain the father's property. The accused and his father had quarreled. The defendant's alibi that at the time of the crime, he had been at home with his wife, was doubted. The Court of Appeals, however, saw in the enmity between father and son no sufficient evidence for the crime.
Another relevant case is the so-called Gunma police-officer murder case. In the night of 3 December 1904, in a village in Gunma Prefecture, policeman Maehara stopped two suspicous men; since they ran away, he pursued them. He succeeded in arresting one of them, when the second stabbed him to death. Early the next year, three men were arrested. They categorically denied the crime. In late March 1905, however, the youngest of them confessed during the preliminary hearing at the Maebashi District Court: 'Only I fled into a different direction, but my father and brother Kôjirô killed the policeman.' The father continued to deny the charge, but the brother got entangled in contradictions. The District Court sentenced both to death; their appeals (Tokyo Court of Appeals 31 October 1905, Imperial Court of Cassation 16 January 1906) were dismissed. The application for retrial was dismissed on 5 February 1906, and both death sentences executed on 9 September 1908.
Later, Sawabe Nagayoshi, who had been held for a different crime, confessed to have committed the murder together with already deceased Ômori Kama.
Noteworthy for the *Taishô* period is the Suzu-ga-mori Oharu-murder case. In the night of 29 April 1914 in Tokyo 25-year-old bath-house employee Tanaka Haru was found dead, with bruises and stab-wounds covering her body. 35-year-old Komori was arrested; he confessed on 30 May. During the preliminary hearing on 23 June he protested his innocence, claiming the police had coerced him to confess by torture.

The most prominent case of the *Meiji* Period was the *Taigyaku* case. For the alleged plan to assassinate *Meiji* Tennô, several suspected anarchists and socialists were arrested and indicted for high treason. On 18 January 1991, after a non-public trial without a single witness, the special criminal bench of the Imperial Court

---

In January 1915, 42-year-old Ishii appeared, claiming to be the murderer. Ishii on 25 January 1915 was indicted for the murder of Haru. The Tokyo District Court on 4 December 1915 ruled Komori not-guilty. But the prosecution appealed the verdict, since Ishii's committing the crime had not been proven. On 30 March 1917, the Tokyo Appeal Court sentenced Ishii to death. He was executed on 17 August 1917. On 27 September 1917, two-and-a-half years after Ishii's appearance, Komori was finally acquitted.

In the Fukui money-lender murder case, on 25 December 1913, in Fukui Prefecture, money lender Shimizu Tomokichi was killed, his pawn tickets and bills were stolen. His dead body had been thrown into a river. As suspects, his older brother, who had borrowed money from him, was arrested, as well as six other persons. All were indicted, all protested their innocence. During the hearing, they insisted that they had been coerced into confession under torture. Nevertheless, the brother on 23 June 1914 was sentenced to death, the others to imprisonment between 15 years and life. The Nagoya Appeal Court on 12 March 1915 acquitted all of the defendants.

In the Osaka mother murder case, on 26 January 1915, 65-year-old Mizoguchi Kura was murdered in Osaka. Her son (26) and a certain Naitô Ukichi (44) were indicted for the crime. In the first instance, Naitô was sentenced to death, the son to ten years in prison. The son served his sentence, while Naitô on 22 July 1916 was acquitted by the Osaka Appeal Court.

In the Hakodate-Maruyama brothel proprietor case, on 28 July 1919, in Hakodate brothel proprietor Yamada Seiichi was murdered. His adoptive son-in-law Yamada Noboru (45) was indicted, but the Hakodate District Court found him not guilty on 14 September 1920. The appeal court followed the prosecution's demand and on 12 September 1921 sentenced Yamada to death. The Imperial Court revoked the decision, and on 20 December 1922 the Sendai Appeal Court aquitted Yamada.

For the early *Shôwa* period, the Osaka-Juso fishing pond case must be mentioned. In the night of 1 March 1931, the guard house of a fishing pond in Juso burnt down. Out of the ashes, the charred remains of guard Takematsu Furuya (52) were pulled, showing signs of serious injury. Police arrested his wife Miyo (47) and her alleged lover Morita (44). After initial denial, both confessed, but Morita during the second preliminary hearing denied his involvement. In the main hearing, both protested their innocence. The Osaka District Court on 26 November 1931 sentenced Miyo to death and Morita to life in prison. The appeal was rejected by the Tokyo Appeals Court on 5 July 1932, and so was the second appeal by the Imperial Court on 8 March 1933. Miyo was executed on 28 June 1935.

Among the numerous cases in postwar Japan, in the Fukuoka-case, Nishi Takeo and Ishii Kenjirô in April 1956 were sentenced to death for a murder, allegedly committed in Fukuoka in 1947. Five requests for retrial were rejected. Nishi was executed on 17 June 1975, Ishii's sentence the same day mitigated into imprisonment for life.

On these and further cases see SCHMIDT Part A ote 29 pp. et seq.

sentenced 25 people to death.[144] From the first hearing until the last, only 20 days had passed, 40 days had passed from the first heating until the ruling. On 24 January, 11 men, and on 25 January the only woman, were executed in Tokyo prison. Four of the convicts indeed seem to have planned the killing of the emperor. The others most likely had nothing to do with this.

Fifty years after the death sentence, the only survivor, Sakamoto Kiyome, as well as Sakako, sister of the executed Morichika Kazuhira, applied for retrial. The motion was rejected by the Supreme Court on 1 February 1965. On 5 July, the Supreme Court also rejected a special complaint. Strong doubts remain whether there really had been no innocent people among the executed after a non-public trial without a single witness.[145]

Moreover, the risk of false decisions can be shown in the course of a trial. Indeed, there are no known cases of executions of innocent people. However, the possibility that a number of such cases remain undetected cannot be denied. One must bear in mind that, for example, cases where death sentences from lower courts in appeal trials were mitigated or the accused was even acquitted, may be regarded as false judgments.

One of the cases that occurred during the *Taishô* Period (1912-1926) was a fourfold murder in Tôkyô-Yanagijima:[146]

---

144 12 death sentences were mitigated by the Tenno into imprisonment for life the following day.

145 see MIHARA Part A note 5 p. 393; SATÔ SHIGEHITO (ED.), Soshite, shikei wa shikkô sareta – moto shikei-shû-tachi no shôgen (The Death Sentence was Executed – Testimony by Former Death Row Inmates) p. 273 (Tokyo 1990)

146 Other cases included for example the following:
On 30 December 1931, in Niigata Prefecture, the blood-soaked body of farmer Hosokawa (50) was found in his home. Since there were no traces of intrusion, the police assumed that the culprit came from within the family, and arrested the victim's mother, Mita (66), his wife Masa (45), his oldest son Yôtarô (21) and his second son Kôda (17). Kôda testified: 'The four of us conspired and then killed him', but Yôtarô confessed: 'Kôda has nothing to do with this. I have killed him alone'. Kôda revoked his confession, and so did Yôtarô: he lied, because he wanted to help his mother and grandmother. The Niigata District Court on 2 June 1914 sentenced all four to death on 27 May 1915, the Appeal Court upheld the death sentence for Yôtarô and acquitted the others. Yôtarô appealed, but his action was dismissed on 8 July 1915. The death sentence thus became finalised. His attorneys requested pardon on 16 August 1915, but this, too, was rejected. Yôtarô was executed on 8 December 1916. His attorney later found evidence that hinted at his client's innocence.

The four members of the family of bicycle dealer Okamoto (34) were robbed and slain in their home. Two young apprentices, who at the time of the crime had slept in the house, were ruled out as culprits; Okamoto's mistress had an alibi. Eventually, bicycle parts dealer Hashimoto Heisaburô (36) was arrested as suspect in the case. During interrogation he confessed to the crime. On 15 October 1914, the Tokyo District Court sentenced him to death, although he by now denied everything.

Before the Tokyo Appeal Court, surprising facts were asserted: because Hashimoto did not confess, he was sent to the police on 10 May, who, after fruitless interrogations, sent Yamaguchi Toshio, a man with multiple previous convictions, into Hashimoto's cell. Yamaguchi already had a track record of assisting police in extracting confessions from fellow accused. Such 'confession recruiters' are called *nakako.* Presenting Hashimoto with food and a shirt, Yamaguchi advised him: 'Once police regard you as the culprit, they will coerce a confession ... therefore you better make a false confession, have a quick and thus a fair and just trial.' Hashimoto had done as he was told.

On 14 June 1915, the Appeal Court acquitted him for lack of evidence.

On 24 July 1919, a 20 year old man was apprehended for theft and dealing in stolen goods. Tormented by nightmares, he eventually confessed to the murder of Okamoto. At the time of the crime he had been 15 years old and worked as a boy for a *miso* shop next door to the bicycle shop. Angry about the miserliness and unfriendliness of the bicycle dealer, he broke into the house and killed the whole sleeping family. He also confessed to several rapes and the murder of two 15-year-old girls. He was sentenced to death.

In the prewar and wartime *Shôwa* Period (1926-1945), the so-called Okayama poisoned-dumpling case caused a stir:

In the early hours of 4 March 1928, in Okayama Prefecture, farmer Morita (44) and his uncle (57) died after having eaten poisoned dumpling soup. Five other people suffered serious injuries. Uma, the uncle's wife, was arrested on suspicion of murder and confessed. The Okayama District Court sentenced her to death, but the Hiroshima Appeal Court on 2 February 1929 acquitted her for lack of evidence.

After the Second World War, the number of doubtful cases increased. Among the most spectacular cases was the Tomiura case:

In the night of 29 January 1948, in Shizuoka, the four members of the family of confectionary producer Hagiwara (34) disappeared. Furthermore, since ¥ 70,000 in cash, about 20 items of clothing and a car were missing, investigations for robbery and murder were instigated, and neighbouring farmers Kondô Katsutarô (27), Kondô Gôhei (47) and Koshima Yukio (21) were arrested. Katsutarô confessed the next day to having planned and committed the murder together with the other two men. One day later, the dead bodies of the four family members were found on a nearby beach. The three farmers were indicted for robbery and murder and discarding the bodies. From the first hearing, all four denied the accusations and complained about police torture.

The Shizuoka District Court, Hamamatsu Branch, on 27 April 1950 sentenced all three to death. On 8 May 1951, the Tokyo High Court dismissed the appeal, but on 14 January 1957, the Supreme Court revoked the decision because of doubts about the credibility of the confessions, and sent the case back to the High Court, which on 28 February 1959 returned not-guilty verdicts. The appeal filed by the prosecution was turned down by the Supreme Court on 9 July 1963.

Also noteworthy is the so-called Yagai-case:[147]

---

147 Other cases include the following:
In the Matsukawa case, in the early hours of 17 August 1949, a passenger train of the Tôhoku line derailed. The driver and two assistants died, about thirty passengers were injured. At the scene, bolts and joint plates had been removed. Police suspected that the culprit came from among the railway union, the union of the Tôshiba Matsukawa factory or from among the ranks of the Communist Party. Based on the confession of a man named Akama, 20 persons were arrested and indicted. On 6 December 1950, the Fukushima District Court sentenced five of the accused to death, the others to penal servitude for various terms, including life. The Sendai High Court on 22 January 1953 upheld four of the death verdicts, but acquitted three of the accused. These three previously had been viewed as the leaders of the attack. Because of doubts on the confessions, the Supreme Court revoked the high Court's decision and sent the case back to the Sendai High Court, which on 8 August 1951 acquitted all of the accused.
In the Kimagase case, in the morning of 7 May 1950, real estate agent Furuhashi (35), his wife and two children were brutally slain in Chiba. Also, ¥ 2,300 in cash

In the night of 24 January 1951, in Yamaguchi Prefecture, farmer Hayagane Sôhyôe (64) was slain, and his wife Hisa (64) fell and broke her neck. About ¥ 10,000 in cash were stolen. Two days later, Yoshioka Akira (22) was arrested. After initial denial, he confessed to having committed the crime alone. Police believed that more than one person was involved, and pressed Yoshioka until he named five alleged accomplices, who were quickly arrested. One of the men was soon released. The other four confessed, but rescinded soon thereafter, claiming they had been tortured by police to confess. On 2 June 1952 the Yamaguchi District Court, Iwakuni Branch, on 2 June 1952 found all defendants guilty and sentenced one of the alleged accomplices to death, the others to imprisonment for life. The Hiroshima High Court on 18 September 1953 principally upheld

---

were stolen. Investigations stagnated. After intensive questioning of the whole neighbourhood, on 27 November 1950, out of 600 suspects, 19-year-old Honda was interrogated, after being arrested in a different case of theft. He denied the murder, but was indicted for the theft on 17 December 1950. The Chiba District Court acquitted him on 27 February 1951, but simultaneously he was arrested on suspicion of robbery and murder. After forty days of interrogation he confessed to have entered Furuhashi's house with the intent to steal; when discovered by the family, he killed them. After the crime, he fled with the victim's car. On 12 April 1951 he was indicted for robbery and murder.

In the hearing he protested his innocence, asserting that the confession had been made under police torture. In December 1954, the prosecution demanded the death penalty. But when six specialists failed to agree on the murder weapon, Honda's attorney on 24 July 1957 demanded his client's release, since such long detention constituted a violation of Honda's human rights. Honda was released on bail. The Chiba District Court on 22 September 1958 sentenced Honda to death, since the confession was credible. However, the Tokyo High Court on 30 May 1961 revoked the decision, and acquitted Honda for a lack of evidence and coercion of the confession.

In the Niho case, on the morning of 2 October 1954, in Yamaguchi Prefecture the six members of the family of farmer Yamane Tamotsu were brutally slain and cash was stolen. Police investigations provided no conclusion. One year after the crime, on 19 October 1955, Okabe Tamotsu (37) from Niho, who then lived in Osaka, was arrested in a different case and handed over to the Yamaguchi police. After four months of continuous interrogation, he confessed the crime and on 30 March 1956 was indicted for robbery and murder. During the trial he denied the crime. There was no material evidence.

The Yamaguchi District Court viewed the confession as voluntary and credible and sentenced him to death on 15 June 1962. On 14 February 1968 the Hiroshima High Court rejected his appeal. However, on 31 July 1970, the Supreme Court revoked this decision due to doubts on the credibility of the confession and misinterpretation of facts, and referred the case back to the Hiroshima High Court, which on 14 December 1972 acquitted Okabe.

this decision and sentenced one of the accused to death, Yoshioka to life in prison, and the others to imprisonment for 12 and 15 years. All men appealed. Yoshioka retracted his appeal on 15 March 1954, finalising his sentence. On 15 October 1957, the Supreme Court revoked the sentences for errors in facts and sent the case back to the Hiroshima High Court. After renewed investigations the court found that Yoshioka must be the sole culprit, and acquitted the other four on 23 September 1959.

The prosecution again appealed, and the High Court decided on 19 May 1962 that there must have been more than one culprit, sentencing the four men to between 12 and 15 years in prison. The accused appealed to the Supreme Court, which quashed the previous judgment, acknowledged Yoshioka as the sole culprit and acquitted the other four for a lack of evidence.

In the Matsukawa case, Satô Kazu and four other persons were sentenced to death on 6 December 1950 by the Fukushima District Court for the derailing of a train causing death. Five other accused received life sentences, ten more prison sentences. In the appeal, the Sendai High Court on 22 December 1953 handed down four death sentences, two life sentences and eleven other prison terms and acquitted three. On 10 August 1959 the Supreme Court quashed this judgment and referred the case back to the Sendai High Court, which on 8 August 1961 acquitted all accused. The prosecution's appeal was turned down on 12 September 1963.

It was only after the Second World War that for the first time criminals with finalised convictions were found not guilty in retrials.[148]

---

148 Other noteworthy cases:
In the Taki case, Taki Junnosuke in June 1953 was sentenced by the Tokyo District Court to prison for life for 19 cases of robbery and murder and robbery and bodily injury. He appealed, but withdrew later. He argued that he had an alibi for eleven cases, and that there was new evidence. His application for a retrial with the Tokyo District Court in January 1974, was rejected in February 1976. After immediate complaint, the Tokyo High Court in October 1980 ruled for a retrial in one of the cases, for which Taki in March 1981 was found not guilty.
In the Kanamori case, on 26 October 1942 Kanamori Kenkô was sentenced to fifteen years in prison for arson which he was alleged to have committed on 2 October 1941 in Kanayama. The retrial was opened on 28 June 1969, the not guilty verdict handed down on 28 January 1970.

The first prominent retrial case was the so-called Yoshida-Gankutsu-ô-case:[149]

In the Katô case, on 7 November 1916, Katô Shin'ichi was sentenced to life in prison for an alleged robbery and murder committed on 11 July 1915 in Yamaguchi; after the sixth request, retrial was opened on 18 September 1976, and Katô acquitted on 7 July 1977.

In the Umeda case, on 22 December 1957, Umeda Yoshimitsu was sentenced to prison for life for robbery-murder, which he allegedly had committed on 10 October 1950 in Hokkaido. The first request to reopen the trial was filed in October 1962 and dismissed in 1968. The second request was filed in December 1979 with the Kushiro District Court, which three years later decided to reopen the case. The immediate complaint by the prosecution was rejected by the Sapporo High Court in February 1985. The trial was reopened on 8 February 1985, and Umeda was found not guilty on 8 September 1987.

In August 1953 Yoneya Shirô was sentenced to ten years in prison. He had been found guilty of raping and killing a woman in 1952. After the apprehension of the real culprit, in August 1957 Yoneya filed for retrial with the Aomori District Court. The application was rejected in March 1973, but granted by the Sendai High Court in October 1976 after immediate complaint. A not guilty verdict was handed down in July 1978.

In detail on these and other cases see SCHMIDT Part A note 29 pp. 287 et seq

149 Also see, for example, the following cases:

In the Hirosaki case, Nasu Takashi was sentenced to imprisonment for fifteen years for a murder which he was accused of having committed on 6 August 1949 in Aomori. Although he had been interrogated intensely for two months, he denied having committed the crime and eventually was acquitted due to a lack of evidence (Aomori District Court 12 January 1951). The prosecution appealed, and on 31 May 1952 the Sendai High Court found him guilty of the murder and sentenced him to fifteen years in prison. The judgment was finalised on 19 February 1953.

After Nasu had served his sentence, a man appeared who confessed to having committed the crime and cited numerous details which seemed to prove his assertion. Still, the Sendai High Court rejected Nasu's application for retrial, since the man could have gained his knowledge from media reports (13 December 1974).

Eventually, on 13 July 1976 the Sendai High Court opened the retrial, acknowledged the other man as the real culprit and on 15 February 1977 found Nasu not guilty.

Yonetani Shirô on 22 August 1953 was sentenced to ten years in prison by the Sendai High Court (original trial: Aomori District Court, 5 December 1952) for attempted rape and bodily injury.

In 1966, eight years after Yonetani's release on parole, a nephew of the victim confessed the crime. The prosecution started the case again and indicted the nephew. But he withdrew his confession and was acquitted by the Tokyo District Court (2 July 1968). The prosecution appealed, but the nephew committed suicide. In the meantime, Yonetani requested a retrial of his case; but since the nephew's confession was not evaluated as a sufficiently new evidence, the Aomori District Court rejected the request in 1973. Eventually, the trial was reopened on 30 October 1976, and a not-guilty verdict handed down on 31 July 1987.

Yoshida Iematsu, based on the testimony of two alleged accomplices, on 4 November 1914 had been sentenced to life in prison for a robbery-murder he was accused to have committed on 13 March 1913 in Nagoya. Although the two renounced their testimony, four requests for retrial by Yoshida were turned down. After the fifth application, the retrial was opened on 30 October 1962, after vehement public protests, and after the Japanese Federation of Bar Associations had established a special committee for Yoshida's support. On 28 February 1963 he was found not guilty.

One of the best-known retrial cases was the Tokushima radio shop case:[150]

For a murder allegedly committed on 5 November 1953 in Tokushima, Fuji Shigeko was sentenced to thirteen years in prison. In 1958, the two main witnesses of the prosecution confessed that they had given false testimony under pressure by the prosecution. Nevertheless, the Tokushima District Court found, when examining the second request for retrial, that these confessions were new evidence, but it could not be asserted whether the witnesses had lied in their original testimony or not. The request was dismissed on 9 December 1960. For the third request, it was no longer new evidence (9 March 1963). When the fourth request was filed, the district court regarded the testimony of the witnesses as new, but not as sufficiently definite. The dismissal was ruled on 20 July 1970. Fuji applied a fifth time, but died in 1979. However, on 23 December 1980 the Tokushima District Court accepted a request filed by her siblings. The prosecution's complaint was dismissed by the Takamatsu High Court on 12 March 1983, and the trial reopened. Fuji was found not guilty on 9 July 1985.

Only a few convicts have succeeded in opening the door to a retrial; even fewer have successfully protested their innocence. Until the early 1980s, not a single convict on death row had been among those acquitted. From 1983, four convicts, all on death row for decades, regained their life and liberty in retrials. The road had been paved by

150 SATÔ note 145 p. 274

the Shiratori case.[151] Murakami Kuniyasu, who had been sentenced to imprisonment for life for the murder of a policeman, requested the reopening of the trial after finalisation of the sentence. While largely ignoring previous decisions as well as the debate, the judgment accepted the criteria 'overall appreciation' of evidence and 'justified doubts' and reduced the requirements for retrial from 'high possibility' to 'possibility' of the convict's innocence. However, in this particular case, after a long procedure, the Supreme Court rejected Murakami's application for retrial in May 1975. Nevertheless, this decision exerted great influence on judicial practice and opened the door to retrials in death sentence cases.[152]

Between 1952 and 1984, a total of 120 requests for retrial were made by death row convicts. Five were accepted, including two filed by Menda Sakae.

---

151 In 1952, policeman Shiratori Kazuo was shot to death in Sapporo, while cycling home. Nine months after the crime, Communist Party member Murakami Kuniyasu was arrested. After having been held by the police for a total of three years for fourteen different delicts, in late 1955 he was rearrested for the murder of the policeman, indicted, and in 1957 sentenced to life in prison by the Sapporo District Court. The Sapporo High Court confirmed the verdict in 1960, but mitigated the sentence to twenty years. The Supreme Court on 17 October 1963 rejected his appeal (17 Keishû p. 1795). In 1965, a request for retrial was rejected by the Sapporô District Court (558 Hanji p. 14). On 16 July 1971, the Sapporo High Court dismissed the case (3 Keisai Geppô p. 869). Murakami appealed to the Supreme Court. The court's first petty bench, which with justices Kishi Seiichi and Dandô Shigemitsu comprised two members who for decades had called for a reform of the retrial system (in detail s. FOOTE note 124 pp. 429-430, 429 fn. 291, 440-442). The decision of 20 May 1975 contains the following passage: 'The expression 'definite evidence which demands an assertion of innocence' should relate to such evidence which leaves room for justified doubt on the facts of the original judgment and sufficient possibility to assume that these findings would be disproved. The evaluation whether the evidence is new should be based on an overall evaluation as well as of all new further evidence. This should be made from the point of view whether the facts of the original judgment would have been reached even under the submission of the new evidence. This procedure should be conducted under the principle 'in doubt for the accused', i.e. in the sense that it is the appearance of justified doubt whose submission suffices for a reopening of the trial.' 29 Keishû p. 177; see FOOTE note 124 pp. 442-443

152 DANDÔ Part A note 13 p. 148

The first death penalty case to be retried was the so-called Saitakawa case:[153] In the early hours of 28 February 1950, in Saita village in Kagawa Prefecture, black market rice dealer Kagawa Shigeo (62) was stabbed to death. About ¥ 13,000 were stolen. Kagawa seemed to have fought with his killer: futon, clothing and tatami were soaked in blood. After the interrogation of some 130 suspects, investigations stagnated. On 3 April 1950, 19 year old Taniguchi Shigeyoshi was arrested as a suspected accomplice in a case of robbery and bodily injury. He confessed the crime and on 15 June was sentenced to three years and six months in prison by the Takamatsu District Court, Marugame Branch. During the three months in detention, he was also interrogated in the Saitakawa case, but did not confess. There was no evidence.

One day before the finalisation of his sentence in the other case, on which Taniguchi was to be transferred to prison, police rearrested him for suspected theft, and continued the interrogation in the Kagawa case until 11 July. Since on that day the longest possible period of detention in this case ended, Taniguchi again was rearrested in yet another case of theft. At the end of that month, Taniguchi had eventually confessed to the murder of Kagawa, and on 1 August he was arrested for this crime. He remained in detention at the police station until the indictment on 23 August.

From the beginning of the hearings before the Takamatsu District Court, Marugame Branch, Taniguchi denied the crime. Besides his earlier confession, the prosecution presented a forensic report according to which blood of the victim's type had been found on trousers allegedly worn by Taniguchi at the time of the crime. The defence claimed that the trousers had belonged to Taniguchi's brother and stressed that neither the murder weapon nor Taniguchi's shoes had been found. Despite these doubts, as well as inconsistencies and the general unbelievability of Taniguchi's confession, the court recognised its voluntariness and credibility, and on 12 February 1952 sentenced him to death. Taniguchi appealed, but on 8 June 1956 this appeal was turned down by the Takamatsu High Court. Taniguchi the same day launched a second appeal.

---

153 For material on the case, see, for example, 929 Hanji pp. 53 et seq, 995 Hanji pp. 3 et seq, 1107 Hanji pp. 15 et seq; 30 Keishû pp. 1680 et seq; NIHON BENGOSHI RENGÔ-KAI (NBR), Zoku saishin (Retrial pt.ii) pp. 70 et seq (Tokyo 1986); DANIEL H. FOOTE, *From Japan's Death Row to Freedom*, in 1 Pacific Rim Law and Policy Journal pp. 35 et seq (1992); FOOTE note 124

This, too, on 2 February 1957 was rejected by the Supreme Court for a lack of grounds for appeal. The death sentence became finalised.

On 26 March 1957, Taniguchi requested a retrial with the Takamatsu District Court, Marugame Branch, based on Art. 435 Nos. 1,2 Code of Criminal Procedure. After only one hearing, the court rejected the request on 20 March 1958. A letter from Taniguchi to the district court in March 1964, in which he had protested his innocence, was found years later by Judge Yano Ikichi, who resolved to treat the letter as a request for a retrial, which was officially launched with that court on 4 April 1969. After intensive investigation, the court acknowledged that there were numerous doubtful points, but nevertheless rejected the request on 30 September 1972 for lack of proof on forgery or alteration of evidence by the prosecution. Taniguchi's counsel (Judge Yano), launched an immediate complaint, which was also rejected on 5 December 1974. The defence filed a special complaint. The Supreme Court's First Petty Bench ruled on 12 October 1976 that the High Court's investigations had been insufficient and many doubtful points remained. Especially a graphological report on the handwriting of the confessions, allegedly produced by Taniguchi himself, showed considerable doubt as to the author and provided evidence as demanded by Art. 435 No. 6 Code of Criminal Procedure. The Supreme Court revoked the judgments of the District and High Courts, and referred the case back to the Takamatsu District Court. This court on 7 November 1977 opened the case, but mainly concentrated on blood tests as well as on documents previously kept secret, which showed that at the time of Taniguchi's confession the police had known that Kagawa had died from two stabs in the heart. Previously, it had been assumed that only the culprit could have known this fact. Therefore, the court on 7 June 1979 resolved to reopen the trial. Simultaneously, the court decided to stay the execution of the death sentence. Imprisonment, however, continued. The trial was reopened on 20 March 1981. The Takamatsu District Court did not elaborate on the voluntariness of the confession, but acknowledged justified doubts as to its credibility. On 12 March 1984 the court ruled that there were stains of blood type 0 on the trousers, but that it had not sufficiently been proven that Taniguchi had worn those trousers on the day of the crime. Taniguchi was acquitted. The prosecution waived an appeal.

The decision became finalised on 26 March, 32 years after the death sentence and 27 years after its finalisation.

The second and most prominent retrial case of a death row convict is the Menda case.[154] In Hitoyoshi, Kumamoto Prefecture, around 11.30 p.m. on 29 December 1948, 76-year-old healer Shirafuku Kakuzô and his wife Tokie (52) were killed in their home with some kind of axe and a knife; both their daughters were seriously injured. The blood-soaked house had been turned upside down, but nothing had been taken. The culprit had left no traces. According to the statements of the daughters, he had been a dark little man between the ages of 20 and 30 with slick hair, wearing traditional clothing.

Investigations by a special commission of the Hitoyoshi police made no progress. In early January 1949, police in nearby Yatsushiro received word about an alleged private investigator who claimed to be investigating in the Shirafuku case. The man was 23 year old Menda Sakae, the son of a farmer, who told police he had spent the night in question in a guesthouse with a prostitute. Police concluded after further investigations that the description of the murderer matched Menda, who in further interrogations confessed the theft of rice in a different case. On 14 January 1949 Menda was arrested in that latter case. Immediately after his release on 16 January, he was rearrested in the Shirafuku case. After uninterrupted interrogations until 16 February, Menda confessed. When, after denying, he repeated his confession on 19 February before the prosecution, he was placed in detention.

On 28 February, Menda was indicted for unlawful entry, robbery and murder and attempted robbery and murder as well as for the theft of rice. During the first hearing before the Kumamoto District Court, Yatsushiro Branch (17 March 1949), Menda confessed, and his counsel stated that the defence would only protest his intent, but not the crime itself. During the second hearing, prostitute Fumiko testified that Menda had stayed with her on the night of 30 December. Menda, however, told the judge that he thought he had spent the night of the 29th with her. On 14 April, Menda eventually renounced his confession before the court. He now insisted to have

---

154 For material on the case, see, for example, 828 Hanji pp. 95 et seq, 939 Hanji pp. 22 et seq, 984 Hanji pp. 41 et seq, 1090 Hanji pp. 84 et seq; NIHON BENGOSHI RENGÔ-KAI (NBR), Saishin (Retrial) pp. 343 et seq (Tokyo 1977); NBR note 153 pp. 47 et seq; FOOTE note 153 pp. 21 et seq

spent the night of the crime with Fumiko. The District Court, based on the credibility of the confession and some material evidence, on 23 March 1950 handed down a guilty verdict, and sentenced Menda to death. The Fukuoka High Court on 19 March 1951 rejected the appeal. The death sentence was finalised on 25 December 1951 with the rejection of the second appeal by the Supreme Court, Third Petty Bench.

Menda repeatedly requested a retrial to prove his innocence. On 18 May 1954, he filed a third request with the Kumamoto District Court, Yatsushiro Branch, which decided to reopen the trial since it thought the authenticity of Menda's alibi possible. After a special complaint by the prosecution, the Fukuoka High Court on 15 April 1959 quashed the District Court's judgment, whose investigations had exceeded the frame of the procedure and thus endangered the stability of judgments and the existence of the judicial system as a whole. Menda filed a special complaint, which on 6 December 1961 was rejected by the Supreme Court. The immediate complaint against this decision was turned down on 4 May, as was the special complaint on 7 July. On 17 April 1972, the sixth request for retrial was filed with the Kumamoto District Court, but was rejected on 30 April 1976. On 4 May 1976, Menda filed an immediate complaint. On 27 September 1979, the Fukuoka High Court elaborated: 'The contents of the applicant's confession do not conform with [the facts of the crime], and according to the forensic report there are doubts as to the credibility of the confession.' Despite doubts about the alibi, the court revoked the district court's decision, and based on the submission of 'new and definite evidence', introduced a retrial, staying the execution of the death sentence. On 2 October 1979, the prosecution filed a special complaint, since the produced evidence was not new or was insufficient. The Supreme Court's First Petty Bench rejected it on 11 December 1979. The Menda case was reopened on 15 May 1981 before the Kumamoto District Court, Yatsushiro Branch. Although the court rejected as inconceivable the testimony of a new witness of the prosecution who claimed to have seen Menda on the morning after the crime in the home of his parents, wet and dirty, the prosecution in its indictment on 5 November 1982 still demanded the death penalty. On 15 July 1983, the Kumamoto District Court, Yatsushiro Branch, acknowledged Menda's alibi. Since Menda consequently could not be the culprit, the court refrained from examining in detail other evidence, but sharply criticised the conduct of the investigating officers during interrogation. The court also did not judge the confession's voluntariness, but expressed doubts about its credibility. The prosecution refrained from appealing and 33 years and four month after the death sentence, on 29 July 1983 Menda was released.

The Matsuyama case:[155] In the early hours of 18 October 1955, in Matsuyama, Miyagi Prefecture, the four members of the Ohara family were brutally murdered. Their home was set on fire. A special commission of the prefectural police took up investigations for murder and arson. Five lovers of Ohara's wife as well as Saitô Sachio, the 24-year-old son of a lumber dealer, came under suspicion. On 2 December 1955, Saitô was arrested in Tokyo in a different case of bodily injury. He was interrogated in the Ohara case and after his transfer to the Yoshikawa police three days later and further interrogation, he confessed on 6 December. On 8 December, he was arrested for this crime. After having confessed in writing and on tape, he denied everything from 15 December.

The Sendai District Court, Yoshikawa Branch, upheld the voluntariness and credibility of the confession, and recognised circumstantial evidence. On 29 October 1957, it sentenced Saitô to death. His appeal was rejected by the Sendai High Court on 26 May 1959. The Supreme Court's Third Petty Bench, too, on 1 November 1960, turned down the second appeal. The death sentence was finalised on 24 November 1960.

After a first request for retrial had been rejected, on 26 October 1971 Saitô filed a second request with the Sendai District Court, Yoshikawa Branch, citing new forensic reports on blood traces. However, on 26 October 1971, the court turned down the request, since it was not 'new evidence' and it was not part of the court's authority to evaluate evidence and facts of a finalised judgment. Saitô's counsel filed an immediate complaint. The Sendai High Court acknowledged this on 18 September 1973, among other reasons, for procedural mistakes, and referred the case back to the district court. The Yoshikawa Branch of the Sendai District Court on 6 December 1979 decided to reopen the trial because of doubts on

---

155 For material on the case, see, for example, 949 HANJI 11 et seq, 1067 Hanji pp. 3 et seq, 1127 Hanji pp. 38 et seq; NBR note 153 pp. 143 et seq; SATÔ note 145 pp. 252 et seq; FOOTE note 153 pp. 45 et seq

the original report on traces of blood and whether there had ever been blood on Saitô's clothes at all. Further, the circumstances under which Saitô's confession had been gained seemed dubious to the court. The prosecution's immediate complaint was rejected by the Sendai High Court on 31 January 1983, and the trial was reopened. On 11 July 1984, the Sendai District Court ruled that due to an unusual correlation between evidence and confession, and a strong likelihood that there had never been blood stains on Saitô's clothing, as well as the uncovering of an earlier analysis which had found virtually no traces of blood, it could be concluded that the evidence had been fabricated. The arrest under the pretext of a different crime had constituted an inappropriate and unlawful act by the police. But despite the recognition of the unusual duration of interrogation, the court found no evidence for the application of physical violence by the police against Saitô. Rather, the confession was held to have been made under psychological pressure by the police and his cellmate. Nevertheless, the court saw the confession not as involuntary, but held its credibility as extremely doubtful. The court found Saitô not guilty. The prosecution refrained from appealing and the ruling was finalised on 25 July 1984. 26 years after the first death sentence, Saitô was released.

The last retrial in a death penalty case so far was the Shimada case.[156] On 10 March 1954, during a children's festival and bazaar on the grounds of a temple-kindergarten in Shimada, Shizuoka Prefecture, seven-year-old Sano Hisako was lured away by a stranger. Three days later, police found her abused and strangled body in a wood at the river south of town.

About ten days later, 25-year-old intellectually disabled Akabori Masao was put on the list of suspects. Akabori, who after the completion of several terms of imprisonment for theft lived with his brother in Shimada, allegedly had been seen waving at a schoolgirl. On 24 May 1954, Akabori was arrested in Gifu and transferred to the Shimada police. On the 26th, a local newspaper wrote that he could not have been the culprit since at the time of the crime he had been in Tokyo. Two days later, Shimada police arrested him on suspicion

---

[156] For material on the case, see, for example, 1079 Hanji pp. 11 et seq, 1193 Hanji pp. 31 et seq, 1227 Hanji pp. 3 et seq, 1316-30 et seq; NBR note 153 pp. 264 et seq; SAITÔ note 145 pp. 258 et seq

of stealing several items (i.e. clothing) from a girls' school in Shimada. After two days of intensive interrogation, he confessed to the rape and murder of Hisako.

The indictment was launched on 17 June. Based on his confession and several items of evidence, the prosecution demanded Akabori's death. Although he by now denied the crime, claiming that he had been walking from Tokyo to Yokohama at the time in question, and despite the defence pointing out that the confession only included facts which the police had already known, the Shizuoka District Court on 23 May 1958 sentenced Akabori to death. The Tokyo High Court on 17 February 1960 dismissed Akabori's appeal, since there were no doubts as to the voluntariness and credibility of his confession and the alibi could not be acknowledged. The Supreme Court turned down the second appeal on 15 December 1960.

Claiming to have found new evidence proving his alibi, Akabori on 17 August 1962 requested a retrial, but was turned down by the Shizuoka District Court on 28 February 1962. After two more failed requests, Akabori on 9 May 1969 applied for the fourth time with the help of the Japanese Federation of Bar Assocotiations, asserting that according to new medical reports, Akabori's statements did not conform with the facts and that there was new evidence for the alibi. When the Shizuoka District Court rejected the application on 11 March 1977, Akabori filed an immediate complaint. On 23 May 1982, the Tokyo High Court revoked the District Court's decision, referring the case back to it. On 29 May 1986, the Shizuoka District Court decided to reopen the case, for the only evidence in this case was Akabori's confession made in detention, which could not be considered credible. This decision on 26 March 1987 was confirmed by the Tokyo High Court. The Shizuoka District Court on 19 October 1987 reopened the trial. The prosecution insisted on the authenticity of the confession and again demanded the death penalty. After new reports on the order and causes of the child's injuries, the defence argued that Akabori's confession was not only unbelievable, but also had been made involuntarily. Further he had an alibi. The court expressed doubts as to the murder weapon and elaborated that there was the possibility that the under-intelligent, very emotional and easy-to-influence Akabori had delivered a confession, as desired by the police, when he realised that nobody would believe his alibi and the truth. Therefore, strong doubts existed about the credibility of the confession, albeit not its voluntariness. But since there was no other evidence against Akabori, the Shizuoka District Court on 30 January 1989 found him not guilty. Akabori was released 34 years and eight months after the arrest.

The four cases have much in common. All occurred during the postwar turmoils, when the violent investigation methods of prewar times were still applied. Police, prosecutors and judges had been trained under the old system, and a confession was still regarded as the most important and absolute evidence. Moreover, the techniques of forensic science had not yet been very highly developed.[157]

As has been shown, in the first years after the war there were numerous cases of false accusation, which were later revoked by higher courts or in retrials. In the four cases presented above, the severe penalty to which innocent men were sentenced is noteworthy. If one takes into consideration the cruel and brutal crimes committed in these cases, one does not wonder why the courts chose the highest penalty. The men did not give a good impression, had previous convictions and drank, came from dysfunctional family backgrounds, and were of low intelligence or mentally weak. Daniel Foote[158] in his study on the retrial cases furthermore points out that by denying that they had committed the crimes, the men lost all sympathy from the judges. Had they pretended and faked repentance, they could have received lighter sentences.

In all four cases, investigations stagnated; public expectations put the police under immense pressure. The four men became suspicious by committing other crimes or, like Menda, posing as investigators. Under the pretence of being suspected of involvement in other crimes, Taniguchi and Saitô were arrested, and Menda and Akabori were encouraged to accompany police to a 'voluntary' interrogation - and eventually arrested for other crimes.[159] During investigation, all four were interrogated about the crimes for which they later were sentenced to death. After confession, they were re-arrested for those crimes and interrogation continued. Most of all, the cases had in common the pressure applied by police to coerce a confession. The suspects were held in detention cells within police

---

157 SATÔ note 145 pp. 143-144

158 note 153 pp. 69-71; note 124 p. 460

159 On the problem of pretextual detention in the *Teigin* Case see e.g. RAMSEYER & NAKAZATO Part B note 13 pp. 170-171

stations, where they were at the investigators' disposal at any time, and easily put under pressure. This treatment continued for at least several days, in Taniguchi's case several months. Interrogations often lasted from the early hours of the morning until late at night. Apart from this psychological pressure, the use of physical force has not been proven, but all four men made statements attesting to its use.[160]

Whether the investigators were convinced about the men's guilt and believed to be doing the right thing by detaining them, or whether the pressure by the media and public caused the police to present somebody – anybody - as culprit, will never be known. The same applies to the evidence, where in all cases there is suspicion of falsification, forgery and tampering. In all cases, the confession records do not contain the exact wording of the suspects' statements, but a summary of several interrogations in the words of the police. During the various stages of investigation, these records were first produced by the police, later by the prosecution. Also, the suspects' various confessions were often contradictory every time detailed records were made.

The credibility of the confessions, under Japanese Law (Art. 38.3 Japanese Constitution, Art. 319.2 Code of Criminal Procedure) has to be corroborated by other evidence. In all four cases, guilt was mainly proven by expert testimony on blood stains or autopsy reports. There was suspicion of forgery, alteration of or tampering with evidence, which was at least partially the foundation for the guilty verdicts. All four men later renounced their confessions. Due to a lack of support by their counsels, an effective defence was not possible.[161] The few arguments which the defence did present were generally ignored by the courts, whose blind faith in the prosecution

---

160 FOOTE note 153 pp. 64-65

161 Under the Japanese system, the suspect has a right to counsel only from indictment. But even thereafter, meetings between the defendant and his counsel can be restricted. The counsel can not participate in interrogations by police or prosecution. Moreover, the defence had no access to the files of the prosecution. Also, so FOOTE (note 153 p. 67), in all four cases the defence in the initial stages of the trials did not seem to be overly zealous. Menda's counsel especially seemed to be convinced of his client's guilt. It is interesting to mention that Menda after his first confession did not even protest his innocence to his counsel. Menda's explanation that at the time he had not known about the difference between police, prosecution, judges and defence, was recognised by the court at retrial. 1090 Hanji p. 94

as well as the literal observation of procedural provisions was also criticised in all cases.[162]

The four convicts had spent decades on death row; while their fellow inmates were executed one after the other, they feared for their lives day after day, year after year. Why were they not executed? Customarily, death sentences are not executed while requests for retrial or pardon are pending, although in many cases executions were carried out immediately after the rejection of such a request. Also, the increased efforts of the counsel provided by the Japanese Federation of Bar Associations need to be mentioned.[163]

The Supreme Court's decision of 20 May 1975 in the Shiratori case was essential for the eventual reopening of the cases. The same First Petty Bench on 12 October 1976 decided on the first retrial in a death sentence case, in the Saitakawa case. Because of the new and eased criteria, which merely require 'new' evidence supporting justified doubts on the convict's guilt, Menda, Taniguchi, Saitô and Akabori succeeded in having their cases reopened. Although all courts acknowledged the voluntariness of the confessions, they found justified doubts about their credibility and the possibility of 'inducement' to confession by the investigation.

Since Akabori's acquittal in the Shimada case, there have been no further retrials of death row convicts. There is suspicion that Japan's judiciary again has adopted a harder stance in such cases to protect itself from doubts about its – and the whole legal system's - credibility and stability, which was shaken by the false judgments. Although the number of retrials for all crimes and cases in recent years had been at 15 to 20 per year, Daniel Foote[164] fears they might merely be the tip of the iceberg. The proponents of capital punishment usually argue that the cases of Menda et. al. had occurred in the turmoils and extreme social situation after the war, and would not be possible today. The opponents of capital punishment, however, see in such cases a common and unchanged pathology.[165] Indeed, in the years after the war, the changes in the legal system caused numerous problems from competency quarrels within the police to the courts' difficulties in applying the new Code of Criminal Procedure. The doubtful interrogation methods of the

162 FOOTE note 153 pp. 66-67, 72
163 SATÔ note 145 p. 143
164 Note 153 pp. 68 et seq
165 FOOTE note 153 pp. 13

police used at the time would be unthinkable today, it is often said. According to the Prosecutor General, back then, small, understaffed and inexperienced prosecutors handled the cases with little or no control over the police. This too could not happen today, where there is close cooperation between police and prosecution.[166]

The Menda, Saitakawa, Matsuyama and Shimada cases caused a wave of activity throughout Japan, discussed in numerous monographs, articles, media reports and analyses. Daniel Foote published a detailed English-language study on the issue. Even the Japanese Prosecutor General began to study the matter, but remains far removed from admitting any mistakes. The prosecution rather seems to aim at the prevention of further 'mistakes' of that kind.[167] Foote[168] believes far more extensive changes are necessary. Especially the dominance of the investigation and indictment procedures by the prosecution urgently needs a reform. No less criticism is aimed at the defence. The prosecution frequently admonished the lack of engagement of the defence, which in turn is rejected by the counsels, who have no choice due to their weak position within the Japanese judicial system. The judges are not spared either. In the words of a former Japanese judge, the situation at the Japanese courts is best described as follows:

> [W]hen a judge issues an acquittal, the faces of his superiors and the displeased faces of prosecutors with whom he's become friendly, will appear in his mind. Those sorts of psychological pressures exist at the

166 FOOTE note 153 pp. 73-74

167 After intensive studies on the Menda, Saitakawa and Matsuyama cases, the Prosecutor General concluded in an internal report that e.g. a jury system as well as limitations on exertion and use of confessions are needed. There must be a more thorough investigation of accused, to gain more precise and complete confessions. The report furthermore seems to criticise the prosecution in the four retrial cases for the insufficiently energetic stance and makes proposals about how this 'defeat' could have been prevented. FOOTE note 153 pp. 72, 78 fn. 332

168 Due to the prosecution's dominant position, the Japanese trial system often is called 'prosecution justice'. FOOTE note 153 pp. 75-77. The prosecution can control the investigations of the police. The accused has a court-appointed counsel only from the time of indictment (Arts. 35, 272 Code of Criminal Procedure). At that time the investigation has been concluded. If the accused can afford to appoint a counsel, then the prosecution is authorised to restrict and control meetings to a certain degree (Art. 39.3 Code of Criminal Procedure). In no case can the counsel be present during interrogations. Neither is he entitled to access the prosecutions' files.

> subconscious level, and there's a psychological brake at work that leads judges to issue as few acquittals as possible.[169]

Some critics hold that Japan's judges tend to identify themselves with their prosecutor colleagues, whose education and careers equal their own. And surely there is a certain unworldliness to many judges, who live a life of almost complete segregation from the average people, thus lacking the ability to understand the accused. The main criticism, though, is directed at confessions. Confessions had convinced the courts of the guilt of Menda, Taniguchi, Saitô and Akabori. In Japanese law, like in so many other legal systems, an accused first of all has the right to remain silent. According to Art. 38 Japanese Constitution, a confession must be voluntary and corroborated by other evidence. A confession exacted involuntarily or after unreasonably long arrest or detention or for other doubtful reasons cannot be used as evidence. Nevertheless, to the present day a confession is regarded as the most important piece of evidence. The maximum detention period of 23 days between arrest and indictment is almost exclusively exhausted to gain a confession. In the four death penalty retrial cases, the accused had either been asked to voluntarily accompany police or was arrested. The voluntariness of the confessions exacted in the ensuing interrogations was not negated by the courts, but in all cases they had raised concerns. Critics pointed out that the investigating authorities should not rely on gaining new evidence through testimony of the accused, but rather conduct more thorough investigations before the interrogation. For otherwise, erroneous judgments like in the Menda case would be the result.

The proponents of capital punishment point out that these cases had occurred during an unusually tumultuous period, and that similar conduct by the investigators could not happen any more; if it did, it at least would be unlawful. Foote is of a different opinion. He reminds us that in the past years there have repeatedly been cases where the courts had not acknowledged confessions because of doubts about their voluntariness. Furthermore, some of those past practices are not unlawful even under current law. Actual court decisions found no fault with 'voluntary accompaniment' – as in the

169 LAWRENCE W. BEER & HIROSHI ITOH, The Constitutional Case Law of Japan, 1970-1990 pp. 27 (Seattle 1996) quoting Daniel Foote who quotes a former Japanese judge.

Menda case – and the additional arrest in a different case has been held unlawful by various courts. The Sendai District Court viewed Saitô's arrest in a different case as an obvious pretence in order to extract a confession for the murder case and thus as unlawful. However, in Saitô's state compensation case the court concluded that the arrest did not constitute an unlawful act for which the state has to pay compensation to Saitô.[170] When at least the appearance is preserved and the accused is also interrogated on the case for which he has been arrested, the courts tend to recognise this as lawful.[171]

Finally, there is the question of the extraction of a confession. Art. 38.2 of the Japanese Constitution prohibits the courts from using confessions gained by force, application of violence or pressure, and Art. 319.1 of the Code of Criminal Procedure forbids the court to use as evidence confessions where there is doubt that they have not been extracted voluntarily. What does 'voluntariness' mean? In the Shimada retrial, the court defined a confession as not voluntary when 'physical or mental coercion of an illegal nature, or other inducement rising to an equivalent level, during questioning' had been applied.[172] Other courts arrived at similar conclusions when the accused had been interrogated in handcuffs or when he was promised leniency if he confessed.[173] In the four retrial cases it did not suffice to the courts that the men had been beaten with fists, did not receive sufficient food, were interrogated day and night, and were not allowed to sleep.

To find the truth is difficult in so far as interrogations are held behind closed doors, and regularly the statements of the interrogated and those of the investigators are contradictory. No one knows what really happens in the 'substitute prisons' (*daihyô kangoku*) within the police stations, where the accused, who should be transferred into custody, are often held until indictment. For years there had been criticism and speculation of human rights violations. According to Art. 203.1 Code of Criminal Procedure, police must not detain a case for longer than 48 hours or otherwise must send him to the prosecution, which has to request his committal within 24 hours (Art. 205.1 Code of Criminal Procedure). The prosecution can detain the accused for ten days, extendable by another ten. After this

170 FOOTE note 153 p. 89 fn. 389

171 FOOTE note 153 p. 90, 1127 HANJI 60

172 1316 Hanji p. 33; transl. FOOTE note 153 p. 91

173 Various cases cited in RAMSEYER & NAKAZATO Part B note 13 p. 48

period has lapsed, the suspect must be indicted or released (Art. 208 Code of Criminal Procedure). It must be noted that this restriction of detention by police is limited to a 'case' but not to the person of a suspect, that is, the police has to transfer a 'case' after 48 hours; the suspect himself can remain in the hands of the police.[174] The Prison Law (Art. 1.3), too, provides for this explicitly. Critics point out that the substitute prison system keeps suspects ready for interrogations at all time; abuse cannot be detected, nor prevented. Also it is difficult for a counsel to contact his client. A suspect who confesses, and who wants to revoke his confession, which has been made under police pressure, often will refrain from doing so for fear of being sent back to the police. However, even the Japanese prosecution has understood the deplorable state of affairs within the Japanese police. The prosecution recommends that, at least in cases of grave complaints about police interrogation, a suspect is transferred into custody and investigations are continued by the prosecution.[175]

Although in all four retrial cases of death row convicts the courts hesitated to openly question the voluntariness of the confessions, they at least found 'reasonable doubt' about their credibility and acquitted the accused. These cases initiated a tendency for closer scrutiny of confessions. Regularly they are cited as proof that although the accused had not made involuntary confessions, they were induced to make false statements. An examination by the courts, however, is only possible if the accused protests his innocence before the court and revokes the confession. Surely, the prosecution is well aware of the need for greater scrutiny in this context, but, as Foote[176] points out, there is the danger of the opposite effect, i.e. that the prosecution will make an even greater effort to produce more credible confessions by improving interrogation techniques.

---

174 See generally DANIEL H. FOOTE, *Confession and the Right to Silence in Japan*, in 21 Georgia Journal of International & Comparative Law p. 415 (1991)

175 FOOTE note 153 pp. 91, 94; MIHARA Part A note 5 pp. 500-501. The latest discussion which has cented on the substitute prisons rather than on the four retrial cases is based on efforts by the Justice Ministry and the police to formally institutionalize the system, although this far draft bills presented to the Diet have not succeeded. In detail see IGARASHI FUTABA, DAIHYÔ KANGOKU (Tokyo 1981); FRANK BENNETT, *Introductory Note on Pre-Trial Detention in Japan,* in 23 Law in Japan p. 67

176 note 124 pp. 96-98

The subject of false accusations for the first time gained widespread attention - surprisingly - from the Prosecutor General, who in 1954 conducted a study on such cases. The Japanese Federation of Bar Associations (JFBA) took up the issue from 1959, by establishing teams within its Human Rights Committee. These, among others, supported the retrial efforts of Menda, Fuji and Yoshida. Legal science, however, had not yet discovered the issue. Due to the widespread publicity of the above-mentioned Yoshida case, the retrial issue also gained wider public attention. The Lower House Legal Affairs Committee established a special committee to inquire into the retrial system. This committee in 1962 and 1963 heard from scholars, attorneys, prosecutors and judges.[177] The *Nihon Keihô Gakkai* (Japanese Criminal Law Society) took up the matter in 1962.[178] A flood of treatises followed. Throughout the country, support groups for various convicts were formed. In 1972, the JFBA established a study group on the retrial system. The following year, a national coordination committee was formed from among the federation, scholars and various support groups, and in 1974, the *Nihon Keihô Gakkai* formed a study group.[179]

In February 1968, socialist Lower House member Kamichika Ichiko, with the support of the JFBA, presented to the Diet a Draft Bill on Retrial Procedure for Death Row Convicts (*Shikei-shû saishin hôan*) which provided that all death row convicts who had been indicted between 2 September 1945 and 28 April 1952 and whose sentences had been finalised before the enforcement of the current law, should be granted retrials of their cases. It was reasoned that Japan at that time had been under Allied occupation, and had undergone a change in its criminal procedure system. During that period, more dubious judgments occurred than at any other time. To benefit from the proposed law, by name were mentioned: Yamamoto Hiroko, Menda Sakae, Yamasaki Shotarô, Hirasawa Sadamichi, Nishi Sadao, Ishii Kenjirô, Taniguchi Shigeyoshi, that is, seven 'veteran' death row inmates in six cases: more than ten years after the finalisation of their sentences, the convicts still had not been executed.[180]

---

177 ODANAKA/ÔDE note 126 pp. 100-101

178 ODANAKA/ÔDE note 126 p. 97

179 ODANAKA/ÔDE note 126 pp. 109-110

180 Kamichika stated as reasons for submitting the bill: 'Retrial is a bridge to the rescue of a convict sentenced upon false judgment. But is, in current practice, the

This draft bill, however, was vehemently criticised by the judiciary, the ruling Liberal Democrats and the Justice Ministry as an intrusion into the realm of the judicature. The draft could not withstand this concerted opposition and failed. A similar draft of a Law on the Partial Reform of the Retrial Law (*Saishin-hô kaisei-an; keiji soshô-hô no ichibu kaisei-an*) was submitted to parliament in autumn 1979, but was rejected after only one day of deliberations.[181] The Socialist

---

system of retrial properly applied in this sense? ... In the heart of our people, a strong desire burns for the system of retrial ... The humanist movement for retrial by attorneys, representatives of science, religion etc. ... is committed to the idea that the individual life is not lost without reason ... As an answer to such a movement of the people it is our task as the people's representatives to grant this wish...' SATÔ note 145 pp. 264-265

The mains points of the bill were as follows:

1. The law provides for exceptions for persons, who were indicted between 2 September 1945 and 28 April 1952 and whose death sentence was finalised before the enforcement of the current law, but has not yet been executed.

2. Regarding a request for retrial of the persons mentioned under 1., in Art. 435 No. 6 as well as Art. 485 No. 6 Code of Criminal Procedure, 'clear evidence' is reread in 'appropriate' evidence, and this provision applied.

3. Requests for retrial must be submitted within one year from the enforcement of the law.

4. Requests for retrial must be submitted with the Tokyo High Court.

5. Decisions on requests for retrial will be made by lay judges (*sanshin*) as determined by special laws.

6. An objection against a decision to reopen a trial is not permissible.

SATÔ note 145 pp. 267-268

181 The contents of the draft were as follows:

1. For a harmonisation of requirements for retrial and to extend reasons for retrial, Art. 485 No. 6 Code of Criminal Procedure will be thoroughly revised:

Regarding the requirement of novelty and definition of evidence, the judiciary's interpretation so far has been too strict. Thus the Supreme Court in the Shiratori decision elaborated: 'If there are rational doubts about the facts in a finalised decision, this suffices to reopen a trial: in this sense the iron principle of criminal law, *in dubio pro reo* will be applied. In Art. 435 No. 6, 'new definite evidence' is altered into 'evidence where there is doubt about an error in and/or of facts.'

2. Clarification of legal protection of the applicant for retrial on the procedural side:

For the phase of application for retrial a system of court-appointed counsel will be created, furthermore the right to secret communication with the counsel, of access to all files, publicity of investigations and the right to state grounds of application of applicant and counsel as well as protection of the right to apply for determination of facts will be introduced.

3. Judges who had participated in earlier trials will be excepted.

4. The prosecution's counter-proof will be partially restricted in the phase of application for retrial, based on the idea that the system of retrial shall merely serve the interest of an accused with a finalised conviction, and the prosecution cannot

Party continued to make efforts to amend the retrial law, and in autumn 1989 presented the Diet with yet another draft on the reform of a part of the Code of Criminal Procedure, which, however, also did not succeed.[182] The JFBA within the frame of its activities for the protection of human rights, also produced several unsuccessful drafts on an amendment of retrial law ('Draft Reform of Retrial Law', *Saishin-hô (eiso-hô daiyon-hen) kaisei-an*).[183]

6. *Public Opinion*

Well aware that the perennial discussion of deterrence, retaliation or mistrial will never lead to a conclusion as to the question of capital punishment, the proponents of the death penalty today focus their attention on public sentiment, which is not yet ready to support an abolition. The opposition rejects this argument, which comprises two elements: the special character of the Japanese people, which does not allow for an application of Western arguments in the discussion, and the will of the people, as expressed in opinion surveys.

---

demand a renewed determination of facts. Here, in the examination of the new evidence produced by the applicant, their authenticity and credibility will be examined.

5. Prohibition of requests to the disadvantage of the convict by the prosecution against a judgment on the opening of a retrial.

6. The costs of a retrial will be secured even before the opening: under current law, only those costs which are incurred in the trial will be compensated.

7. The adduction of forged or altered evidence by the prosecution suffices to reopen a trial.

8. Meaning and purpose of retrials are clarified:

'The system of retrial serves the rescue of innocent and the respect of the human rights of the accused.'

9. Stay of execution

In the case of an application for retrial, the execution of punishment will be stayed upon application. SATÔ note 145 pp. 270-271

182 Opinion on a Partial Reform of the Code of Criminal Procedure and Rules of Criminal Procedure Regarding Criminal Retrial. *Keiji saishin ni kansuru keiji soshô-hô narabini keiji soshô kisoku-chû ichibu kaisei iken-sho)*

183 SATÔ note 145 p. 271. In detail see especially NIHON BENGOSHI RENGÔ-KAI (NBR), *Nichibenren saishin-hô kaisei-an – keiji saishin ni kansuru keiji soshô-hô (dai yon-hen saishin) narabi ni keiji soshô kisoku-chû ichibu kaisei iken-sho) (Draft by the Japanese Federation of Bar Associations on a Reform of the Retrial Law)*, in 28-3 Jiyû to seigi (1997)

Legal scholar Aoyagi Fumio,[184] a frontrunner of the 1970s *Nihon-jin-ron* theory on the peculiar biological and mental characteristics of the Japanese people, and a vehement supporter of the death penalty, more than once pointed out that the international debate on capital punishment is meaningless in Japan, due to the special and unique *kokuminsei* of the Japanese people, the national character. The term *kokuminsei*, which no dictionary can define adequately, is described by Aoyagi[185] as follows: ever since the prehistoric *Yayoi* Period, there has been one people, one culture and one language in Japan, resulting in numerous ethical characteristics which are reflected in various ways in the fields of crime, punishment and criminal procedure. *kokuminsei* in this meaning is not a biological characteristic of a people or a race (*minzoku)*, but the sociological characteristic of a people as the entirety of all citizens (*kokumin*).[186]

Many Western religions form a unity with ethics, founded on the idea of a legal order based on natural law. Crime is not merely a violation of the legal order, but simultaneously of Christian (or, more generally, monotheistic) ethics and the divine order; punishment is revenge for these injuries. Aoyagi believes that this, however, is different in the case of Japan. When Buddhism came to Japan, the concept of 'mercy' had a great impact on the ethics of the people. Aoyagi explains that in the Japanese climate, which is marked by the change of the four seasons and where natural disasters such as earthquakes or typhoons occur frequently, the strongly developed *kokuminsei* melded with Buddhism and skilfully adapted to the surroundings, at the same time easily adopting outward influences. In this process, Mahayana Buddhism was gradually harmonised and transformed.[187] Also, he held, the Japanese group mentality is

---

184 For example in Nihon-jin no tsumi to batsu (Guilt and Punishment of the Japanese) p. 19 (Tokyo 1980)

185 Ibid. p. 20. Aoyagi's views are shared by HONDA MASAYOSHI, *Nihon-jin to hanzai (The Japanese and Crime*), in 295 Kenshû pp. 9, 12-13 (1973)

186 Since the *Meiji* Period one theory stresses special biological characteristics of the Japanese and their superiority; this theory blossomed in the early *Shôwa* period, at the end of the Second World War and saw a revival in the early 1970s in the *Nihon-jin-ron.* But this, even AOYAGI (note 185 p. 20) holds, could not be called anything but an illusion.

187 AOYAGI FUMIO, Hanzai to waga kokumin-sei (Crime and our National Character) p. 125 (Tokyo 1969). In 1980, Aoyagi (note 185) wrote that when compared to other parts of the world, Japanese special characteristics must be considered: Japan - one people, one culture, one language. This is unique throughout

closely related to a lack of individualism and the irresistible urge to apologise. Every act contradicting tradition is regarded a crime or sin (*tsumi)*, while in the West, it is conscience that decides questions of 'good' and 'evil'. This group pressure usually forces a criminal to confess shortly after the crime.

Ruth Benedict categorised Japan as a culture of shame, in contrast to the Western culture of guilt. If one applies Benedict's thoughts on crime, then in the West, committing a crime is a sin against God, and the conscience of the sin has a strong general preventive effect. Alternately, in Japan a crime is not a sin, but a source of shame not only for the culprit, but for his whole kin or group. Here, shame has a general preventive force. Since the consciousness of 'sin' is closely related to religion, especially Christianity, with the weakening of religiosity, crime prevention grows weaker. The consciousness of 'shame', however, is still strong in Japan, despite the disintegrating group cohesion and weak religiosity. The strong Japanese consciousness of shame is typical for a rice-agricultural people, says Honda Masayoshi.[188] Since rice agriculture requires a large number of workers, it needed the intensive joint work of all members of a village. The individual's dependence on this community is so great that in former times an expulsion from the village community had equalled a death sentence. To prevent his, every single person naturally was very keen to form harmonious human relations within the group. Nothing was feared as much as bringing shame over the group by one's own actions. Since this consciousness of shame is a special characteristic of a rice-agricultural people, Honda says, it is limited to the Japanese! Among the Chinese, too, such a consciousness exists, for Confucius regarded it as a virtue. The Japanese, who have never been conquered by another people, and mostly lived peacefully, are a people with a simple, straight character, and to the present day are highly dependent on the group. This dominating characteristic still provides fertile soil for a general preventive effect.

The acceptance or endurance of one's own fate, such as natural disasters or war, and on the other hand the desire to prevent and

---

the world, it is not a society like the U.S., a melting pot of several races and religions. Although there are numerous crimes threatened with death by the law, in practice, every year only some ten death sentences are handed down. Most such cases are robbery-murders, planned serial murders or especially brutal homicides.

188 Note 185 pp. 13-14

suppress it, are antithetic positions. The first aspect accepts the loss of objects as well as of life as destiny, while the latter applies various activities and methods for prevention. The former has had great influence on the Japanese character, the latter on that of the peoples of Europe and Northern America. This is related to the Buddhist concept of cause and effect and the Christian concept of the dignity of man.[189]

Furthermore, in Aoyagi's opinion, Japan's rather high suicide rates demonstrate that Japanese disregard not only the lives of others, but also their own. This does not mean, however, that the threat of capital punishment is meaningless. Even to those who might choose their own death, capital punishment can function as a threat.[190]

With the demise of Aoyagi and other representatives of the *Nihon-jin-ron,* today *kokuminsei* no longer plays a central role in the discussion of the death penalty in Japan. In the attempt to rationalise the debate and to apply more 'fool-proof' scientific arguments, it is focused on the seemingly objective 'will' of the people, rather than on their innate characteristics.

The Japanese Government argues for the retention of capital punishment using this 'will of the people'. In its judgment of 12 March 1948, the Supreme Court, too, cited public opinion as one of the main reasons for capital punishment, and a draft Penal Code reform refrained from suggesting an abolition of capital punishment for the same reason, which was also used to counter international criticism on Japan when it refused to sign the so-called Convention against Capital Punishment, i.e. the Second Optional Protocol to the ICCPR, adopted by the United Nations on 15 December 1989.[191]

In light of the actions of the governments of Great Britain and France, which decided to abolish capital punishment in spite of the declared will of the general public, Kikuta Kôichi[192] believes that it is the task of Japan's parliament and government not to blindly follow

---

189 AOYAGI FUMIO, *Shikei sonchi-ron (On the Retention of the Death Penalty)*, in 37-1 Hôgaku kenkyû pp. 15, 16-18 (1958)

190 AOYAGI note 187 pp. 129-133. Also see HONDA note 185 pp. 9-10.

191 In detail on this aspect see KIKUTA KÔICHI, *Shiryô – Shikei haishi e no kokusai-teki dôkô (Materials: The International Trend towards the Abolition of Capital Punishment*), in 62-3 Hôritsu Ronkô p. 85 (1994)

192 Part B note 36 pp. 14 et seq. This opinion is shared by MIYAZAWA KOICHI, *Die Todesstrafe in Japan*, in Strafgerechtigkeit – Festschrift für Arthur Kaufmann zum 70. Geburtstag pp. 729, 723 (Fritjof Haft et. al. (eds.), 1993)

the will of the people, but rather to guide it morally and educationally. In this way they would be able to solve criminal-political questions rationally and not emotionally. Also, public opinion is unstable and easy to influence. Reports about violent crime regularly cause the pendulum of public opinion to swing towards capital punishment, while news about executions can influence the sentiment in the opposite direction.[193]

What is this highly valued public opinion? First of all, it is not clear what exactly the conviction of the people is, who forms it and how it is measured. Is it appropriate when evaluating public opinion, as Kikuta[194] does, to limit it to a small group of experts and ignore the majority of the people? Or rather, as seems to be the view of the Japanese Government, should public opinion be regarded as the opinion of a representative cross-section of the whole people (that is, of every age, sex, educational level or occupation, independent from the competence on the issue). Takigawa Haruo,[195] in contrast to Kikuta a supporter of the death penalty concludes that a thought, which cannot be disregarded for its great influence on the *zeitgeist*, is

---

193 DANDÔ (Part A note 13 p. 343) thinks that government and politicians must not neglect the public, whose will on the other hand is not binding either; one must not follow without criticism or use it as a cover for conservative politics. In a functioning democracy, the elected representatives must lead the public opinion. Sometimes it is appropriate to conduct policies contrary to the public opinion. In politics there must be philosophers and ideals. Real politicians like former French President Mitterand with alert consciousness and real ideas have led the people to change opinions.
Outside Japan, too, public opinion mostly wants to retain or reintroduce the death penalty. In many states where the death penalty has been abolished, the governments reacted in a different way from that of Japan. In Great Britain in 1969, the year capital punishment was abolished, 85% of the people polled just before the enactment of the law on abolition supported the retention of the death penalty. Nevertheless, Parliament passed the bill. Then Prime Minister Callaghan said that at times Parliament must lead public opinion. This determination to be a model, bore fruit in England: between 1969 and 1983 a total of seven draft bill for the reintroduction of capital punishment were introduced, all failed. In a poll conducted in 1983 by the BBC, 53% wanted a reintroduction, even 77% in a poll conducted by a newspaper the same year. Similarly in France, directly before the abolition of capital punishment in 1981, 62% of the French people declared their support for the death penalty.

194 Part B note 36 p. 52

195 *Shikei haishi no mondai-ten (Problems of an Abolition of Capital Punishment)*, in 10-9 Keizai-jin p. 96; also see TAKIGAWA HARUO, Keihô kôwa (Criminal Law) pp. 96-97 (Tokyo 1951)

called public conviction. For example, it is the conviction of the people that a civilised society cannot endure public executions. If this conviction is not exactly measured quantitatively, however, it cannot be simply seen as the will of the whole people. Former Prosecutor General Yasuhira Masayoshi,[196] known as a decided proponent of the death penalty, postulates that justice and the law must be based on the legal conviction of the public, and therefore there must be the death penalty for certain severe crimes. Capital punishment is not merely demanded by the idea of retaliation. It is the only appropriate method of repentance, which does not have a subjective function of retaliation, but is founded on an objective feeling of justice within the people. From this Yasuhira concludes that the people's legal conceptions are the only and appropriate reason for the retention of capital punishment.

Even the supporters of the death penalty, however, admit that the public opinion does not have to remain unchanged forever. Fuwa Takeo[197] explains that there is a worldwide trend to abolish capital punishment, and at the proper time this will have to take place even in Japan. In contrast to the West, however, the roots of the Japanese penal system lie in the national character, whose traditional concepts of punishment must not be disregarded. The idea that the nature of punishment is retaliation based on justice rules even in present-day Japan and forms the foundation for retention and application of capital punishment. When a time has come when the judges reject the use of the death penalty and society no longer recognises this punishment, then it will disappear without special efforts. Only after such a period of non-application can the legal provisions be repealed. History shows that this is the only appropriate way. Before the background of the current social conviction of the Japanese people, however, which attaches a great deterrent and retaliative effect to the

---

196 *Shikei wa haisubeki ka – kakukoku no shikei seido ni kansuru (Must the Death penalty be Abolished? On the System of Capital Punishment in the Nations of the World)*, in 10-6 Keisatsu Jihô p. 17; also see OKANO MITSUI, *shikei seido no dôkô (trends in capital punishment)*, in Keihô sôron II p. 28 (Fukuda Hira et.al. eds., Tokyo 1968); FUWA TAKEO, *Shikei ni tsuite (On Capital Punishment)*, in Keiji-hô-jô no sho-mondai p. 50

197 FUWA note 196 p. 50; also see TAKIGAWA HARUO, Keiji hôgaku jiten (Lexicon of Criminal Law) p. 355 (Tokyo 1957). Very similar the opinion expressed in ÔTANI MAKOTO, Keihô kôza (Criminal Law) p. 510 (Tokyo 1991)

death penalty, it must be retained. Yasuhira Masayoshi[198] believes that the people's conviction could surely change if the state provides an adequate substitute for the death penalty. For the people's moral conceptions are satisfied only by preserving the social order through the death of a violent criminal. If this could be achieved by other means, the people would abandon this conviction.

The view is often expressed that the death penalty must be retained because the people demand it. Even those who oppose this view do not deny the existence of this claim. They doubt, however, whether the people are able to decide such a question. Kimura Kameji[199] pointed at the history of Germany and Italy, and warned of the abuses of capital punishment. For under those National-Socialist and Fascist regimes, the death penalty was revived, strengthened and abused 'in the name of the people'. Other opponents of capital punishment, such as Abe Shinnosuke, insist that the public should be educated or, rather, re-educated, to alter this unstable public opinion.[200] This, however, is only possible if one does not merely call for an abolition of the death penalty but simultaneously strives for a reduction of crime rates and the elimination of the causes of crime. For by creating a peaceful society, the reasons which cause the people to call for the death penalty would disappear. Mihara,[201] though, criticises the idea that there could be a 'natural' abolition since the repeal of legal provisions requires human action. If the public has not yet reached such a level of consciousness that it can be taught the value of life, then there will never be an abolition.

To a certain degree, public opinion has always played a role in the modern controversy about capital punishment. Proponents and opponents concern themselves with it in numerous lengthy treatises, and the legislator likes to cite this argument as a reason for the death

198 YASUHIRA MASAYOSHI, Shin-keiji seisaku (Criminal Policy) p. 333 (Tokyo 1953)

199 Part B note 80 p. 176

200 ABE SHINNOSUKE, *Shikei haishi to kokumin ishiki (Abolition of Capital Punishment and Public Conscience*), in Sandee Mainichi 3 July 1958 p. 46; also see TAKEDA note 52 pp. 33-34

201 Part A note 5 pp. 34-35. Mihara finds support in ONO SAKAHIRO (*Shikei (Capital Punishment)*, in Keiji sôron (Criminal Law) p. 260 (Ôtani Makoto ed., Tokyo 1983)), and YOSHIOKA KAZUO, Keiji-gaku (Criminal Law) p. 260 (Tokyo 1980)), who traces today's calls for the death of a criminal back to the extensive use of capital punishment in the past, and therefore sees a lack in convincing force of the people's will.

penalty's retention. To the present day, however, there is no generally accepted definition of this term and no agreement about its content. One way to trace the will of the people, opinion polls. Since 1953, such polls have been conducted in Japan some thirty times. These polls ranged from those restricted to the mere question 'pro or con' to meticulously detailed studies. Some asked only a few dozen people, others thousands. While the government surveys attempted especially to poll a representative cross-section of the population, others studied only certain professional or age groups.

Every one of these surveys contained the abstract question about whether the respondent was for or against capital punishment. In almost all cases, a majority expressed support for the death penalty. An average 53.1% voted in favour of a retention of the death penalty, while 26.9% voted against it; the highest percentage supporting capital punishment was 76% in the 1982 Asahi Shinbun survey. The record for opponents in legitimate surveys was 45.8% in the 1991 poll conducted by the Bar Federation.[202]

202 The results of the poll by the 'Committee on the Stop of the Execution of Capital Punishment', conducted among parliamentarians in 1989 must be disregarded for statistical doubtfulness.

Table C-2: Opinion Polls on Capital Punishment in Japan[203]

	Year	Poller	Pro	Con	Other
1	1953	Japanese Bar Federation	61.7%	36.0%	2.3%
2	1953	Masaki Akira	72.3%	27.2%	0.5%
3	1956	Prime Minister's Office	65.0%	18.0%	17.0%
4	1956	Mainichi Shinbun	59.3%	21.8%	15.5%
5	1966	Kanagawa University	54.1%	33.0%	12.0%
6	1967	Prime Minister's Office	70.5%	16.0%	13.5%
7	1969	Meiji University, Kikuta-Seminar	68.0%	27.0%	5.0%
8	1969	Sankei Shinbun	55.8%	35.9%	8.2%
9	1969	Sankei Shinbun	48.2%	46.2%	5.7%
10	1970	Kokugakuin University	57.6%	32.3%	10.2%
11	1972	Sankei Shinbun	53.5%	30.2%	16.2%
12	1975	Prime Minister's Office	56.9%	20.7%	22.4%
13	1976	Rikkyô University	42.0%	31.0%	27.0%
14	1977	Sankei Shinbun	61.0%	19.0%	20.0%
15	1980	Prime Minister's Office	62.3%	14.3%	23.4%
16	1981	Tokyo Bar Association	60.4%	39.6%	0.0%
17	1982	Asahi Shinbun	76.0%	19.0%	5.0%

203 For details see SCHMIDT Part A note 29 pp. 357 et seq, 621 et seq; KIKUTA Part B note 36 pp. 124 et seq, 158 et seq, 299; MURANO Part A note 14 p. 129; Mainichi Shinbun 27 March 1956; KANAGAWA DAIGAKU SHIKEI MONDAI KENKYÛ-KAI, Shikei haishi ni kansuru kokumin ishiki chôsa bunseki kisoku shiryô (Analysis, Rules, Materials on an Opinion Poll on the People's Consciousness concerning Capital Punishment) 1966; NAIKAKU SÔRI DAIJIN KANBÔ KÔHÔ-SHITSU, Shikei ni kansuru seron chôsa (Opinion Poll on Capital Punishment) 1967, NAIKAKU SÔRI DAIJIN KANBÔ KÔHÔ-SHITSU, Hanzai to shobatsu ni kansuru seron chôsa (Enquette on Crime and Punishment) 1975, 1980, 1989; KOKUGAKUIN DAIGAKU HÔRITSU-GAKU KENKÛ-KAI, *Shikei ni kansuru ankeeto* (*Enquette on Capital Punishment*), in 7 Jûhô (special issue) 1971; TÔKYÔ BENGOSHI-KAI JINKEN YÔGO IN-KAI, Shikei ni tsuite ankeeto (Enquette on Capitral Punishment) 1981; Asahi Shinbun 3 January 1981; NHK HÔSÔ SERON CHÔSA-SHO, Dai-jûsan-kai Sangi-in senkyo dai-ni-ji zenkoku chôsa (13th Upper House Elections, 2nd Nationwide Poll) 1983; HANZAI TO HIKÔ NI KANSURU ZENKOKU KYÔGI-KAI (JAPANESE COUNCIL ON CRIME AND DELINQUENCY), in 37 JCCD PP. 8-13 (1986); SEINAN GAKUIN DAIGAKU KEIJI-HÔ KENKYÛ-KAI, SHIKEI NI KANSURU ANKEETO CHÔSA (ENQUETTE POLL ON CAPITAL PUNISHMENT) 1987; A.I. NIHON SHIBU SHIKEI HAISHI NETTOWAAKU SENTAA, *Shikei haishi ni kansuru ankeeto* (*Enquette on the Abolition of Capital Punishment*), in a.i. Nyuusuretta 10 (April 1989); SHIKEI SHIKKÔ TEISHI RENRAKU KAIGI (1989); TÔKYÔ SHINBUN, *Hyakunin ankeeto shikei seido wa ze ka hi ka* (*100 Persons Poll: Pro or Con Capital Punishment?*), TÔKYÔ SHINBUN 18 April 1990; A.I. NIHON SHIBU, *Shikei haishi ankeeto* (*Enquette on the Abolition of Capital Punishment*), a.i. Nyuusuretta 16-17 October 1990; NIHON BENGOSHI RENGO-KAI SHIKEI SEIDO TOKUBETSU CHÔSA IINKAI, in 62-46 Hôritsu Ronsô pp. 17 et seq (1990); KAWASAKI KAZUO, *Shikei haishi e mukete (Towards an Abolition of Capital Punishment),* in 38-10 HÔGAKU SEMINAA 41 (1993); Hiragana Times 1994 at 22; <http://www.elis.sk/hum/full/hum196g.pdf>

18	1983	NHK	70.2%	13.4%	16.4%
19	1985	JCCD	63.4%	35.9%	0.7%
20	1987	Seinan Gakuin University	44.3%	22.5%	33.3%
21	1989	Amnesty international			
22	1989	Meiji University, Criminological Institute	50.8%	42.6%	6.5%
23	1989	Prime Minister's Office	66.5%	15.7%	17.8%
24	1989	Committee on the Stop of Capital Punishment	9.8%	80.0%	11.2%
25	1990	Tôkyô Shinbun	53.0%	34.0%	13.0%
26	1990	Amnesty international			
27	1991	Special Committee Japanese Bar Federation	49.7%	42.3%	8.0%
28	1991	Meiji University, Criminological Institute	47.6%	45.8%	6.6%
29	1992	Forum Shikoku	35.1%	38.8%	26.8%
30	1993	Terebi Asahi	62.1%	20.6%	20.9%
31	1993	Yomiuri Shinbun	63.9%	28.3%	7.8%
32	1994	Hiragana Times			
33	1994	Prime Minister's Office	73.8%	13.6%	12.6%
34	1994	Asahi Shinbun	40.2%	47.2%	12.6%
35	1999	Prime Minister's Office	76.3%	8.8%	14.9%

Pro: support for capital punishment
Con: Opposition to capital punishment

One of the major flaws, which can be frequently observed in the evaluation of these polls by the Japanese Government, academia as well as the media, is that attention is focused almost exclusively on the overall yes-no question. However, the meaning of the above-mentioned results, on which both sides in the Japanese discussion nowadays rely, becomes doubtful when the opinions of the pollees are questioned in greater detail. Indeed, fourteen of the polls went beyond the general question for or against capital punishment, and requested the pollees to explain the reasons behind their attitude. As a matter of fact, further probing into the people's opinion showed that, for example, a statement 'pro capital punishment' does not necessarily mean favouring the retention of the death penalty forever. On the other hand, even opponents of this punishment do not always want an immediate abolition. Independent from the differences in number for and against, in five out of six polls (Table C-2), about one-third of the pollees supported a gradual or future abolition. The share of absolute pros and cons was clearly below the total result, which proves that in both groups many are neither radically for nor against capital punishment, but wish for a gradual abolition.

Some polls studied the distribution of opinions for and against in case of a gradual or future abolition, also showing clearly that only just over one-third of all those who wished for an abolition of the death penalty wanted an immediate and complete repeal of all provisions on capital punishment. Surprisingly, the vast majority rejected such a radical solution; more than two-thirds regarded immediate measures as premature and preferred a gradual abolition (Table C-3).

The same phenomenon can be observed among the proponents of capital punishment. Although a clear majority support a retention, one out of five in this group would prefer a gradual or future abolition. Consequently, in between the groups for and against exists a third group which considers an abolition premature now, but desirable for the future. It is remarkable that the proponents of capital punishment are more consequent in their 'no' to an abolition, while more than half of the opponents can imagine its abolition only for the future (Table C-4).

Table C-3: Opinion on the Future of the Death Penalty

Poll No.	Total result: Pro	Total result: Con	Future treatment: Immediate abolition	Future treatment: Gradual abolition	Future treatment: Retention
5.	54.1%	33.0%	17.2%	59.7%	17.8%
6.	70.5%	16.0%	3.0%	37.0%	45.0%
18.	70.2%	13.4%	2.8%	39.3%	41.5%
22.	50.8%	42.6%	15.4%	33.2%	45.3%
24.	10.2%	82.7%	45.9%	32.7%	6.1%
27.	47.6%	45.8%	20.7%	34.9%	39.4%

Irrespective of the current attitude towards the death penalty, many Japanese undoubtedly would prefer a gradual, future abolition. The pollees in some surveys were given several alternatives regarding the practical execution of such a step. Between one-quarter (Bar Federation, 1991) and one-half (Prime Minister's Office, 1967) of those who wanted to retain the death penalty agreed that its application should be suspended on a trial basis.

Table C-4: Proponents of an Abolition of the Death Penalty and Attitude towards a Gradual or Future Abolition

Poll	Total result		Future (out of con 100%)	
No.	Pro	Con	Retention	Gradual abolition
7.	68.0%	27.0%	50.0%	42.0%
15.	62.3%	14.3%	21.0%	63.0%
16.	60.4%	39.6%	53.7%	45.3%
19.	63.4%	35.9%	49.1%	47.9%
20.	44.3%	22.5%	26.3%	59.3%
23.	66.5%	15.7%	27.5%	65.6%

Table C-5: Support for Capital Punishment and Attitude on Future Abolition or Retention

Poll	Total result		Future (out of con 100%)	
No.	Pro	Con	Retention	Gradual abolition
7.	68.0%	27.0%	78.0%	14.0%
15.	62.3%	14.3%	77.4%	12.9%
16.	60.4%	39.6%	57.3%	40.0%
19.	63.4%	35.9%	75.1%	21.4%
23.	66.5%	15.7%	76.8%	15.6%

The results in response to the question of which punishment should be substituted for the death penalty in the case of an abolition or suspension, however, were mixed. Support for an absolute life sentence without the possibility of release on parole varied between 15 and 35 percent throughout the surveys, while the support of a life sentence with a chance for early release fluctuated between 30 and 65 percent. However, clearly a life sentence is seen as the only acceptable alternative to capital punishment, with opponents of the death penalty generally tending to consider a limited life sentence sufficient, while supporters of the death penalty would agree to a substitution only if capital punishment was to be replaced with an absolute life sentence without parole.

The non-existence of an unshakeable opinion on the death penalty in Japan is further shown in the views on punishment for certain crimes. The pollees in the Prime Minister's Office's 1967 poll and the survey conducted by Meiji University in 1969 were given examples of various crimes. The attitude towards capital punishment in these cases showed considerable deviations, with support varying between 26% and 78%. Opposition was lowest in case of murder of a child kidnapped for ransom, or of arson on structures where people are present. The abhorrence of crimes is greatest in cases against women and children. It is so great that even many opponents of the death penalty are ready for exemptions, even for crimes, which under current law are not threatened with death. On the other hand, for political crimes threatened with death, support of capital punishment is comparatively low. It is further of interest that although a vast majority favoured retention for homicide, the pollees were willing to accept exceptions according to the person of the victim. While six out of ten demanded death for the murderer of a policeman, only four out of ten wanted to see the killer of a minister-of-state or parliamentarian hang. An interesting qualification of the value of human life![204]

The inaccuracy of the apparent black-and-white picture presented by the polls' results is further shown by the choice of arguments for or against the death penalty, as presented by the pollees. As stated above, one of the main arguments provided by the proponents of this penalty in the general discussion, is its deterrent, general preventive effect. The supporters of this penalty fear that in case of abolition, violent crime would rise. Following this trend, in polls where multiple answers could be given, on average over half of all pollees cited the general preventive, deterrent effect as the main reason to retain the death penalty. It is noteworthy that only two out of ten cited special prevention, that is, the prevention of a crime by eliminating the culprit.

Respect for the feelings of the victims or their bereaved families was cited as one reason to retain capital punishment in most polls; however, great deviations between the various surveys could be observed, with support for this argument ranging from 10 to 60 percent. On the other hand, support for the closely related argument of retaliation - a person who kills must atone with his own life - was constantly high in all polls with half of all pollees choosing it on average.

---

204 This point is only rarely taken up in the academic discussion. However, MOTOE (note 58 pp. 88 et seq) argues for the retention of capital punishment especially using the need of its deterrent effect for the protection of police officers.

Table C-6: Reasons for the Retention of Capital Punishment: Deterrence, General Prevention

Single answers		Multiple answers	
Poll	**Share**	**Poll**	**Share**
7.	48.0%	**7.**	15.0%
13.	62.0%	**13.**	28.0%
15.	46.0%	**15.**	28.0%
16.	43.6%	**16.**	21.1%
20.	43.3%	**20.**	26.0%
23.	53.1%	**23.**	37.9%
24.	60.0%	**24.**	10.0%

As has been shown, when the respondents had the opportunity to give multiple answers, a majority chose general deterrence as an important reason for their attitude, followed by the need for the criminal to atone with the own life for having taken another, respect for the feelings of the victims, and prevention of repetition.
Hardly surprising, when only one answer could be chosen, priority was given to deterrence and retaliation (Table C-7).

Table C-7: Reasons for the Retention of Capital Punishment (Multiple Answers): Victims' Feelings, Retaliation

Victims' feelings		Retaliation	
Poll	**Share**	**Poll**	**Share**
7.	30.0%	**7.**	43.0%
13.	12.0%	**13.**	43.0%
15.	10.0%	**15.**	37.0%
16.	51.1%	**16.**	56.1%
20.	54.6%	**20.**	54.6%
23.	29.7%	**23.**	56.0%
24.	60.0%	**24.**	50.0%

A regularly high percentage, averaging more than 50 percent, believed that killing is inhuman and barbaric, that man does not have the right to kill man. As to the academic debate's crucial argument of miscarriages of justice, the polls' results here range from 12 to 82 percent, making a reliable statement on the average choice of this argument meaningless. Apart from this difficulty, a constant rise in the importance of this aspect in the forming of people's opinions can be observed since the 1980s.

Table C-8: Reasons Pro Capital Punishment (Single Answers)

	A	B	C	D
Total	50.0%	21.4%	35.3%	48.6%
3.	49.2%	23.0%	6.1%	16.9%
6.	43.0%	21.0%	7.0%	24.0%
10.	45.8%	-	-	36.6%
16.	16.2%	6.3%	21.6%	33.6%
22.	23.3%	15.5%	25.8%	29.4%
Average	35.5%	16.5%	15.1%	28.1%

A = Deterrent Effect; B = Special Prevention; C = Feelings of the Victims; D = Retaliation

While the results on this question varied to a high degree, replies were unanimous when the pollees were presented with the argument that there is a chance for correction even in case of the very worst violent criminals. In all surveys, about one-third expressed their belief in a possibility of correcting criminals as an argument against capital punishment. A somewhat smaller percentage based their attitude on the belief that a culprit must atone for his crime alive.

The opponents of capital punishment were also asked their reasons for their opinion.

Whereas the proponents of the death penalty regularly base their view on the alleged general preventive force, this argument, or rather its negation, is of comparatively small importance for the opposing view. Less than one-third in all polls chose this as a reason against the death penalty. Unfortunately, one of the central topics in the postwar and current academic discussion, the constitutionality of the death penalty, was studied in only three surveys. Still, a remarkable 35.1 percent on average believed that capital punishment must be abolished because it violates of Art. 36 of the Japanese Constitution

One aspect, which so far has not caused political problems in Japan and has been discussed only on the fringes of the academic debate, is the danger that the state might abuse the death penalty against political opponents. It is therefore surprising that more than half of all pollees in the three surveys which listed this argument chose this alternative. Similarly, the postulation that a state, which prohibits killing, must not kill, given as an optional answer in the same three polls, found rather wide support.

In further ignorance of the academic debate, only one survey (Tokyo Bar Association 1981) provided as an optional answer that instead of killing a violent criminal, a compensation system for victims of crime should be introduced. However, only one in twenty pollees thought this aspect decisive for their opinion against the death penalty. In addition, some other choices were provided in individual polls. For example, when asked by Amnesty International in 1984, almost half of those surveyed agreed that capital punishment must be abolished because it causes psychological damage to all persons in contact with it. Two out of five of the pollees in the Japan Bar Federation's 1991 survey pointed at the violation of the convicts' human rights.

Table C-9: Reasons Against Capital Punishment (Multiple Answers)

Killing is inhuman and barbaric		**Erroneous judgments**		**Possibility of correction**		**Atoning alive**	
Poll	**Share**	**Poll**	**Share**	**Poll**	**Share**	**Poll**	**Share**
6.	50%	**6.**	18.8%	**6.**	31.3%	**6.**	18.8%
7.	60%	7.	71.0%	7.	57.0%	7.	13.0%
13.	58%	**13.**	33.0%	**13.**	37.0%	**13.**	21.0%
15.	43%	**15.**	12.0%	**15.**	20.0%	**15.**	26.0%
16.	55%	**16.**	69.7%	**16.**	37.3%	**20.**	47.5%
20.	63%	**20.**	48.9%	**20.**	33.3%	**23.**	32.5%
23.	43%	**21.**	82.6%	**23.**	34.2%		
		23.	45.8%	**24.**	38.0%		
		24.	62.0%				
		26.	78.1%				

No general preventive effect		**Cruel punishment**		**Abuse against political opponents**		**State must not kill**	
Poll	**Share**	**Poll**	**Share**	**Poll**	**Share**	**Poll**	**Share**
6.	18.8%	**16.**	23.2%	**21.**	64.6%	**21.**	43.4%
7.	46.0%	**24.**	37.0%	**24.**	29.0%	**24.**	40.0%
13.	37.0%	**26.**	45.0%	**26.**	66.3%	**26.**	54.7%
15.	9.0%						
16.	47.3%						
20.	20.2%						
23.	27.5%						
24.	27.0%						

Table C-10: Reasons Against Capital Punishment, Single Answers

	A	B	C	D	E	F
Total	53.1%	52.1%	36.0%	26.5%	29.1%	35.1%
Poll No.						
3.	11.1%	22.2%	-	-	-	-
10.	-	10.5%	39.3%	-	11.6%	-
16.	37.0%	31.3%	15.3%	-	10.6%	4.2%
22.	19.2%	24.0%	14.0%	-	18.0%	11.5%
Average	22.4%	22.0%	22.9%	-	13.4%	7.9%

A = Barbarity; B = Miscarriages of Justice; C = Possibility of Correction; D = Atoning Alive; E = No Preventive Effect; F = Cruelty

As in the case of the proponents of the death penalty, the opponents of this punishment, too, were asked to choose the single foremost reason underlying their attitude. Remarkably, in all polls, the single most frequently cited reason was 'barbarity', followed by miscarriages of justice, possibility of correction and cruelty. It is furthermore of interest that, while the deterrent effect was the most often cited reason for retention, less than 30 percent of the opponents of capital punishment argued that the death penalty must be abolished because no such preventive effect exists. Also, while many of the proponents of the death penalty wanted to retain this punishment in consideration of the victims' feelings, this proved to be an argument of minor importance for the opposition, put forward only in the context of an introduction of a system for the compensation of victims to replace the death penalty.

As has been mentioned above, in the academic debate, many opponents of the death penalty reject the argument that the public wants this punishment, for the people have only insufficient and often no information at all about this issue and therefore must not be a decisive factor. Consequently, several polls inquired into the pollees' knowledge about the death penalty. While it was shown in the Prime Minister's Office's polls that a vast majority was familiar with several prominent actual cases, it was revealed that the Japanese people have little if any knowledge about the legal provisions relevant for the death penalty: most pollees were not aware that the laws threaten leadership in civil war, inducement of external war, lending assistance to the enemy, arson on structures where people are present or derailment of trains causing death with capital punishment.

Surprisingly, while two-thirds of the students polled by Kanagawa University knew the exact number of execution sites in Japan, hardly any of the pollees were able to state who carried out executions; almost half did not know what method of execution is in use in Japan today. Overall, concrete knowledge about capital punishment is extremely limited and is mostly restricted to the mere existence of this penalty and the facts of cases sensationally presented by the media.

When evaluating opinion polls, it is indispensable to analyse who had been polled, to find out if the results of the surveys can be regarded as representative for the whole people, and if or how the views differ according to age, sex, religious denomination, origin, education or occupation.

While none of the recent polls include young adults in their survey – a group known from similar North American and European polls to be overwhelmingly opposed to capital punishment – the results of the Japanese polls among adults (20 years of age and above) without fail demonstrates that with increasing age, support for the death penalty rises, and opposition decreases.[205]

Furthermore it has been repeatedly shown in overseas surveys that women tend to favour a retention of the death penalty more than men do. However, the Japanese surveys which provide relevant data show inconsistent results, rendering a representative analysis impossible.[206]

---

205 The surveys conducted by the Prime Minister's Office are conducted only among adults, that is, pollees have to be at least 20 years of age. Studies abroad often onclude young adults (14-19 years), who frequently oppose capital punishment. To study this question in the Japanese context, the poll conducted in 1966 by the Kanagawa University included minors from the age of 15. The results showed that with increasing age, support for the death penalty rises, opposition decreases. Although the supporters are still in the majority among those below the age of 20, it is the lowest percentage among all age groups.
Although the Prime Minister's Office's polls did not include minors, the results here show, too, that support for capital punishment increases with age. The results in the other polls are similar.

206 To find out whether, as is frequently the case in European polls, in Japan, too, women support the death penalty rather than men, Professor José Llompart in 1975 conducted a study among students at Tokyo's Sophia University. Out of 135 male and 51 female students, 59% of the women, but only 36% of the men supported the death penalty, while 27% of the women and 45% of the men opposed it. However, when Llompart in 1970 studied 109 men and 74 women, more men than women had favoured a retention of this punishment (58% and 54%

The data regarding origin, education, social status and religious denomination are insufficient for evaluation.

Professor Kikuta[207] of Meiji University, who himself bases his opinion against the death penalty on the will of the people, asserts that public opinion must not be understood as the will of the general public, but as that of experts with sufficient conscience and knowledge about the issue of capital punishment. Among the above-mentioned surveys, the polls conducted by the various universities and bar associations had legal experts as their target. According to Kikuta's theory, the results in these polls should be decidedly different, that is decidedly more pro-abolition, than those in the surveys conducted by the Prime Minister's Office among a representative cross-section of the allegedly ignorant general Japanese population.

Although the overall approval rate for the death penalty in the polls among experts seems to be somewhat lower, support for this punishment is nevertheless overwhelmingly high among lawyers, legal practicioners, law students etc. However, some idiosyncrasies can be observed. For example, counter to the general trend, attorney support for the death penalty, albeit increasing with age, is strongest among those below 30 and over 50. Also, attorneys who during their career had ever held the mandate in a capital punishment case were more likely to oppose it.

Unsurprisingly, considerable differences in attitudes could be observed in the various occupations. Whereas in all polls, judges, prison wardens and especially prosecutors rejected the idea of abolishing the death penalty with a very substantial majority, university professors and students seem to be increasingly opposed it. As in the case of the general population, among the experts, too, a

---

respectively), 30% of the men and 14% of the women supported an abolition. LLOMPART note 13 pp. 219, 221 fn. 3

Also in 1991, when asked by the Special Committee of the Bar Federation, 59.7% of 134 female pollees, but only 45.2% of 2,589 male wanted an abolition. 32.1% of the women and 48.2% preferred to retain the death penalty. When the same survey asked about the form of an abolition, more men than women (30.6% and 20.2% respectively) wanted an immediate abolition, and 36.6% of the female pollees, 34.7% of the men opted for a gradual abolition. The question, whether capital punishment should continue to be used to respect for the victims' feelings, was approved of by 24.6% of the women, but almost double the number of men (45.0%).

207 See e.g. KIKUTA KÔICHI, *The Death Penalty in Japan: Why Hasn't It Been Abolished*?, in 1 Meiji Law Journal pp. 43, 59 et seq (1994)

large number prefer the idea of a gradual, future abolition of the death penalty. This opinion is especially widespread among judges, but only infrequently favoured by prosecutors.

Again, as with the general population, the Japanese legal experts, too, showed no preference for one single method regarding the practical realisation of a gradual or future abolition, although about half of all attorneys expressed their desire to see the number of capital crimes reduced. A similar percentage among judges and academics favoured the introduction of a stay period after the finalisation of a death sentence. Such a measure, however, was opposed by almost all prison wardens.

As has been seen, in most surveys, the Japanese people see a life sentence with a chance of early release as the preferable acceptable alternative to capital punishment. About one-third in the general polls favoured a life sentence without parole. Like the general population, the experts, too, see imprisonment for life as the only possible alternative punishment. However, only an insignificant minority of generally less than 10 percent would insist on imprisonment until death. This latter figure was, as could be expected, higher among those who demand a retention of the death penalty.

The general polls showed that opinions vary considerably when the pollees are asked about individual crimes, leading to a rather doubtful scaling of the value of life. Differences in views on the appropriateness of the death penalty for certain crimes, however, could also be observed among the experts. Here, too, some of the proponents of the death penalty supported an abolition for some crimes, while on the other hand, some who wished for an abolition, saw no problems in keeping it for certain violations of the law. The from the general polls lies in the fact that the experts tended to draw the line according to the nature of the crime and not necessarily according to the person of the victim of a homicide, although a slightly higher approval for the death penalty for the murder of a child or for rape and murder could be observed. Capital punishment for crimes against the state was also demanded by an overwhelming majority. Overall, the results confirmed the general trend.

What causes the representatives of the various occupations to choose 'pro' or 'con'? As shown above, the general population based its opinion in favour of a retention of the death penalty to a large extent on this punishment's deterrent effect, followed by the idea of retaliation and respect for the victims' feelings. Although these three arguments are also the most frequently cited aspects among attorneys, judges and university professors, most emphasis here is placed on the latter two arguments, with especially the members of the procuracy stressing the importance of the death penalty's function as a means of avenging a crime. Law students, on the other hand, tended to agree with the general populace and saw the deterrent effect of capital punishment as the main reason for its retention. At the other end of the spectrum, the opponents of the death penalty in the general surveys believed that capital punishment constitutes a barbarity contradicting humanism and that the danger of miscarriages of justices necessitates an abolition. Japan's attorneys, judges, and prosecutors against capital punishment in their majority shared this view, while the prison wardens, as can be explained from the nature of their profession, strongly supported the argument that even serious offenders can be corrected. This latter point was furthermore frequently brought up by law students. It is noteworthy that although among the law professors those specialised in criminal law wished for an abolition due to the danger of false judgments or brutality, constitutional law professors cited the unconstitutionality of capital punishment (especially Art. 36 Japanese Constitution) as the foremost reason for abolition, a point hardly raised by others. However, although there are undoubtedly differences in the allocation of arguments, in the overall evaluation the opinions of the general public and the experts are not fundamentally different.

Separately from other occupational groups, the views of Japanese parliamentarians deserve mention. In many nations of the world, governments have ignored the declared will of the people and abolished the death penalty. Thus, many opponents of capital punishment in Japan hold that the Japanese Diet, too, should lead the people in this issue. To find out whether such a tendency exists within the Japanese Parliament, and if so, to what extent, the Japanese Council on Crime and Delinquency (JCCD) conducted a poll among the representatives of both chambers in 1985, and the Committee on the Stop of Capital Punishment carried out a survey in 1989.

After a short interim period when Japan was ruled by a non-LDP coalition government under Prime Ministers Hosokawa and Hata, and then by a SDP-LDP coalition under Murayama, today the LDP under Mori Yoshiro holds the sceptre again. Therefore, the data gained in the polls seem to be still meaningful. In the former survey, 142 out of 753 representatives replied, 98 in the latter. The cause for the JCCD poll had been the coming into force of the International Covenant on Civil and Political Rights. The Committee's survey was conducted shortly after the United Nations had adopted the Second Optional Protocol to the ICCPR, which aimed at the abolition of capital punishment, and which Japan refused to sign, reasoning that the Japanese public wished to retain the death penalty.

When one has a closer look at the results of the two surveys, the first striking characteristic is that they hardly differ from those of other polls. In the JCCD survey, about two-thirds opted for the death penalty, while one-third opted against. A closer look at the party membership at the time of the pollees shows that it largely resembled the composition in the Diet. The distribution for and against, too, roughly mirrored the respective parties' attitude towards the issue. Professor Kikuta,[208] however, is of a different opinion. He believes that these answers do not reflect the real intentions of the parliamentarians with the fact that the Communist Party in the name of the chairman of the Legal Affairs Committee had submitted in reply to the questionnaire the following statement to the JCCD: 'Our Party in its draft for a constitution, published in 1946, included the sentence 'The death penalty is abolished', and we believe that in the future the approval of the people must be gained and the death penalty be abolished.' Kikuta calculates this as the reply of all 40 of the then Communist Party representatives and adds it to the overall result, thus changing the quotas for and against capital punishment to 49.2% and 50.8% respectively. This is surely desirable from Kikuta's point of view, but statistically insupportable. For such an interpretation over-evaluates the opinions of the small opposition party and thus in no way can be regarded as an accurate reflection of the Diet's intentions. Undoubtedly, the views stated by the replying LDP representatives could be held as exemplary for all or most LDP parliamentarians. If calculated in the same manner, this would lead to a far above-average support for capital punishment.

---

208 KIKUTA Part B note 36 pp. 154, 198; also see KIKUTA KÔICHI & TSUJIMOTO YOSHIO, *[Ankeeto] Shikei mondai ni kansuru kokkai giin no ishiki ([Enquette] The Conscience of Parliamentarians about Capital Punishment)*, in 372 Hôgaku seminaa pp. 30, 31-33 (1985)

Even less representative for the whole Diet are the results of the Committee's study. Here, 81 out of 98 respondents supported an abolition of the death penalty. It must be noted that out of the respondents, 56 belonged to the SDP, and 16 were Kômei Party members. Both parties support an abolition. On the other hand, only 16 LDP members answered the questionnaire, leading to a gross under-representation of this party, which supports the retention of capital punishment. Even at first glance at the results one can see that in the former poll, seven out of ten of the supporters of the death penalty also want to retain it in the future, while the camp of the opponents is split in half between those who want an immediate abolition and others who would be content with a gradual one. This reflects the general trend. The 1989 survey did not include a concrete question regarding one's opinion for or against capital punishment, but addressed the entirety of the pollees. It is striking that while asked in the abstract, ten respondents had supported a future retention, now only six wanted an immediate one. Similarly, the number of opponents of capital punishment, who previously with 81 votes favoured abolition, had fallen to 45, when asked about an immediate and complete abolition. The remainder of both groups probably can be counted among the group supporting a gradual abolition. Due to the statistical doubtfulness, the results of this poll will only be analysed regarding some general aspects.

It is more interesting to consider why the parliamentarians' apparent interest in this matter is so low. Surely one can assume that the LDP representatives had no reason to engage themselves for the retention of the death penalty, since there was no danger of its abolition. It is known that the opponents of this penalty, however, fight for their goal. In addition, most parliamentarians hold it not only to be unimportant, some even believe it would be damaging to take up the issue in an election campaign. 77.8% said in the 1985 poll that raising the matter in a campaign would have no effect on the election result. A similar question had not been included in the 1989 survey. Here it is remarkable that despite majority approval for an abolition, only 55 of the respondents said that they had 'great interest' in the subject, 42 had 'some interest'.[209]

209 Here, too, KIKUTA'S (Part B note 36 p. 215) interpretation seems doubtful when he points out that almost 100% had some sort of interest. As can be derived from the lack of responses to the survey, it is obvious that only those who in one way or another have an interest in capital punishment take it upon themselves to

The low interest among politicians furthermore became evident when a majority of both groups stated that both the Diet and the parties hardly deal with the issue. Almost none of the respondents cited capital punishment as one of the main topics of his party's policies, although most stated that it is often debated.

A situation like that in France, where in 1981 the abolition of the death penalty had become the topic of the presidential election campaign, is at present unthinkable for Japan. Rather, Japanese parliamentarians devote their energy in election campaigns to promise tax, finance and bureaucratic reforms, for this, the majority in both camps know are more promising topics for gaining votes than the death penalty.

If there ever should be a parliamentary vote on the death penalty, 60.6% of the pro and 82.7% of the con group would wish for a free vote, where the representatives are bound only by their conscience and not by the decision of their factions. Since the declared will of the parliamentarians mainly coincides with general public sentiment, surprises in such a vote could hardly be expected.

One problem related to the polls remains to be studied. For one of the weakest points of such surveys lies in the danger of manipulation, that is, that the ones responsible for the surveys steer the results in a certain direction by influencing the subjects of their study in various ways and means. Both opponents and proponents of the death penalty in Japan regularly criticise the other side stating that their polls are influenced, biased, and thus the results are not representative.

Many of the death penalty's opponents have repeatedly pointed out that the argument that the people are against an abolition of capital punishment, as proven in polls, is irrelevant, for the people only receive insufficient, partially incorrect and altered information about capital punishment. Because of this lack of objective information, many opponents of the death penalty hold the view that public support for capital punishment first of all is based on one-sided media coverage, secondly on traditional and uncritical acceptance of its deterrent effect, and finally on influence by politics.

answer and return the forms. In reverse interpretation it thus could be rather concluded, that all other roughly 500 representatives had no interest at all.

Fujiyoshi Kazushi[210] points out that the available information is totally insufficient. For example, although the media have reported in detail on retrial cases, there are virtually no reports about the causes of erroneous judgments, about the suffering of the convicts in prison or about international trends regarding the death penalty. If one wants to make laws based on the public opinion, first of all one must give the people as much information as possible, that is, not emotional, but scientifically founded information.

To find out whether accurate information changes public opinion on capital punishment, and to prove that the so-called public sentiment cannot be relevant because of the lack of information so far, Professor Kikuta, head of the Criminological Institute at Meiji University, carried out a study among students in 1989. At the beginning of the semester he had third and fourth year students, who had no expert knowledge of the matter, and thus were no different from the average Japanese, fill out a questionnaire. After the completion of a lecture on capital punishment, he conducted another survey.[211] The results: Kikuta found out that after the completion of the lecture ('after') more students advocated an abolition than at the beginning of the course ('before'). It is unclear how he reached this conclusion. For although the approval rate fell from 47.6% to 42.4%, it still exceeded the percentage of those who opposed the death penalty, which also fell, from 41.1% to 40.7%. Thus, the input of information did not convert a majority into opponents of the death penalty. Rather, it caused insecurity, demonstrated in an increase of 'don't know' replies from 11.1% to 16.9%. Furthermore, Kikuta discusses the results in such a way as to imply that after the completion of the course, a majority supported either an immediate complete or a gradual abolition. Indeed, the share of those who wanted a future retention had fallen by 6%. In conformity with this result, a clear majority of the students 'after' advocated an introduction of stay of execution or a practical non-application. On the other hand, the number of those who thought that the death penalty will disappear even when the current system is retained fell drastically. It is problematic that Kikuta subsumed all replies of

210 FUJIYOSHI KAZUSHI & MATSUI CHIAKI & MINATO KAZUO, SERON CHÔSA NI OKERU SHIKEI *(Capital Punishment in Opinion Polls)*, in Shikei no genzai (Capital Punishment Today) pp. 150, 154-155 (Ibaraki Rieko et.al. eds., Tokyo 1990)

211 See in detail KIKUTA Part B note 36 pp. 185 et seq. It is not known whether the contents of the enquettes were identical.

'gradual abolition' uncritically under the heading of 'against death penalty'. For, as has already been pointed out, support for a future abolition can also be regarded as a rejection of an immediate abolition and thus as 'pro capital punishment.'[212] This difference is further shown in the 1989 Prime Minister's Office's poll, where the respondents were asked about their opinion on a complete and immediate abolition. Although the percentage of its supporters rose by four points, and that of the opponents fell by six points, the number of opponents was still three times that of the proponents. Especially remarkable is that in both surveys, almost 40% replied 'don't know'. Kikuta also supports his opinion with the replies of the pro-group to the question about the future of capital punishment. Here, about 10% of those who 'before' had answered with 'retaining current provisions', replied: 'to reform the current law so that as few as possible crimes are punished with death'. However, again, Kikuta's interpretation does not hold up. For even the approval to a reduction in the end means opposition to abolition now. Overall, Kikuta sees in almost all results a change in favour of abolition. This seems insupportable. On the contrary, these findings appear extremely inconsistent and fluctuating. Moreover, the strong influence exerted by Kikuta's agitation against the death penalty can be drawn from the many results in the poll, which comprise the classic points of the discussion. For example, when asked about the changes in crime rates after an abolition of capital punishment, 'after' far less students answered that violent crime would probably increase. As has been pointed out above, there is no evidence for either possibility. It is a question of conviction, which is strongly influenced by one's attitude towards capital punishment. This attitude can be influenced and was influenced in the present example. The information which the students received in the lecture had hardly been objective, for otherwise the information that there is no proof for or against general prevention should have led to an

212 Overall, Kikuta sees in almost all results a change to favouring abolition. This is insupportable. On the contrary, these findings appear extremely inconsistent and fluctuating. For one, the exact contents of Professor Kikuta's lecture are not known. It can be safely assumed that the passionate crusader for an abolition, who after the 1993 executions even staged a hunger strike, held strictly anti-capital punishment lectures. Neither must it be forgotten that in Japan, if one does not want to endanger his own success and career, it is not advisable to contradict one's teacher's opinion. This assumption can already be drawn from the steep increase in 'don't know' answers, which show a clear insecurity on the part of the students.

overwhelmingly large percentage of 'don't know' answers. The same applies to the questions on causes for crime and the possibility of correcting serious offenders.

In Kikuta's opinion,[213] his survey had made clear that through more information a different result can be reached. In other words, public opinion, represented by Meiji University students, thus can be manipulated according to the goals of those conducting a poll. It is exactly this accusation Kikuta had made against the government polls. There is no doubt that Kikuta as a very engaged opponent of the death penalty vehemently tried to convert the students to his view. It is this fact through which his survey loses all convincing force in the point which Kikuta wanted to prove: that the people's real opinion is against capital punishment. The only statement that remains is that the public's opinion can be influenced so easily that one could think it doesn't have one. This causes doubt about the credibility of all polls. As Sophia University's Professor José Llompart has said, the people's conviction in questions of criminal policies is irrelevant.

At this point it seems appropriate to turn to another point of criticism brought up by Kikuta. He believes that the reliability of opinion polls is most of all doubtful, since results can easily be influenced by polling method, kind of contact, sound of voice etc. Yamaguchi Masanori[214] also criticises in his analysis of the 1989 poll conducted by the Prime Minister's Office that it contained numerous catch questions. That respondents to a poll can be influenced by the attitude of the conductor of a poll, has already been shown. As has been pointed out above, the order of questions is of great importance. Kikuta[215] criticised the 1989 poll conducted by the Prime Minister's Office, especially regarding the first three questions:

- Is violent crime increasing?
- Would violent crime increase if the death penalty was abolished?
- Do you agree to the view that the death penalty in Japan must be completely abolished now?

---

213 Part B note 36 p. 192

214 YAMAGUCHI MASANORI, *Shikei seido iji ni katan suru masu media* (Media, Supporting the Retention of Capital Punishment), in: IBARAKI RIEKO et.al. [ed.], Shikei no gendai (Capital Punishment Today) pp, 138, 139 (Tokyo 1990)

215 Part B note 36 p. 157

Kikuta sees here a clear case of manipulation, and criticises especially the last question as very inductive. This opinion rings true when the pollee answering the first question recalls especially brutal and sensationally reported crimes of the past, he will be emotionally influenced in such a way that one can almost speak of a preparation for the answers 'yes' and 'no' to the following two questions. Influencing can hardly be denied here. Dandô Shigemitsu[216] first of all finds fault with the contents of this survey. The 1967 poll had included the question of what the pollees think about someone who intentionally set fire to a building where persons are present. It does not come as a surprise that 70% demand death for the culprit. Although polling methods have improved since then, many misleading points are still included. In particular, the issue of miscarriages of justice is still only indirectly mentioned as a possible reason for opposition against the death penalty. Dandô believes that the second question in a poll should rather be: 'Do you think that the death penalty should be retained and that it should be accepted that in the worst case innocent people are executed as convicted murderers?' This suggestion leads to the opposite extreme. A better first question might be 'Could you accept as unavoidable that an innocent person is executed?' Kikuta[217] sees as the main problems of Japanese polls the way in which the questions are asked and the choice of words. For example, it is natural that a question such as 'Do you agree to the death penalty for all violent criminals or do you oppose it?' is more likely to be replied to in the positive than an abstract 'Are you for or against the death penalty?' However, there is so far no proof for such assumption. Kikuta[218] provides another example from the 1989 Meiji University poll. 'Should the death penalty in present-day Japan be abolished in any case?' This question, he believes, induces a reply in favour of capital punishment. However, the actual result was rather balanced, with 50.8% for and 42.6% against capital punishment. Kikuta furthermore believes that the question about an increase in violent crime in the case of an abolition is problematic. In the Prime Minister's Office's 1989 survey, a total of 28.6% replied in the negative or gave no answer. On the other hand, in the Meiji

216 Cited in A.I. note 111 p. 5
217 Part B note 36 p. 40
218 Part B note 36 p. 173

University study the same year, 71.8% answered 'no' or 'don't know'. How can such differences occur? Kikuta explains this, saying that in the former poll it had first been asked 'Do you think that violent crime is increasing?' and thereafter 'Do you believe that violent crime would increase if the death penalty was abolished?' Furthermore, just before the poll, in June 1989, sensational murder cases had rocked the nation. If one asks such questions before such a background, naturally 'crime will increase' will be the majority opinion.[219] Based on an analysis of the Prime Minister's Office's 1989 poll, Fujiyoshi draws the same conclusion. After giving the example of patricide, it is asked whether the pollees believe that violent crime has increased and if such evil crime would be on the rise if the death penalty was abolished. This order, says Fujiyoshi,[220] psychologically induces approval of severe punishment as an answer to the question 'Do you agree to the view that the death penalty must be completely abolished?'. The order of questions: knowledge about aggravated punishment for patricide - necessity of such a provision - other crimes than patricide - knowledge about the 1973 Supreme Court decision - need for aggravated punishment for the killing of a child - gravity of homicide within and outside the family - views on crime tendencies in recent years - increase of crime in case of abolition of death penalty - must death penalty in Japan today be completely abolished directs the answers a certain direction by building up within the pollees a feeling of *angst* and disgust.[221]

This matter deserves a closer look at the relevant points in the polls. The following tables compare the various asking methods of the abstract question and the results thereof.

A. Do you think it is better in practice not to punish a violent criminal with death?

Poll 15.	Yes 42.0%	No 25.0%

B. Do you think that the death penalty is necessary?

Poll 25.	Yes 53.0%	No 34.0%

219 This view is shared by AMESAKA note 154 pp. 92-94

220 Note 210 pp. 151-154

221 Also see KIKUTA Part B note 36 p. 215

C. Are you for or against the death penalty?

Poll 5.	Pro 54.1%	Con 33.0%
Poll 6.	Pro 68.0%	Con 27.0%
Poll 19.	Pro 64.8%	Con 37.3%
Poll 22.	Pro 50.8%	Con 42.6%
Poll 23.	Pro 42.4%	Con 40.7%
Poll 24.	Pro 10.2%	Con 82.7%

D. Are you for or against an abolition of the death penalty?

Poll 2.	Pro 59.3%	Con 23.8%
Poll 27.	Pro 45.8%	Con 47.6%

E. The death penalty is the severest penalty in Japan. Must it be abolished?

Poll 17.	Yes 19.0%	No 76.0%

F. How do you think about the future of the death penalty?

Poll 16.	Retention 53.6 %	Abolition 39.6%
Poll 18.	Retention 68.0%	Abolition 13.4%

G. Are you for or against an immediate and complete abolition?

Poll 6.	Pro 16.0%	Con 71.0%
Poll 3.	Pro 18.0%	Con 65.0%
Poll 12.	Pro 58.0%	Con 42.0%
Poll 13.	Pro 31.0%	Con 42.0%
Poll 15.	Pro 14.0%	Con 62.0%
Poll 20.	Pro 22.5%	Con 44.3%
Poll 23.	Pro 15.7%	Con 66.5%

The average of the results of the various questioning methods provides the following picture:

	Pro death penalty	**Con death penalty**
A	42.0%	25.0 %
B	53.0%	34.0%
C	49.4%	42.1%
D	35.7%	52.6%
E	56.1%	25.1%
F	61.9%	26.5%
G	76.2%	19.0%

The results show clear differences. Whether these stem from the way of questioning or if they are based on other factors cannot be established conclusively. However, the results of the polls which use the pro/con question are remarkable; when taking into consideration the high percentage of those who advocate an abolition now or in the future, the opponents of capital punishment clearly dominated. The meaning of this result gains further weight by the fact that in other methods (E, F, and G), which require an absolute decision, the majority opposed an abolition.[222]

Another issue is pointed out by Fujiyoshi:[223] the attitude of the interviewers can convince the pollees or lead their answers in a certain direction.

Dandô:[224] finally, sees one more weak spot. For example, in the 1967 poll conducted by the Prime Minister's Office, the pollees'

222 The question 'Do you approve of an abolition of the death penalty or are you against it?' in poll 27 was assented to by 45.8% and disagreed with by 47.6%. Usually, KIKUTA (Part B note 36 p. 230) says, in this place the question 'Are you for or against the death penalty?' is asked. He thinks that the high percentage for abolition can partially be explained with the negligence of many pollees in reading the questionnaire, whose opinion became evident in later questions. But such ambiguities had not been planned. At the same time he says (Id. p. 231) that the sudden change of mind among the attorneys in the previous polls could be explained by the increasing discussion of the topic in recent years. Other reasons are the adoption of the Second Protocol of 1991 and the fact that in Japan, at the time, there had been no executions for a while, there had been sensational retrial cases, repeated campaigns against the death penalty etc. His train of thought, however, seems contradictory in itself, as has been pointed out before.

223 note 210 p. 154

opinion on several individual crimes was asked. He believes the reason that approval here was rather high in most cases, has was by the fact that the danger of erroneous judgments was not pointed out. Although the form of the poll in 1989 was improved, Dandô points out that here, too, only those who had already expressed their opposition against the death penalty were asked about their view on erroneous judgments ('reasons for abolition'). He believes that here it is necessary to ask the following question: 'Suppose one out of ten thousand executed is innocent. Do you think this cannot be helped and it is still better to retain the death penalty for murder?' Will a respondent not tend towards the opposite extreme if the interviewer were to cite such an extreme example? Surely, more objectivity is needed in the survey questions, although the argument that the proponents of the death penalty been asked about their opinion on the problem of erroneous judgments certainly is weighty.

---

224 DANDÔ SHIGEMITSU, *Naze shikei haishi e no ketsui o tsuyoku shita no ka (Why has the Intention on an Abolition of the Death Penalty become Stronger?)*, in Shikei no genzai (Capital Punishment Today) pp. 30, 35 (IBARAKI RIEKO et.al. eds., Tokyo 1990)

CONCLUSION

CONCLUSION

The history of capital punishment in Japan can be traced back to the legendary times of Japanese prehistory and stood, as in many other parts of the world, in closest relationship with an animistic religion, in this case Shintoism. With the penetration of Chinese culture since the *T'ang* Period, Japan underwent an extensive Sinisation in all aspects of life. Although the legal system was formed upon the Chinese model as well, the ancient Japanese system of sanctions was characterised by greater leniency than its Chinese model. During the *Heian* Period capital punishment was not applied for three-and-a-half centuries. The reasons for this occurrence, which is unique in world history, today no longer can be traced with certainty, but one can suspect a combination of the Japanese rulers' deep Buddhist faith and the fear of evil-minded spirits of revenge. It was only from the Middle Ages that the Japanese penal system underwent a process of extreme brutalisation, mirroring the general trends of Japanese society at the time. This period today is erroneously often regarded as exemplary of pre-modern Japanese penal law. After centuries of the harshest sanctions for the most trivial offences and a cruel variety of execution methods, eventually the multitude of foundations of the sanctionary system were standardised during the *Tokugawa* Period and certain crimes and punishments codified in a 1792 collection of precedents entitled *Osadamegaki Hyakkajô*. Since sanctions were exclusively of a punitive character, sentences were oriented predominantly on the gravity and reprehensibility of the act as according to the Confucian value system, which served as the foundation for the Japanese state. However, after Japan's opening in the nineteenth century, this law proved to be totally inadequate for this sudden confrontation with the West. The first codification attempts in the field of criminal law after the 1868 Meiji Restoration were once again modelled after the laws of the glorious Chinese dynasties, thus creating a vast number of precedents and archaic punishments varying according to class and position. Eventually, though, the inevitability of dealing with the Western world and therefore of thoroughly westernising Japan's state system took the upper hand. In the early years of the *Meiji* Period the most cruel execution methods as well as additional degrading punishments were abolished. The so-called *Kyû-keihô*, or Old Penal Code of 1882 contained hanging as the sole method of execution, and the code no longer distinguished between the choice of punishment according to the social position of culprit and victim. The sole exception to this rule were crimes against the Emperor or the Imperial family, which, according to Japanese ideology at the time, were prosecuted relentlessly. Although the influence of German law grew steadily, and dominated the 1907 reform of the *Keihô*, neither the rather liberal provisions of the new code nor the vehement discussions among scholars of criminal law succeeded in preventing the penetration of the code by militaristic and ultra-nationalistic tendencies, leading to an increase of the number of crimes sanctioned with death.

After the defeat in World War II, no thorough reform of the penal system was carried out. Nevertheless, all provisions related to the Imperial Household and the wartime regime were abolished. Despite continuing reform work and decades of passionate debate, a fundamental revision of the code has yet to come.

The discussion on the death penalty has a long tradition in Europe and the United States, beginning with Beccaria's and Bentham's utilitarian theories of abolition. Scholars of criminal law and politicians, philosophers and clerics have been arguing for and against it for centuries. In Japan, the first timid beginnings of this debate can only be found from about the middle of the *Meiji* Period, but these hints at Western tendencies of abolition and punishment's character as education (*Erziehungsstrafe*) did not fall on fertile ground in prewar and wartime Japan. Only the nation's extensive democratisation after the Second World War provided the proponents of an abolition of capital punishment with the security and self-confidence needed for the discussion, and Japan's new Constitution (*Nihon-koku kenpô*) of November 1946 paved the way for a new line of arguments. Although the constitution does not clearly express an opinion on the issue, numerous opponents of capital punishment refer to its Article 36: 'The infliction of torture by any public officer and cruel punishments are absolutely forbidden.' As early as 12 March 1948, the Supreme Court (*Saikô saibansho*) decided on the compatibility of capital punishment with this provision, while ignoring the actual legal problem. Compared to the execution methods of the past, the Supreme Court elaborated, capital punishment carried out by hanging could not be considered cruel. Art. 31 reads: 'No person shall be deprived of life or liberty, nor shall any other criminal penalty be imposed, except according to procedure established by law.' In 1961, the Supreme Court took up the issue of the constitutionality of the death penalty for a second time; this time its compatibility with Art. 31 had been questioned. Although Japan's legal academia repeatedly pointed out the dubiousness of the legal validity of an Imperial Rescript dated 1872, which serves as the basis for executions, the Supreme Court acknowledged this antiquated rescript as a law in a formal and material sense and thus as the constitutional basis of a penal sanction taking human life. Also, the Supreme Court has on several occasions made it clear that in its opinion it is of subordinate importance that today's execution method of subterranean hanging does not comform with the provisions of the forementioned rescript. Art.13 of the Constitution is often said to be incompatible with the death penalty: 'All the people shall be respected as individuals. Their right to life, liberty, and the pursuit of happiness shall, to the extent that it does not interfere with the public welfare, be the supreme consideration in legislation and in other government affairs.' Once again the Supreme Court in its 1948 decision pointed out the necessity of a subordination under public welfare.

Besides these and other issues in constitutional law, the Japanese discussion on capital punishment is mainly dominated by those arguments, which have always stood and still stand in the centre of all and any discussions of the subject. Especially the possibility of general prevention, meaning deterrence from and prevention of crimes through imposition and execution of death sentences, to the present day provides material for heated debates between proponents and opponents of capital punishment. Sellin's and Ehrlich's theories have as many supporters in Japan as they do in the United States, and in Japan, too, it is attempted to present 'the' characteristic criminal, statistics or alternative punishments as a proof of counter-proof of general or special prevention. So far, however, no generally accepted proof has been demonstrated. The same applies to the argument of capital punishment being a means of vengeance and retaliation. The position of the victims' feelings, compensation by the culprit and consideration of remorse time and again materialise as one of the central points of the debate.

However, there is one argument which is by far more concrete, closer, and in its specific materialisation more Japanese than the aforementioned traditional issues: mistrials, and the fear of miscarriages of justice. Unlike the case of the United Kingdom, where a proven case of the execution of an innocent man directly led to the abolition of the death penalty, official Japan to this very day denies that there had been a single such case since the beginning of the *Meiji* Period. Nevertheless, Japan's modern penal history is comprised of a number of cases, where the suspicion of mistrials can hardly be erased, but can not be proven either. It was only in the 1980s that after a revision of the interpretation of prerequisites for retrials by the Supreme Court, four convicts, who in the 1950s had been sentenced to death because of homicide or robbery-murder, were found not guilty in sensational retrials. Although in all these cases there had been clear hints at abuse of the suspects and of inducement and coercion of a confession, none of the courts involved in the retrials took a concrete position on these issues. Despite or maybe rather because of the fact that the surfacing of these four cases nourished anxious suspicions over miscarriage of justice, the probability of any further retrials and eventual releases of prisoners is minuscule. Prosecution and especially the Justice Ministry have clearly tightened restraints after these 'defeats'.

Another important aspect in the Western discussion on capital punishment is the relationship between the death penalty and religion, morality and ethics. This issue, however, plays only a minor role in Japan's debate. Although at various times in Japanese history Shintoism, Buddhism and Confucianism shaped the foundations and application of capital punishment, today only remains of these influences can be traced.

Since eventually none of the perpetually presented arguments serves as proof for or against capital punishment, both sides nowadays repeatedly refer to public opinion as expressed in opinion polls. These polls, it is believed, in present times when only scientific facts and watertight statistics are acknowledged as evidence, will lead to a solution of the endless debate. The analysis of dozens of polls conducted in postwar Japan, however, only shows once more that proof is impossible. The results of the polls regularly match the wishes of their conductors, influenced by polling method or terminology and frequently stirred up by sensational media reports on spectacular cases. Other than this, the average Japanese knows nothing about capital punishment, and is not really interested in this subject. If, in addition to this, the results of such polls are interpreted in an unbiased manner, one finds that neither among the general population nor among experts can a clear majority for or against capital punishment can be found. Thus the will of the people cannot be valid as the decisive criterion for the future treatment of the death penalty in Japan.

The Japanese Criminal Code provides for six main and two additional penalties: death, penal servitude, imprisonment, fine, penal detention and minor fine as well as confiscation as an additional penalty (Art. 9 *Keihô*). The death penalty as the gravest penalty is carried out by hanging in a prison, with the delinquent being confined in prison until the execution of the penalty (Art. 11 *Keihô*). Currently the Japanese Criminal Code provides for capital punishment as a sanction in the following cases: homicide (Art. 199 *Keihô*), robbery causing death (Art. 240 *Keihô*), robbery and rape, causing the death of the woman (Art. 241 *Keihô*), arson of structures used for residence or containing people (Art. 108 *Keihô*), being the ringleader of a riot (Art. 106 No.1 *Keihô*), inducement of external war or assistance to the enemy (Arts. 81, 82 *Keihô*), as well as various qualifying crimes such as causing the death of the victim (Arts. 117 I, 126 III, 127, 146 No.2 *Keihô*). Furthermore, a number of crimes are sanctioned with capital punishment in certain special laws. Capital punishment is mandatory only in the case of inducement of external war.

After a more than three-year long execution moratorium between 1989 and 1993, Japan is presently undergoing a 'renaissance' of capital punishment with 39 executions between 1993 and 2001, although in general a continuous decline in finalised death sentences as well as executions can be observed since the early *Meiji* Period. Whether the recent increase marks an end to this trend or just a temporary anti-cycle has yet to be seen.

Another tendency is that of the almost complete exclusion of the application of capital punishment in cases other than homicide or robbery causing death. However, the criteria for sentencing are unclear. During decades of discrepancies in the judiciary, the only generally accepted criterion was that of the number of victims. In a decision dated 8 July 1983 in the Nagayama Case, the Supreme Court explained on the issue of criteria for the selection of imprisonment for life or the death penalty, that not merely the number of victims but also the degree of cruelty must be taken into consideration. What matters, the court explained, is whether the culprit is remorseful and whether the bereaved families forgive him. Even this ruling, however, could not provide for a generalisation or standardisation of sentencing. This apparent dependence of judgments on fate increases even further after the finality of a sentence, when the ambiguity of the criteria for the selection of convicts for execution almost appears to be a grotesque but lethal game, with the losers those who pull the shorter straw.

According to Arts. 475 *et seq* of the Japanese Code of Criminal Procedure (*Keiji soshô-hô*), a death sentence has to be carried out within six months from the finality of the judgment upon orders of the Minister of Justice. Since this period can be extended through appeals, applications for retrial or clemency, or interrupted by still pending trials of accomplices, the period between finality of a judgment and execution in practice usually amounts to between fifteen and twenty years. If all obstacles have been removed and all checks have been concluded by the Ministry of Justice, the Ministry prepares an execution order and submits it to the Justice Minister for signing. It remains unclear why some certain convicts are chosen for execution from amidst several with identical conditions. Another uncertainty lies in the position and person of the Minister. Since the end of the war, Japan has seen more than six dozen ministers of justice. Although the majority of Japan's justice ministers so far have kept silent about the issue of capital punishment and especially on the question of if and why they themselves have signed execution orders, many of them have called the act of signing their inevitable duty, which has to be kept strictly separated from their individual opinion on the matter. Miyazawa, minister under the LDP-SDP-Sakigake coalition, stated this view after the execution of three convicts on 11 July 1996. Nevertheless, there are examples of former ministers who in fact allowed their personal opinions to influence their conduct in office. Minister Tanaka Isôji for example declared in front of journalists his horror over the crimes committed by the convicts, and even boasted about having signed more than twenty execution orders in a single day. Satô Megumu on the other hand, minister of justice between November 1990 and December 1991, refused to sign such orders because of his Buddhist faith.

This general ambiguity of criteria for executions as well as the Justice Ministry's omnipotence become further evident when viewed in light of the ministry's strategy of absolute secrecy of executions. Although one of the ministry's main arguments in favour of capital punishment is its general preventive effect, no official information at all is given on executions pending or carried out. Since November 1998, the Justice Ministry has announced the date and number of executions after the fact. Apart from this, merely some 'leaks' in the ministry keep the media informed about details, without such reports even being confirmed by the official side. The only time executions appear officially in Japan is as numbers in the yearly statistics. This practice is usually explained by the ministry as being for the protection of the convicts' families, whom one wants to spare the shame and humiliation of having their relationship to a serious offender publicly known, and also to prevent criticism of the minister.

At a time when not only the opponents of capital punishment expected its abolition within the near future because of a three-and-a-half year stay of executions, executions under then-LDP justice Minister Gotôda Masaharu's in March 1993 came as a shock. New hope for abolitionists, represented by some fifty citizens' groups,[1] appeared on the horizon with Hosokawa's coalition cabinet, which included parties such as the Social Democrats, who clearly advocated the abolition of the death penalty in their party program. Again all hopes were destroyed, however, in December 1993. The historic coalition of LDP and SDP did not bring about the much hoped-for reform, but rather even more executions instead. Within eight years from 1993, a total of 39 persons were executed, almost twice the numbeer than in the 1980s in total. The reasons for this new trend can only be suspected: after the short moratorium in the early 1990s, which in all likelihood had been caused by the retrial cases of innocent men who had been sentenced to death, the government wanted to make a clear statement that it did not intend to abolish capital punishment. The move was a clear slap in the face of the abolitionists and a message that the government did not intend to allow them to dictate policy. At a time of political change, another

1 These groups include large-scale organisations such as Amnesty International or the Forum 90, various committees set out by the Federation of Bar Associations or regional bars, as well as religious groups. Most include only a small number of members and remain rather obscure, as is the case with the Katatsumuri no kai (Snail Society), Kyoto's Blue Sky Society, or the Women's Association for the Abolition of the Death penalty.

reason might have been a demonstration of power by the LDP and, eventually, most certainly in the government's affirmation of security and stability to calm the people, who had started to feel anxious because of the increase in violent crime in general.
The generally more and more conservative attitude of the Japanese toward capital punishment has resulted from a series of organized crimes by Aum Shinri Kyo, a new religious organization that had pervaded since the 1980s. In addition to numerous kidnappings and confinement, in March of 1995, the religious organization carried out an indiscriminate massacre using poisonous sarin gas in the crowded subways in Tokyo, which took 12 lives and injured thousands of commuters. Now the principal offenders who were involved in the crimes are on trial, and such was the impact of the terrorism on Japanese people that they expect for punishing them severely. Indeed, the death sentences handed down in the Aum case so far, were welcomed by the public. This sentiment is further reflected in the latest public polls, showing the high approval rate of capital punishment.[2] The full effect of the worst serial killing since the Aum case, the murder of eight elementary school children in Ikeda, Osaka, by mentally disabled Takuma Mamoru, on public opinion remains to be awaited, but will, in all likelihood, lead a further increase in the public's support of the death penalty in Japan. But in a country such as Japan, where revulsion against particularly heinous crimes of violence, especially against women and children, is immense, in the weeks following this latest mass killing, public favour for the death penalty for Takuma was almost unanimous[3]

Certainly the issue will not be solved with a typically Japanese consensus. One thing, however, is for sure: the oft-cited argument that the Japanese people want the death penalty to remain for good, lacks any foundation. As in many other countries, revulsion against institutionalised killing is widespread among the people of Japan.

---

2 This tendency might be seen in the second death sentence handed down by a court of first instance against a member of the Aum cult on 30 September 1999 – despite the fact that that particular defendant's actions during the Sarin gas attack on the Tokyo subway system had not caused any deaths. DAILY YOMIURI ONLINE 1 October 1999. The public's expectations were not disappointed in the other trials, either; as of May 2001, a total of six former AUM members have been sentenced to death by Japanese district courts.

3 JAPAN TIMES ONLINE, 15 June 2001, <http://www.japantimes.co.jp/cgi-bin/getarticle.pl5?ed20010615al.htm>

But this sentiment is countered by revulsion against heinous crimes, which regularly cause the public to cry out for the gallows for serious offenders.[4] Whether the Japanese government will abolish the death penalty or not is thus a secondary issue. Of much greater importance is the problem of the extent to which the penal system is being ruled by personal moods of judges, ministers and the bureaucrats of the justice ministry.

4 See e.g. ibid.

INDEX

INDEX

BRILL'S JAPANESE STUDIES LIBRARY

Edited by K.W. Radtke & H. Bolitho

Brill's Japanese Studies Library is concerned with the languages, history and culture of Japan in past and present. Among the subjects included are history – political, social, economic – based on primary sources, including biography; religion; classical literature and performing arts; law; language; philosophy; history of science; et cetera. Geographically the series covers the Japanese isles as well as manifestations of Japanese presence abroad. Chronologically, the period from the beginnings of written history until the present is covered. The series includes monographs on substantial subjects, thematic collections of articles, handbooks, text editions, and translations.

1 Plutschow, H.E. *Chaos and Cosmos.* Ritual in Early and Medieval Japanese Literature. 1990. ISBN 90 04 08628 5
2 Leims, Th.F. *Die Entstehung des Kabuki.* Transkulturation Europa-Japan im 16. und 17. Jahrhundert. 1990. ISBN 90 04 08988 8
3 Seeley, Chr. *A History of Writing in Japan.* 1991. ISBN 90 04 09081 9
4 Vovin, A. *A Reconstruction of Proto-Ainu.* 1993. ISBN 90 04 09905 0
5 Yoda, Y. *The Foundations of Japan's Modernization.* A Comparison with China's Path Towards Modernization. Translated by K.W. Radtke. 1996. ISBN 90 04 09999 9
6 Hardacre, H. & A.L. Kern (eds.). *New Directions in the Study of Meiji Japan.* 1997. ISBN 90 04 10735 5
7 Tucker, J.A. *Itô Jinsai's* Gomô Jigi *& the Philosophical Definition of Early Modern Japan.* 1998. ISBN 90 04 10992 7
8 Hardacre, H. (ed.). *The Postwar Development of Japanese Studies in the United States.* 1998. ISBN 90 04 10981 1
9 Hanashiro, R.S. *Thomas William Kinder and the Japanese Imperial Mint, 1868-1875.* 1999. ISBN 90 04 11345 2
10 Teitler, G. & K.W. Radtke (eds.). *A Dutch Spy in China.* Reports on the First Phase of the Sino-Japanese War (1937-1939). 1999. ISBN 90 04 11487 4
11 Mortimer, M. *Meeting the Sensei.* The Role of the Master in Shirakaba Writers. 2000. ISBN 90 04 11655 9

12 Scholz-Cionca, S. & S. L. Leiter (eds.). *Japanese Theatre and the International Stage.* 2000. ISBN 90 04 12011 4

13 Saltzman-Li, K. *Creating Kabuki Plays.* Context for *Kezairoku*, 'Valuable Notes on Playwriting'. 2001. ISBN 90 04 12115 3

14 Ozaki, M. *Individuum, Society, Humankind.* The Triadic Logic of Species according to Hajime Tanabe. 2001. ISBN 90 04 12118 8

15 Bentley, J. R. *A Descriptive Grammar of Early Old Japanese Prose.* 2001. ISBN 90 04 12308 3

16 Higashibaba, I. *Christianity in Early Modern Japan.* Kirishitan Belief and Practice. 2001. ISBN 90 04 12290 7

17 Schmidt, P. *Capital Punishment in Japan.* 2001. ISBN 90 04 12421 7

ISSN 0925-6512